951.
C43

P9-CMF-349

UNIVERSITY OF WASHINGTON PUBLICATIONS ON ASIA

Sponsored by

THE FAR EASTERN AND RUSSIAN INSTITUTE

This book is a product of the Modern Chinese History Project carried on by the Far Eastern and Russian Institute of the University of Washington. Members of the group represent various disciplines in the social sciences and humanities. The work of the project is of a cooperative nature with each member assisting the others through critical discussion and the contribution of ideas and material. The responsibility for each study rests with the author.

DS759.5
C 5
1954

THE NIEN REBELLION

by

SIANG-TSEH CHIANG

1954

UNIVERSITY OF WASHINGTON PRESS

SEATTLE

NOV   '54   47726

Copyright 1954

by the

University of Washington Press

Printed in the United States of America

PREFACE

This study of the Nien Rebellion was written by Chiang Siang-tseh as a doctoral dissertation at the University of Washington in 1951. It was recognized as a valuable contribution to the understanding of the changes which took place within China during the nineteenth century, and plans were made for its publication in a revised form which would be of interest to the general student as well as to the specialist in problems of nineteenth-century China. Such revision was rendered impracticable, however, by Mr. Chiang's return to his home in China. His study is now presented in its original dissertation form. To facilitate its use by the more general student, it seems advisable to preface it with a few statements which, it is hoped, will help to orientate the reader to the scene in which the Nien drama was enacted.

The nineteenth century in China was a period of decline. The central government had become weak and corrupt and the whole machinery of administration was functioning less and less effectively. The exploitation of the peasants by the scholar-gentry and the officials, who belonged to the same privileged upper class, had increased until the economic burden of the peasants had become almost insupportable. At the same time there occurred a series of natural catastrophes which were to a large extent the result of administrative neglect. A vital function of the Chinese government was the maintenance of waterworks which were essential for irrigation and flood control as well as for transportation. By the middle of the nineteenth century the waterworks were not being adequately maintained. Flood waters broke through weakened river dikes, destroying crops and driving people from the surrounding land. Government granaries and other relief measures failed to relieve the suffering from famines which followed in the wake of the floods. Gangs of bandits arose to roam unchecked over wide sections of the countryside, reaping their profits from looting, kidnapping, and extortion; into their ranks they drew many of the peasants who had been forced to leave their lands. These bands of outlaws were able to expand their forces and widen their areas of activity because the government police machinery had become too weak to restrain them.

Unable to obtain protection from the government, the local communities were forced to take into their own hands the functions of local defense. The result was the emergence of local military corps. These corps were organized and led by local leaders and were supported by the community for whose defense they were established. Such local corps took over the responsibility of local police action when the government machinery failed to operate. To secure funds to maintain their forces, local corps leaders taxed the people of the community, and administrative authority as well as military control gravitated away from the officials into the hands of local corps chiefs.

Such encroachments on its local authority were troublesome to the central government and they seriously endangered its tax revenue, but they did not in themselves present a real threat to the existence of the dynasty. Local corps were not new in the nineteenth century; they had existed in varying degrees throughout the dynasty and had been used by the government as a supplement to its regular forces. After 1800, and particularly after the Opium War, however, the local corps became increasingly independent units, for whose political support the government was frequently forced to barter. Besides dealing with the problem of how to utilize and control the local corps, the government was forced to decide which corps formation it would support and sanction in those situations where several corps competed for local control.

These problems were intensified when the "defense" corps were combined and developed from local groups into organizations covering wider areas. Such regional forces constituted a real threat to central authority. Such expansion was a logical develop- ment in the existing chaotic situation. As the conditions of disor- der expanded, the problems of defense, as well as the ambitions of local leaders, could not be confined to the home community; and the struggle for control of a community prompted the competi- tors to seek additional sources of strength outside their own community. The success of such expansion depended on more than the personal ambitions of a local corps chief; it required a higher degree of organization and a broader financial basis. Local corps were best able to grow into regional organizations when their leadership was linked with broader organizational elements in Chinese society. Two groups in particular were in a position to provide the framework of widespread organization; these were the scholar-gentry and the secret societies. These two groups represented different interests, reflecting the different positions of their members in the social structure. Although the interests of the gentry were not always in accord with the interests of the central government, the gentry were more inclined to defend the existing government because it guaranteed their privileged position. The secret societies, on the other hand, though some- times including gentry, drew their membership largely from the commoners. They aimed not merely at resisting the abuses of officialdom, but at overthrowing the government and setting up their own political organizations. Local and regional forces did not follow any clearly defined political alignment, however, partly because their membership and leadership were both drawn from various social strata, partly because ambitious leaders were mainly concerned with advancing their own positions.

The government could not prevent the establishment of such local and regional forces; neither could it crush them after their emergence. It could only hope to utilize them in such a way as to prevent any one of them from achieving a concentration of power which might overthrow the dynasty. Regional forces with an openly anti-dynastic policy presented the most immediate threat to the existence of the dynasty; in its struggle against these, the central government was willing to align itself with any forces that would aid in the struggle. Generally these were the regional armies under scholar-gentry sponsorship. To gain the support of these gentry-controlled armies, however, the government was forced to accept their essentially autonomous status and to bring their leaders into the ranks of higher officialdom. The process eliminated those forces which were in open rebellion against the dynasty, but it did not restore the monopoly of power to the central government.

The Nien Rebellion, the subject of this study, follows this general pattern of the nineteenth-century struggle between central and regional forces. The Nien first emerged as community defense groups and local bandits who exploited the prevailing conditions of distress and disorder; then in the 1850's they developed into a regional power unit in open rebellion against the central government. This development of Nien power and objectives was facilitated by secret-society affiliation and was promoted by clan leaders and members of the lower gentry who came into the organization. The government had no success in dealing with the Nien until it enlisted the aid of the Huai Army and other regional forces. Consequently, the eventual defeat of the Nien in 1867-68, while eliminating an immediate threat to the existence of the dynasty, was at the same time a further step in the consolidation of regional powers within the framework of the existing government.

The process by which local forces were combined and organized on a broader, regional level, and the government's efforts to handle these forces, present a complex problem, involving not only military, but also economic, political, social, and ideological factors. This study of the Nien Rebellion, by analyzing one phase of the struggle between regional and central power, helps to clarify the issues involved in the struggle as a whole.

Mr. Chiang has divided his study of the Nien Rebellion into two main parts; the first part deals with the emergence of the Nien regional force in open defiance of the government; the second with the measures adopted by the government to deal with the Nien. These two main parts are preceded by an introduction in which the author delineates the conditions of famine, insecurity, and official corruption which prevailed in the Huai-pei area in the 1850's.

In the first section of the first part Mr. Chiang traces the connections between the Nien and the famous White Lotus Society. It was this secret society relationship which gave the Nien a spirit of "national consciousness" and an objective greater than mere brigandage. This "greater enterprise" motivated a number of Nien bands to join together to raise the flag of rebellion in 1853. The program of rebellion required a tighter organization than existed in the scattered, elastic, and essentially independent Nien bands before 1853. The military aspect of the new Nien organization which emerged is discussed in the second section, and the territorial and economic aspects are treated in the third section. In organizing and consolidating their territorial domain, the Nien utilized two elements in the local situation: the local corps and the earthwall communities. The nature of the local corps has already been briefly discussed; it may also be useful for the general reader to note at this time that the so-called earthwall communities were simply villages surrounded by fortified earthen or brick walls which not only served as defense against bandit raids, but also made possible the storage of all the villages' agricultural products within a guarded enclosure so as to leave only barren fields for the plundering bandits. This use of walls was, of course, not new, but it had been particularly developed, under government promotion, in Anhwei as a measure to deal with the Taiping penetration into that province. When these earthwall communities came under Nien control, they became the basis of Nien defensive tactics; they also became the basic units in the decentralized Nien organization. Control over the earthwall communities could be secured by winning the allegiance of the local corps chiefs, but the retention of this control demanded the support of the peasants. To win this support the Nien assisted the people in their opposition to officials and brought in foodstuffs to relieve the sufferings of famine. These food supplies were obtained from raids on more prosperous neighboring areas and on government supplies.

Membership, and more particularly leadership, in the Nien organization is analyzed in the fourth section. In general, Nien leadership was drawn from the large clans and from the gentry. The gentry in particular contributed their experience in organizing and planning. The third major component in the Nien forces, the peasants, provided the bulk of manpower.

In the Nien system, looting was an essential operation, upon which the maintenance of both the Nien fighting forces and the home communities partly depended. It was consequently natural for the Nien to emphasize their cavalry. The sources from which the Nien procured their horses is discussed in section five, and

viii

the manner in which the cavalry was used in the offensive tactics of the Nien is discussed in the following section.[1] This latter section also examines the way in which the earthwalls were utilized as the basis of Nien defensive tactics, and emphasizes the dual nature of a Nien band--its function as both a military and an agricultural unit.

The second part of this study is concerned with the efforts and eventual success of the loyalists in crushing the rebellious force of the Nien. The term "loyalist" is used to designate any force which operated in support of the existing regime; it includes, therefore, both central and regional forces. The first two sections deal with the fruitless military and political policies adopted by the government before 1865 in its effort to return the Nien domain to central control. The failure of the central government forces on the military front showed the general decay and ineffectiveness of these regular forces; it also reflected a lack of understanding of the nature and source of Nien strength. Nien power was manifested in the defensive strength of the earthwalls and in the mobile striking power of the cavalry; the true base of this power, however, was the support of the peasants. Even when the government forces were successful in driving the Nien out of their "nests," they could not win the support of the people in those areas. Even in areas to which Nien control had not yet extended, the government was generally unsuccessful in its efforts to gain local support. This last aspect of the struggle between the government and the Nien is discussed in the third section, in which Mr. Chiang examines the "policy of pardon" which was adopted in an attempt to win to the government's side the rebellious leaders of local forces. The author shows how this policy created the danger of rear attacks on the government forces which were advancing to attack the Nien. Furthermore, it increased the jealousy and rivalry which existed between the Imperial forces and the regional forces which were in a position to give assistance to the loyalist cause.

The appointment of Tseng Kuo-fan as Imperial Commissioner in 1865 and the entrance into the Nien conflict of the Huai regional army, which had been organized under Tseng, mark the beginning of a new phase in the Nien problem, a phase which ended with the suppression of the rebels in 1867 and 1868. This last part of the Nien story is discussed in the fourth and fifth chapters of the second part. Here Mr. Chiang emphasizes the significance of Tseng's policy of converting the Nien "nests" to the loyalist cause,

---

1. The mobility of the Nien forces is a special point of study in the work of Lo Erh-kang, Nien-chün yün-tung-chan, which was not available at the time Mr. Chiang wrote his thesis.

of using the earthwalls to resist the return of the Nien, and of incorporating the loyal inhabitants into the Huai Army. It was the Huai Army which largely accomplished the suppression of the Nien. Since the Huai Army was a regional force, however, its triumph did not indicate any rejuvenation of the declining power of the dynasty. Furthermore this triumph did not solve the problems which gave rise to rebellious outbursts, as subsequent rebellions were soon to testify.

For the general reader who has not had a previous occasion to consider the Nien Rebellion, a brief chronicle of the main events may be of value.

In the winter of 1852-53 a group of Nien leaders gathered at Chih-ho, near the junction of the three provinces, Honan, Anhwei, and Kiangsu; here they conducted a sacrifice to a flag and proclaimed Chang Lo-hsing as their leader. This action marked the beginning of the Nien "rebellion." Before this time the activities of the Nien "bandits" had not differed significantly from those of other outlaw groups engaged in general brigandage in various parts of China.

The 1853 concentration of Nien forces at Chih-ho drew official attention to that spot, and in the following year troops under the prefect of Ying-chou dispersed the Nien. At this time Chang Lo-hsing, along with several other Nien leaders, surrendered to the assistant commissioner of the Anhwei local corps. Chang was pardoned and granted a post in the local corps. This defeat and the removal of their newly chosen leader did not, however, seriously deter the other Nien leaders, who continued to strengthen their local positions and to expand their forces. In the early part of 1855 Chang Lo-hsing, following the disbandment of the local corps which he had commanded, returned to Chih-ho and resumed activities with the Nien. Chang's return stimulated the development of the Nien organization. In 1856 the Nien leaders established a systematic military organization, and in the same year conferred on Chang Lo-hsing the title, "Lord of the Alliance." This development in military organization and leadership facilitated the expansion of Nien activities during the next few years. The Nien intensified their looting raids throughout the neighboring areas. They cooperated with the Taipings in Anhwei, helping the latter to capture Liu-an and to occupy a number of cities along the Huai River. Most significantly, Chang Lo-hsing succeeded in building up a tightly knit domain in the area north of the Huai River; in this region the Nien concentrated on winning the support of the people and on gaining control of the local corps organizations. By 1859 the region between the Hui and Sha rivers had been integrated into a solid defensive core. Concurrent with the expansion of Chang Lo-hsing's power in the central part of the Huai-pei (that is the area north of the Huai River), another force under an ambitious local corps chief, Miao P'ei-lin, was wresting the southeastern part of the area from Imperial control. In 1857 Miao erected earthwalls at Hsia-ts'ai, a town north of Shou-chou; from here his influence radiated until it encompassed more than three thousand communities.

When it became evident that the disturbances in the Huai-pei area were too large to be handled by any one of the infested provinces, the government attempted to effect a cooperative policy. In 1855 Wu-lung-o was appointed provincial commander in chief for the three provinces, Anhwei, Kiangsu, and Honan. While Wu-lung-o procrastinated and petitioned for more troops, the Nien seized the offensive. Wu-lung-o fled before the advancing rebels; he lost five districts in ten days. The command of the provincial forces was then entrusted to the governor of Honan, Ying-kuei, assisted by Yüan Chia-san. In the middle of 1856 the government troops succeeded in taking Chih-ho, the center of the Nien domain, but were soon pushed out again by returning Nien forces. A second attempt to penetrate the Nien domain was even less successful.

In 1856 the Manchu general, Sheng-pao, was sent out to suppress the Nien. However, Sheng-pao never set foot in the Nien central domain. Between 1856 and 1859 he concentrated his efforts to retake the cities along the Huai which were jointly occupied by the Nien and the Taipings. In 1860 he was placed in charge of the military affairs of Honan. In the period between 1856 and 1862 the actual command of the troops from the three provinces rested with Yüan Chia-san, who was first director of military affairs at the Honan-Anhwei border, later director of pacifying affairs of the three provinces.

In 1860 the Mongol prince, Seng-ko-lin-ch'in, was sent out as Imperial Commissioner for military affairs dealing with the Nien; he did not arrive in the Huai-pei area, however, until the autumn of 1862. Seng-ko-lin-ch'in interpreted Nien strength largely in terms of their highly developed cavalry; his own policy empha- sized pursuit, for which he built up his own cavalry strength. This policy achieved temporary success; in the early part of 1863 the Nien were driven from the Huai-pei area, and a number of Nien leaders, including Chang Lo-hsing, were captured and killed. Seng-ko-lin-ch'in did not have a chance to consolidate his victories, however, because a new outburst of "bandits" in Shantung drew him away from the Huai-pei area. The Mongol prince's absence gave the Nien an opportunity to regroup their forces and to re- occupy their old territory under the leadership of Chang Tsung-yü, a nephew of Chang Lo-hsing. A few months later Seng-ko-lin-ch'in returned to the Huai-pei area, this time to put down an insurrec- tion led by Miao P'ei-lin, who in 1862 had gone over to the side of the government after betraying the Taiping leaders with whom he

had associated himself. In the latter part of 1863 Seng-ko-lin-ch'in
defeated Miao's forces, killed Miao himself, and for the second
time cleaned up northern Anhwei. From here he pursued the Nien
across the borders of Anhwei, Honan, Hupeh, and Shantung.
Although he recaptured several cities and killed some of the Nien
leaders, he achieved no decisive victory. The rebels had developed to a high degree the elusive tactics of ambush and evasion.
In 1864 the Nien inflicted a crushing blow on Seng-ko-lin-ch'in's
forces in the Honan-Hupeh border area, and then led the prince on
an exhausting chase into Shantung. Here, in May 1865, Seng-ko-
lin-ch'in's forces were ambushed and the prince himself was
killed. Seng-ko-lin-ch'in's defeat marked the end of the first phase
of action against the Nien, the end of reliance upon the regular
government troops.

On hearing of the Shantung disaster, the court sent a hurried
mandate ordering Tseng Kuo-fan, distinguished for his recent
work in suppressing the Taipings, to proceed from Nanking to
Shantung to deal with the Nien. Tseng's arrival in Shantung
heralded a new approach to the Nien problem -- the use of loyalist
regional forces to fight a rebellious regional force. Tseng, now
in supreme command of military affairs in Chihli, Shantung, and
Honan, established his headquarters at Tsi-ning in Shantung, and
proceeded to reorganize his forces. Having observed the results
of Seng-ko-lin-ch'in's policy of pursuit, Tseng emphasized the use
of stationary armies to contain the rebels. He closed the Nien out
of a large section of their old homeland by concentrating his
troops at four points -- one each in northern Anhwei, northern
Kiangsu, southern Shantung and western Honan -- and by connect-
ing these points with a system of defenses along the Chia-lu, Huai,
and Sha rivers and the Grand Canal. Within the area encircled by
this cordon, Tseng concentrated on winning back the support of
the people, because unlike his predecessors he realized that the
real basis of Nien strength was neither mobile cavalry nor their
defensive system of earthworks, but rather the loyalty of the
people. Huai-pei natives converted to the side of the government
were taken into the Huai Army, a regional army which had been
organized by Li Hung-chang under the direction of Tseng Kuo-fan
to fight the Taipings, and which had been brought into the Nien
struggle by Tseng. Tseng's policy of winning back the support of
the people and using them to fight against the rebels was not one
which could achieve the immediate elimination of the Nien.
Criticism from impatient officials compelled Tseng to resign his
command in December 1866. He recommended that Li Hung-chang
be his successor in the campaign against the Nien. Li continued
and expanded Tseng's system of defensive blockade; at the same
time he returned in part to Seng-ko-lin-ch'in's policy of pursuit.

From the latter part of 1865 on, the Nien had made a series

of desperate and unsuccessful attempts to break through the defenses and return to their homeland. A few months before Li's appointment as Imperial Commissioner to deal with the Nien, the rebels had been repulsed when they attempted to drive into southwestern Shantung. They then returned to Honan, where they divided into two main branches. One group followed Chang Tsung-yü into Shensi and was known as the West Nien. The other group, known as the East Nien, remained in Honan under Jen Chu and a former Taiping rebel, Lai Wen-kuang. In the middle of 1867 the East Nien, compelled by the need for supplies, broke through the northern part of the government's defense system and penetrated into eastern Shantung to plunder this area. Li Hung-chang then shifted his Grand Canal defense barriers from the east bank to the west bank. The Huai Army forces stationed along the canal joined with other loyalist forces along the Yellow River on the north, and along the Liu-t'ang River in the southeast, to enclose the Nien within the Shantung area. Within this blockade zone the Nien found little popular support, for it was an area which they had previously plundered in raids from their old domain in the west. The effective blockade made it impossible for them to escape the onslaughts of the cavalry led by Liu Ming-ch'uan. Four decisive battles fought in 1867 brought an end to the East Nien. Jen Chu was killed, but Lai Wen-kuang succeeded in escaping across the Liu-t'ang River with a few hundred men, only to be captured alive a month later in northeastern Anhwei.

After the division of the Nien forces in 1866, Chang Tsung-yü had advanced to Shensi, where he apparently hoped to join with the Moslem rebels in that province. Disappointed by the shortage of provisions there, and threatened by loyalist forces under Tso Tsung-t'ang, Chang turned eastward, crossed the Yellow River into Shansi, and then in the first month of 1868 slipped into Chihli and reached the suburbs of Tientsin. To defend the endangered capital from the invaders, the government concentrated a formidable force which pushed the Nien down from the north. Again a blockade was thrown up, this time with the Grand Canal on the west and the Yellow River to the south. Within this trap the combined loyalist forces moved in and crushed the last of the Nien.

Far Eastern and Russian Institute   Renville Lund
March, 1953

TABLE OF CONTENTS

LIST OF MAPS

THE NIEN REBELLION

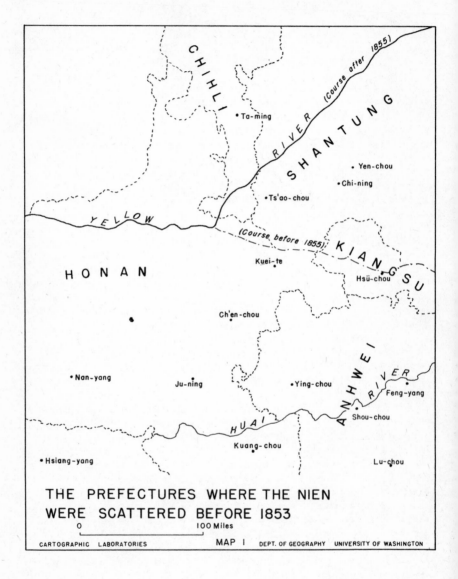

CHIHLI

• Ta-ming

RIVER (Course after 1855)

SHANTUNG

• Yen-chou

• Chi-ning

• Ts'ao-chou

YELLOW

(Course before 1855)

KIANGSU

Kuei-te

Hsü-chou

HONAN

Ch'en-chou

• Nan-yang

Ju-ning

• Ying-chou

ANHWEI RIVER

Feng-yang

Shou-chou

HUAI

Kuang-chou

Lu-chou

• Hsiang-yang

THE PREFECTURES WHERE THE NIEN
WERE SCATTERED BEFORE 1853

0   100 Miles

CARTOGRAPHIC   LABORATORIES   MAP 1   DEPT. OF GEOGRAPHY   UNIVERSITY OF WASHINGTON

INTRODUCTION

1. The Outbreak of Rebellions in the Late Ch'ing Dynasty

The Manchus, who were the last of the dynastic rulers in the
long history of China, represented the culmination of autocratic
imperial rule. The authority of the Ch'ing government, centralized
as it was supposed to have been, never attained perfect centraliza-
tion. It was always potentially open to challenge by regional forces,
even in the earlier days of the dynasty, and as soon as it began to
show signs of decay and weakness, these forces more or less
openly contested for a share of the splendor and wealth which the
imperial government sought to monopolize. These regional forces,
it should be noted, were not merely politico-military complexes.
They had their roots in the social and economic conditions of imperial China. In the primary stages of their growth, they might
take widely different forms, appearing as local "bandits," secret
societies, unruly clans, or even as powerful local officials. But
whatever their bases and forms, they pointed to one important
historical fact: the perennial struggle between central and regional
forces. The Nien (捻) Rebellion, one of several uprisings in nineteenth-century China and the subject of the present study, repre-
sents one phase in this struggle.

The hundred years of peace and prosperity between the suppression of the San Fan (三藩) Rebellion in 1681 and the rising of
the White Lotus (Pai-lien-chiao) bandits in 1796 marked the zenith
of Manchu rule; however, in the latter part of this period the downward course from the peak began. The vitality which had characterized the newly risen Manchus had begun to diminish. Long years
of leisurely and luxurious life inside the Great Wall had emascu-
lated the Banner Army, once an invincible force on which the
Manchu rulers relied for the seizure and continued control of
their Empire. A rapid increase in population threatened the
thriving economy which had succeeded the great upheaval of the
seventeenth century. The ruling machine was rotting from within.
Maladministration destroyed the people's confidence in the capa-
bility and good will of the rulers.

The White Lotus Rebellion already had proved almost too
tremendous for the waning dynasty. During the early years of the
nineteenth century, no signs of regeneration were to be seen. A
general explosion of revolts, ten times more formidable than that
of the White Lotus, occurred in the early eighteen fifties: the

1

Taipings in Kwangsi, the Northwest Moslems in Shensi and Kansu, the Southwest Moslems in west Kweichow and Yunnan, the Miao (苗) and I (彞) in Kweichow, the Eight Diagrams sect (Pa-kua-chiao) in south Shantung, and the Nien in the Huai (淮) Valley.

The Nien was but one wave of the uproaring tide which struck the crumbling sea wall of Manchu rule. As an element in the whole movement, the Nien shared with their contemporaries, as well as with former rebellious groups, certain methods of building power, particularly the organization of local forces into larger regional groupings. In other words, they expanded their influence to a broader area and proceeded to a higher organizational level. However, as an independent group they possessed some charac-teristics of their own, and as such, are deserving of a special study.

2. The Background of the Nien Rebellion

The Huai-pei (淮北) area, the area north of the Huai River, was the central dominion of the Nien "bandits" from 1853 to 1865. Before 1853, the "bad people" under the name of Nien were scattered widely in the districts (chou or hsien) under the pre-fectures (fu) of Hsü-chou in Kiangsu; Ying-chou, Feng-yang, and Lu-chou in Anhwei; Nan-yang, Ju-chou, Kuang-chou, Ch'en-chou and Kuei-te in Honan; Yen-chou, I-chou, Ts'ao-chou and Tsi-ning in Shantung; Ta-ming in Chihli; and Hsiang-yang in Hupeh.[1] These areas were located along the respective frontiers of the various provinces, but if the artificial boundary lines of the provinces were removed, the areas would be found to lie in the heart of China proper. The greater part of them were situated in the North China Plain.

The ascendancy of the Nien in Huai-pei, after 1853, made that area the central territory of the Nien, and consequently attracted people's attention to that corner. Huai-pei lies in the southern margin of the North China Plain. In Huai-nan, that is, the area south of the Huai River, the soil is finer, and because it contains more clay, it is similar to that of the Yangtze Plain. In Huai-pei, north of the river, on the other hand, the soil is sandy and con-sists of the deposits of the ancient Yellow River. Topographically the Huai-pei belongs with the dry millet and kaoliang area to the north. Thus the boundary between the North China Plain and the Yangtze Plain is placed slightly north of the Huai River. The fact that Huai-pei, the homeland of the Nien, belongs to the North China Plain is the key for any understanding of the nature of the

---

1. P'ing-ting Yüeh-k'ou chi-lüeh, 3/34; Wang Ting-an, Hsiang-chün chi, 16/1. See map.

Nien organization. They were rebels of the northern type.[2] For example, they shared the practices of the White Lotus sect and its branches, whose influence prevailed in the north rather than the south. The Nien emphasized the use of cavalry on a large scale. This practice was another peculiar trait shown only by the northern rebels. This was possible because in the Huai-pei Plain, no great mountains and, after 1855, no great rivers stood in the way.

In comparison with Huai-nan, that is, the territory south of the Huai, Huai-pei was a poor area. As a part of the North China Plain, it shared the inadequate rainfall of that area. In times of drought, the land looked like a semidesert. Often the rainfall was so intense that the otherwise dry watercourses overflowed. Owing to the flatness of the area and the high water table, drainage was poor. Sometimes both drought and flood took place in the same year. In addition, the destructive Yellow River, with its muddy torrents, passed through the middle of the Huai-pei region. Floods from that river recurred throughout the years 1851-1853, covering south Shantung, north Kiangsu and north Anhwei.[3] In the sixth month of 1855, after twenty days of hard rain, the flood of the Yellow River wrecked the dike at T'ung-wa-hsiang (銅瓦廂) in Honan.[4] From there the river flowed northward and combined with the Ta-ch'ing (大清) River before emptying into the sea. At the head, where the river bent to the north, there was no definite basin for the newly shifted river. Water overwhelmed an area thirty li wide in the districts of P'u-chou and Fan-hsien. All villages and towns in the flood area were buried in water.

Drought and flood meant famine, and famine bred agitation for revolt. During the early fifties, famine dominated the Huai Valley.[5] It was in 1851 and 1852 that the members of the Nien Society became unusually active, and finally in 1853, at the point where Ying-chou, Po-chou, Meng-ch'eng, and Su-chou adjoin, the Nien formally raised the flag of rebellion.[6] In response to the Nien, hundreds of thousands of displaced people in the Yellow River flood area in south Shantung indulged in banditry, offering themselves as guides to the Nien who were expanding their routes of plundering in that direction.[7]

---

2. Sano Manabu in his Nomin bodo emphatically points out this character. (Shin-cho Shakai-shi, Nomin bodo, 2/30.)

3. Shantung chün-hsing chi-lüeh, 17A/1-2.

4. Ibid., 2A/2-3; Chiao-p'ing Nien-fei fang-lüeh (hereafter referred to as Fang-lüeh), 122/4; 138/12-13.

5. Fang-lüeh, 2/15.

6. Wo-yang feng-t'u chi, 15/8-9; Ch'io-shan hsien-chih, 20/7-8.

7. Huang-ch'ao ching-shih wen hsü-p'ien, 10/9; Shantung chün-hsing chi-lüeh, 2A/2-3; Fang-lüeh, 138/12-13; 230/20.

Natural calamities found in the misgovernment of the local
authorities a partner in provoking the Nien's uprising. In view of
the general decay of the Manchu rule, local maladministration was
nothing strange. According to the censors' accusations, it seemed
that most of the local magistrates in Huai-pei could not escape
from two failings: They were either corrupt, or, if honest, lenient
and incompetent. In 1851 a Nien insurrection occurred in the districts under the Nan-yang prefecture in Honan. The prefect dared
not report the case to the provincial governor until it could no
longer be concealed; the governor, in the same fashion, reported
to the central government only after one year had passed.[8] The
magistrate of Meng-ch'eng led troops to arrest one of the Nien
leaders, but the expedition boomeranged; the magistrate himself
was captured by the Nien.[9] The magistrate of Po-chou, Chang
Ch'ing-yüan (張清元), was charged in 1853 by Yüan Chia-san
(袁甲三)[10] (then commissioner in charge of the military affairs
in Anhwei with the title of censor) with twice irritating the people
to the verge of revolt.[11] When Imperial Commissioner Chou T'ien-
chüeh (周天爵)[12] died at the town of Wang-shih (王市) in 1853,
Chang, according to Yüan, took the liberty of disbanding Chou's
militia in opposition to the wishes of the inhabitants. Since the
provincial frontiers were usually beyond the direct control of the
governors, the adjacent areas of the provinces provided the Nien
with a paradise of opportunities.[13] Even though the provincial
authorities occasionally intensified the suppression of the Nien on
the frontiers, it was very convenient for the Nien to seek safety
by crossing the border to another province, whose governor
seldom bothered to intervene in his neighbor's business. Censor
Chang Feng-shan (張鳳山), therefore, reminded the central
government of the need for the provincial authorities concerned
to take joint action.[14] As a rule, the central government referred
such recommendations to the governors, who simply answered
that they were devoting every effort to the performance of their
duty. That was all. The "joint action" ended at this point.

---

8. Fang-lüeh, 1/4-5, 25. The prefect, not daring to arrest the
Nien leader, seized a tanner with the same name and sent him to the
provincial capital. The governor, though aware of the falsity of
the prefect's accusation, did not punish his under-official until a
year later when the Nien had spread their looting, and the news had
been disclosed to the central government.
9. Hsü-hsiu Meng-ch'eng hsien-chih, 6/4.
10. 1806-1863. Hummel, Eminent Chinese of the Ch'ing Period,
pp. 948-949.
11. Yüan Chia-san, Yüan Tuan-min-kung chi, Memorials, 2/33.
12. Chin-shih of 1811, d. 1853. Hummel, p. 779.
13. Fang-lüeh, 2/11.
14. Ibid., 1/7.

It was said that the magistrate of Huo-ch'iu, Anhwei, even had "treacherous intercourse" with the top Nien leader, Chang Lo-hsing (張樂行).[15] Across the border to east Honan, the magistrate of Lo-shan, Lei Yüan-chao (雷遠照), respected a Nien leader as his sworn brother, while the provincial commander in chief, Po-shan (博山), received from the Nien a bribe of seven thousand liang of silver. Other magistrates such as Chao Teng-chün (趙登駿) of Kuang-chou and Ch'en T'ang (陳棠) of Hsi-hsien did the same.[16] Beneath the magistrates, the yamen-runners had even closer association with the Nien. In the event that the local governments attempted to arrest the Nien leaders, the runners informed them beforehand, thus enabling them to escape or to prepare armed resistance.[17] The chief runner of Hsi-hsien adopted as his son a Nien leader; and the magistrate of Kuang-chou, Chao Teng-chün, hired a Nien leader as chief runner in order to safeguard Chao's own family and property.[18] When the Hsi-hsien troops were besieging the Nien under Li Shih-lin (李士林), the runners of that district deceived the magistrate, Ch'en T'ang, by telling him that this band of Nien had been pardoned by the governor-general of Liang-Hu. The Nien were thus spared annihilation.[19] Ch'eng Ta (程達), a Nien leader of Kuang-shan, took refuge in Lo-shan, where two chief detectives of the local government recommended him as a runner.[20] Most of the above cases are found in the memorials of the Imperial censors. Since irresponsible exaggerations based on mere rumors were not rare, these accounts should be accepted with caution. For example, Ch'en T'ang in one place was accused of receiving bribes from the Nien, but in another he was reported to have led a troop to besiege them. However, the existence of a secret association between the Nien and the yamen-runners in the prerebellion period is indisputable. The governor-general of Liang-Kiang, the governor of Kiangsu, and the governor of Honan all admitted this relationship.[21]

Frequently famine haunted the Huai Valley and banditry would appear in its wake. The tide of the Nien's activity rose and ebbed according to the varying economic pressure from year to year.[22] Since the early nineteenth century, stories about the Nien had appeared in official documents. But the situation which gave rise to the Nien's insurrection in defiance of the existing regime, was

15. Wo-yang feng-t'u chi, 15/12.
16. Fang-lüeh, 6/25-27.
17. Ibid., 1/19-20; 2/6-7.
18. Ibid., 6/25-27.
19. Fang-lüeh, 6/21-22.
20. Ibid., 16/28-29.
21. Ibid., 1/19-20; 2/6-7.
22. Huang Chün-tsai, Chin-hu ch'i-mo, 4/4.

new. In the second month of 1853, the Taiping rebels captured Anking, provincial capital of Anhwei. The Nien in Su-chou, Meng-ch'eng, Po-chou and Shou-chou organized, in response to the triumphant Taipings several hundred li to the south of them, no less than thirty bands. [23] In the fifth month of that year the Taiping expeditionary detachments under Li K'ai-fang (李開芳) and Lin Feng-hsiang (林鳳翔) started from Yangchow, smashed all resistance in their way to the Huai, and captured Feng-yang and Huai-yüan, from which they crossed the Huai. "Wherever they arrived, they were hostile to the officials. To the common people they were harmless. The trading fairs continued to flourish. "[24] The fall of Kuei-te, Honan, to the Taipings encouraged the Nien to raid the city of Yung-ch'eng, and also to rebel in large groups in other districts of that province. [25] In the Ying-chou and Po-chou area, the peasants, whom the officials usually presumed to be timid and peace-loving, banded themselves together in order to plunder along the highways. [26]

The upheaval resulting from the Taipings' arrival in the lower Yangtze basin provoked the Nien Rebellion, an uprising which had been engendered by recurrent economic difficulties and aggravated by traditional administrative corruption long before 1853.

---

23. Wang K'ai-yün, Hsiang-chün chih, 14/1; Shantung chün-hsing chi-lüeh, 2A/2; Fang-lüeh, 3/1.
24. Wo-yang feng-t'u chi, 15/8-10.
25. Fang-lüeh, 3/19.
26. Ibid., 5/15.

6

PART I. THE ORGANIZATION OF THE NIEN

1. The Background of the Nien

The word nien (捻 or 撚) in some cases means a roll of twisted paper strips. Dipped with oil, such a roll can be lighted and will flame like a torch. When celebrating the Chinese New Year, people usually displayed dragon lanterns to drive away the plague demon and lighted paper rolls within the bamboo skeleton of the dragon lanterns. From this usage some storytellers inferred that the Nien bandits must have had their origin in the gathering of a group of people who displayed the dragon lanterns.[1] Some say that the Nien were a gang of "vagrants" who lighted nien-tzu or paper strips when they set out to plunder.[2] Both of these interpretations are based on the assumption that the word nien indicated a roll of twisted paper strips. Both are guesswork. The real reason why the Nien adopted such a queer name remains obscure.

But one thing is definite and worthy of attention, especially in the discussion of the Nien organization. That is the application of the term nien to units of the Nien bands -- one band was called one nien, regardless of its size.[3] One can find a parallel terminology in the "Club Bandits" (Kun-fei 棍匪) who called the unit of their bands fu (幅),[4] meaning a strip of cloth. Therefore the Kun-fei

---

1. Wang Ting-an, Hsiang-chün-chi, 16/1.
2. Wang K'ai-yün, 14/1.
3. Huang Chün-tsai, Chin-hu ch'i-mo, 4/4; Fang-lüeh, 1/26.
4. Along the great canal, there were several hundred thousand irregular sailors earning a living from the grain tribute fleet. Since the tribute transportation was changed from the canal to the sea as a result of the Taiping Rebellion, these laborers were thrown out of work. Banditry became their natural alternative as an occupation. These sailor-bandits were the so-called Fu-fei. The word fu, like nien, is a mysterious expression and many explanations have been worked out to clarify it. Someone surmises that fu was a strip of cloth with which these bandits bound their heads. (Shantung chün-hsing chi-lüeh, 17A/1) But I do not think this is a satisfactory explanation. Other bandits used kerchiefs to bind their heads, too. (I shall discuss the red turban of the Nien in a later part of this section.) If I am allowed to make a guess, I shall take this word fu as a term used to indicate a unit, similar to the use of the word nien, because fu is a unit of cloth. It is likely that the Fu-fei called each of their bands one fu, and then the outsiders called them Fu-fei. In the official code of criminal

were at the same time called Fu-fei. A number of sources have
the same explanation for the word nien being used as a name of
unit. "The brigands combined themselves into a band, called Nien,
swearing to enjoy the same benefits and to suffer the same calamities. "[5] The Nien "associated several members into one nien,
or thirty or even over a hundred into a big nien. "[6] Nien originally
meant "to knead" (揑) or "to pinch. "[7] The character 揑 is pronounced "nieh, " phonetically close to nien which is sometimes also
pronounced as "nieh. " According to the Honan t'ung-chih, nien
indicates the way in which the Nien bands were assembled. The
Nien gathered their members into bands in the same way as
"people knead something together in their palms, but discover that
it breaks up as soon as the hand releases it."[8] This is the fashion
in which the Nien organized themselves. Here is a possible explanation as to why the bandits called the organizational unit of
their bands nien.

This elaboration on the word nien is not prompted by interest
in matters of terminology, but because a correct knowledge of its
meaning facilitates the understanding of the Nien's primary form.
The action described by nien, "to knead," indicates their unique
manner of organizing their fighting forces. Before the loosely
"pinched" bands advanced to a tighter organization, there was a
long and difficult road to travel. Even after the later military
system had come into being, traits inherited from the earlier
stage still lingered on. Hence this term not only implied the manner, but also conditioned the development of the Nien organization.

One should not be misled, however, to expect that from this
word one can trace the origin of the Nien. For that, one must look
elsewhere. For example, what do the similarities between the
Nien and other secret societies tell of the Nien origins?

In the next chapter one will see that the Nien entitled their
leader "Great Han Prince with the Heavenly Mandate" (Ta-Han-
ming-ming-wang 大漢明命王). This title implies that the Nien
defied the Manchu Emperor not only as a ruler but as a non-
Chinese ruler. It is unlikely that national consciousness could
have existed among a mere mob of rural bandits who could do
nothing but light rolls of twisted paper while carrying on robbery.

---

law, the government used the words, "結 幅 ," chieh fu (meaning
that people associated themselves into fu), to describe the behavior of the Fu Society. If fu had signified any headgear of the
bandits, the word chieh or "to associate" could not have been pre-
fixed to it.

    5. Ibid., 320/4.
    6. Ibid., 1/26; 4/17; Wang K'ai-yün, 16/1.
    7. P'ing-ting Yüeh-k'ou chi-lüeh, 3/34-35; Honan t'ung-chih,
73/1861; Ch'ing-pai-lei-ch'ao, 7/9.
    8. Honan t'ung-chih, chüan 73.

8

The same national consciousness existed in some "religious bandits" in Shantung. In 1861 the government officers happened to find in their war booty two seals used by the "religious bandits." On one of them the bandits had engraved four characters, hsing-han-mieh-hu (興漢滅胡), "to revive the Chinese and to eradicate the barbarians (Manchu)"; on the other they had engraved sao-Ch'ing-li-Ming (掃清立明), "to sweep away the Manchu to reestablish the Ming."[9] In the same manner the bandits of Tzu-ch'uan, Shantung, proclaimed their leader "Prince of Han" (Han-wang 漢王).[10] These bandits were not spontaneously organized. They were led by the secret societies originating from the White Lotus sect.[11] Can the Nien, who were also characterized by national consciousness, be similarly classified as a secret society?

Among a number of various secret societies which were located in the area where Shantung, Honan, and Chihli adjoin, there was one called Nieh-tzu-hui (捏子會).[12] According to the Ch'ing-pai lei-ch'ao, "Nien was nieh. Outlaws pinched themselves together into bands and called themselves 'Nien-tzu' (捻子)."[13] Insofar as "nien was nieh" and the Nien were also called Nien-tzu, Nieh-tzu-hui must be a variant name for the Nien organization.

As a secret society, did the Nien have any relationship with

9. Wen-hsien ts'ung-p'ien, 22/46.
10. Shantung chün-hsing chi-lüeh, 20A/6.
11. A Buddhist religious society, named the White Lotus, existed in China in early times. A certain member, bearing the clerical name of Hui-yüan (慧遠) (d. 416), was generally regarded as the founder of the society. To cultivate religious perfection, the members settled somewhere in the Lu (廬) Mountains. The reason they called their friary by the name of White Lotus is described as follows: "Hsieh Lin-yün (謝靈運) arrived in the Lu Mountains, and no sooner had he met with Hui-yüan than he respectfully yielded himself to him, heart and soul. He then built a terrace close to the monastery, translated there the Nirvana-Sutra, and dug a pond, in which he planted white lotus flowers. On this account, Hui-yüan and his sages, who at that time devoted themselves to salvation in the land of Purity, were called the White Lotus Community. [Lien-she kao-hsien chuan (蓮社高賢傳), p. 1.] But the White Lotus sect did not come into being until the beginning of the Southern Sung dynasty. A certain Buddhist monk of Wu-chün (Su-chou), Mao Tzu-yüan by name, started this sect, holding to asceticism. As time passed on, persecutions from the government and other rival sects transformed its doctrines and practices. [Shigematsu Shunsho 重松俊章 , "The White Lotus Sect in its Opening Period," translated by T'ao Hsi-sheng (陶希聖), published in the semimonthly Shih-huo, I, 4, pp. 27-28.] In subsequent dynasties, one rebellion after another was led by the White Lotus sect against the oppressing authorities.
12. Suemitsu Takayoshi, Shina no nimitsu kessha to juzen kessha, p. 123.
13. Ch'ing-pai lei-ch'ao, 7/149.

the White Lotus? In the exact areas where the Nien were scattered,
(Ying-chou, Po-chou, Hsü-chou, Kuei-te, Ts'ao-chou, I-chou and
Yen-chou) the following secret societies existed side by side: the
Shun-tao-hui (順刀會), the Hu-wei-pien (虎尾鞭), the Pa-kua-
chiao (八卦教) and the I-ho-ch'üan (義和拳).[14] The fact that the
Pa-kua-chiao, or the Eight Diagrams sect, and the I-ho-ch'üan,
or the Boxers, definitely originated from the White Lotus sect[15]
suggests that the Nieh-tzu Society must have had some connection
with the latter. Yüan Chia-san,[16] a government official dealing
with the Nien, wrote a memorial to the Emperor in 1854 saying
that the Nien leader, Chang P'eng (張鵬), had been preaching a
heretic creed for many years.[17] Yüan's accusation reveals that
the Nien Society contained some religious traits. But "heretic
creed" is still too vague a term to suggest the kind of religious
society to which the Nien belonged. A definite statement regarding
this can be found in the Chin-hu ch'i-mo, which makes clear the
relationship between the Nien and the White Lotus.

> ...there were some remnants of the White Lotus
> Sect, committing outrages and plundering. With their
> beards dyed red, they were called "Red Beard Bandits."
> Each band of them was given the name of nien. One nien
> included from ten to several hundred bandits. Since the
> reign of Chia-ch'ing, bandits of this type have been active.
> After an interval of several years of good harvest, they
> arose again on occasions of scarcity.[18]

Thus it appears that the Nien were the "remnants" of the White
Lotus. The tie between these two can further be confirmed by

14. I-ho-ch'üan chiao-men yüan-liu k'ao (義和拳教門源流考),
collected in Ch'üan-luan san-chung, p. 2.
15. Nagano Akira, Shina no shakai soshiki, p. 223.
16. 1806-1863. Hummel, pp. 948-949.
17. Fang-lüeh, 5/10.
18. Huang Chün-tsai, Chin-hu ch'i-mo, 4/4. Ch'en Kung-lu ac-
cepts both of the explanations, that is, "paper spills" and "to
pinch up people into a bundle," but does not point out the fact
that the Nien was a kind of secret society. (Chung-kuo chin-tai
shih, p. 202.) Kuo T'ing-i gets on the right track when he confines
the meaning of the word nien to a unit and definitely holds that
nien means a band. But Kuo still fails to make it clear that the
Nien was a secret society. (T'ai-p'ing t'ien-kuo shih-shih jih-
chih, Appendices, p. 120.) Li Ting-sheng, Fan Wen-lan, and Ts'ao
Po-han all ascertain that the Nien was a secret society but do not
trace its origin back to the White Lotus sect. (Li Ting-sheng,
Chung-kuo chin-tai shih, p. 76; Fan Wen-lan, Chung-kuo chin-tai
shih, p. 166; Ts'ao Po-han, Chung-kuo hsien-tai shih tu-peng, p.
15.) Sano Manabu admits that the Nien was a secret society but
asserts that it did not contain any element of heterodoxy. (Nomin
bodo, 2/30.)

some parallels concerning their locations and usages. At the end
of the Yüan dynasty (during the years 1350-1368), the rebellious
forces under the White Lotus standards prevailed in the area of
Hsü-chou (Kiangsu), Po-chou and Hao-chou (Anhwei) and Kuang-
chou (Honan).[19] This was exactly the area in which the Nien were
centered. In the same area, near Kuang-chou, the White Lotus
rebels in the Chia-ch'ing reign of the Ch'ing dynasty started their
preaching.[20] As noted above, the Nien dyed their beards red.[21]
Red was the favored color in the White Lotus Society. In the rebellion at the end of the Yüan, both the western and eastern White
Lotus rebels used red turbans as a sign, and called themselves
the "Red Army." It was this army which Chu Yüan-chang (朱元璋),
later the first emperor of the Ming dynasty, once joined.[22] At the
early stage of the Nien Rebellion, the red turbans were inherited
as badges.[23]

In their nine-year rebellion in the Chia-ch'ing reign, the
White Lotus adopted an art of fighting which was copied by the Nien
fifty years later. The "religious bandits in the 1790's were a military force with a capacity for great mobility. After securing their
recruits and provisions wherever they looted, they always avoided
combat with the pursuing government armies, but never let slip
any chance of raiding the government armies' weak points."[24]
The Nien followed this pattern well and increased their mobility
by stressing mounted troops.

(The Nien and the White Lotus also had something in common
with regard to practices. Since this is related to the Nien organization, we shall deal with it in the next chapter.)

The border areas of Anhwei, Honan, Shantung and Kiangsu
contained many types of secret societies besides the Nien and the

---

19. Han Lin-erh was an inhabitant of Luan-ch'eng. His ancestors had been condemned to perpetual exile because they had
seduced the people to burn incense in White Lotus communities; and
when the Yüan dynasty was drawing to a close, his father, called
Shan-t'ung, had loudly proclaimed abroad the ominous assertion that
a great disturbance was about to break out in the Empire, and that
the Buddha Maitreya would be born in this world. In Honan and the
country between the Yangtze and the Huai, the people generally
believed him. A person from Ying-chou, called Liu Hu-t'ung, spread
the report that Shan-t'ung was a descendant in the eighth degree
from Emperor Hui-tsung of the Sung dynasty, and therefore the
appointed lord of the Empire. Then they took up arms against the
rule of the Yüan in 1350. (Ming-shih, pp. 122-123.)
20. Wei Yüan, Sheng-wu chi, 9/1.
21. Also see Fang-lüeh, 2/6; 320/4.
22. Ming-shih, 1, 2, 3, 122, 123.
23. Yüan Chia-san, Yüan Tuan-min-kung chi, Memorials, 2/32;
3/10; Fang-lüeh, 7/1-3.
24. Huang-ch'ao ching-shih wen-p'ien, 139/21-22.

11

aforementioned Eight Diagrams sect and the Boxers. Among these were the Ta-ch'eng-chiao (大乘教), the Ju-i-chiao (如意教), the Ch'ing-men-chiao (清門教), and the Pai-yang-chiao (白陽教). Their origins can all be traced back to the White Lotus.[25] The Eight Diagrams sect[26] had once been called the Society of the Rules of Heaven (T'ien-li-hui 天理會). This change of title did not indicate any internal transformation in the secret societies. It only served as a clever means to confuse the persecuting government. The History of the Chinese Secret Societies has a good comment in this respect.

> After the defeat of Hsü Hung-ju, the rebellious leader in 1625, the White Lotus Society continued to exist under divergent titles, namely, the "Rules of Heaven," the "White Feather," the "White Incense," the "Eight Diagrams"... In face of the severe persecution of the government, they made efforts to confuse the outside world by changing their names from time to time. [27]

It thus seems possible that the Nien Society was one of the branches of the White Lotus, only under the guise of a different name.

In 1801 the government enacted a supplementary article to the law against heresy:

> Those who propagate the heresies of the White Yang, the White Lotus, the Eight Diagrams, and such sects... shall be condemned to strangulation... The accessories ...shall all be sent to the Mohammedan cities... And persons over sixty, who have been tempted to practice that religion...shall be sent for everlasting banishment to the regions in Yunnan, Kweichow, Kwangtung, or Kwangsi, where malaria prevails.... [28]

The same legislation was applied to the Nien. Huang Chün-tsai assumes that 1814 was the year when the Nien arose.[29] But Wang K'ai-yün sets an earlier period, the K'ang-hsi reign (1662-

---

25. Nagano Akira, Shina no shakai soshiki, p. 223.
26. The Eight Diagrams sect was also called the Lung-hua Society (P'ing-ting chiao-fei chi-lüeh, 26/24.) The Lung-hua monastery was in the neighborhood of Shanghai. It existed before the eleventh century. Later it possessed, in the northwestern corner, a building for the White Lotus religion. (Ku-chin t'u-shu chi-ch'eng, chüan 109.)
27. Hirayama Amane, Chung-kuo pi-mi she-hui shih, pp. 2-6.
28. Ta-Ch'ing lü-li hui-chi Pien-lan, 16/5-6.
29. Huang Chün-tsai, Chin-hu ch'i-mo, 4/4.

1722), as the founding time of the Nien Society.[30] It was not until the Chia-ch'ing reign (1796-1820), however, that the government issued a special edict against those who associated into Nien bands and laid a heavy penalty upon any gathering of three or more persons.[31] In Ying-chou, Anhwei, the government passed regulations stating that any Nien organization which had over three members and who harmed people with weapons would be sentenced to banishment, or its members would be sent to the remote frontiers.[32] Except for specifying the number of the members, the text of this article was merely a repetition of the law of 1801 against the White Lotus. The fact that the Nien received the same treatment as the White Lotus not only displays the difference between the Nien and the ordinary local bandits but helps in establishing direct links between the Nien and the White Lotus.

To ascertain that the Nien was a secret society, a secret society with its origin in the seditious White Lotus, is a task of magnitude. In the first place, it is prerequisite to evaluating the significance of the Nien activities in the prerebellion years.

The Nien story before 1853 is obscure. Occasional narratives appear only in official reports concerning the Nien lawlessness. There are records of 1834 in the government's criminal code concerning Nien brigandage.[33] There are also recorded cases of extortion from civilians by the Nien. Prior to their formal uprising, they usually distributed a notice (t'ieh 帖) to the well-to-do inhabitants of their community as preliminary notification of their intention to collect tribute. This process had a special term, ting-ting (定釘).[34] Sometimes they kidnapped people and forced them to join their secret society. If the captives declined the offer of membership, they would not be released until they had paid the ransom demanded by the captors. Up to the early part of the Hsien-feng reign, cases of depredation involving the Nien continued to increase. One group seized the gates of a rural fair and barred traders until they had paid a fee for the right to pass.[35]

There is no way to distinguish the Nien from the ordinary local bandits who likewise engaged in kidnapping and plunder, unless the fact that the Nien were led by an insurgent secret society is counted. This fact leads us to infer that, for the Nien leaders, riches to be gained from robbery might not be an end but rather a means of inducing more people to join their group. They knew how to attract those who had a lust for gain and those who were compelled by poverty. Moreover, extortion of tribute was a

30. Wang K'ai-yün, 14/1.
31. Fang-lüeh, pp. 1-2; Wang Ting-an, Hsiang-chün chi, 16/1.
32. Fang-lüeh, 2/3.
33. Ibid., 1/1-2, 17-18.
34. Fang-lüeh, 1/17-18; Ta-Ch'ing hui-tien shih-li, chüan 133.
35. Fang-lüeh, 1/18.

common method practiced not only by the Nien but also by other secret societies[36] for raising funds to sustain their organizations.

Aside from robbery, cases of salt smuggling appear from time to time in official and semiofficial records concerning the Nien on the eve of the rebellion. The Nien archrebel, Chang Lo-hsing, was reported as a salt smuggler before 1853.[37] Outlaws of this type were usually called "salt owls." They carried on smuggling in the wide area between Tientsin in the north and Yangchow in the south, with the intersection of the Kiangsu, Anhwei, and Shangtung borders as the center. In the early years of Tao-kuang (the 1820's), Ying-chou, Anhwei was the haven for fleeing "owls."[38] There the "owls" and the Nien collaborated so closely   x that the government could not distinguish one from the other.[39] The salt smugglers, of course, can not be put in the same category as the religious bandits whose influence prevailed in the same area during that period. Their particular profession had already indicated the nature of their association. Yet Chang Lo-hsing was both a Nien leader and a salt smuggler. We do not know whether he was a Nien member first and then adopted the illegal traffic of salt as a means of livelihood because of his contact with the "owls," or whether he was first an "owl" and was then later converted to the Nien Society. Whatever the case, the cooperation between the Nien and the salt smugglers is an indisputable fact.

Since the Nien was a secret society, the Nien's engagement in contraband trade had an important effect. Salt smuggling provided the Nien leaders another outlet for expanding their organization. In pursuing such a dangerous business as salt smuggling, a man had to have a gang of fellow adventurers at his command. When the Nien and the smugglers were once united, the result was that the Nien leader who carried on the smuggling of salt had at his disposal a standing band of marauders, in addition to his fellow members of the Nien Society. In that period the government always held that Nien members were recruited from ignorant people who were deceived by the heretic cults and whose adherence to the Nien was unstable.[40] But no one could deny the devotion of the smugglers for whom association with the Nien promised immediate material benefit. This type of band, with a definite purpose and a permanent organization, was the backbone of the Nien as a fighting force. In shaping the Nien force into numerous bands of vigorous fighters, the gangs of smugglers played a decisive role.

36. Hsüan-tsung Ch'eng-huang-ti sheng-hsün, 84/7.
37. Wo-yang feng-t'u chi, 15/8-9.
38. Wang Hsien-ch'ien, Tung-hua lu, Tao-kuang, 6/9-10.
39. Hsüan-tsung Ch'eng-huang-ti sheng-hsün, 130/30; Hsü-hsiu Meng-ch'eng hsien-chih, 6/4.
40. Fang-lüeh, 6/3; 53/17-18; Shantung chün-hsing chi-lüeh, 2A/2; Ch'üan-an tsa-ts'un, collected in Ch'üan-luan san-chung, A, p.2.

The understanding of the Nien as a secret society descending from the White Lotus gives meaning not only to the prerebellion period activities which are described above but to the Nien activities on the eve of the rebellion.

As described in the Introduction, the relatively tranquil atmosphere in Huai-pei was broken up by recurring famine following Emperor Wen-tsung's accession to the throne in 1851. On the one hand, the Imperial administrative and military machinery deteriorated from within; on the other hand, discontent among the agrarian populace mounted higher and higher. Under these circumstances, a spark could kindle the wildfire of rebellion. Would the Nien Society, which was an organized body in contrast to the disorganized peasants, come forth to take the leadership?

Ever since the Southern Sung dynasty (the twelfth century), the White Lotus had initiated a succession of peasant revolts: in the middle of the fourteenth century at the end of the Yüan dynasty; around 1621 in the Ming; and in 1796-1804 in the Ch'ing. The last one, which had taken place a mere fifty years before, was still fresh in people's memories. From the viewpoint of the government, the reports of the suppression of the bandits indicated, as a rule, the end of each rebellion. But from the viewpoint of the White Lotus Society, the suppression only meant a temporary setback. Once they deemed the time to be ripe again, they would rekindle the flame. The persistence of this struggle was disclosed by a White Lotus member in his confession: "[In peace time, we preached that] by reciting sutras and phrases, one can escape the dangers of swords and arms, water and fire... In time of confusion and rebellion, [we] planned for greater enterprises."[41]

The Nien, as one of the "remnants" of the White Lotus, did not depart from this principle. During the period of robbery and smuggling, they were watching and were always ready to seize the first opportunity to defy the existing authority. The Huai-pei situation in the early fifties presented exactly those conditions which the Nien always hoped to exploit. Indeed, the Nien formally raised the banner of rebellion in 1853; before this, from 1851 on, they had been intensifying their activities in agitating their fellow villagers[42] and availing themselves of every opportunity to seize leadership.

This is specifically expressed by the Nien's activities in the traditional armed battles (hsieh-tou 械鬥) among hostile village communities. This kind of fighting was by no means confined to the Huai Valley, nor did it first draw the government's attention in the Hsien-feng reign. It happened in every part of China throughout Chinese history whenever the central government

41. P'ing-ting chiao-fei chi-lüeh, 26/24.
42. Anhwei t'ung-chih, 102/1-17.

became weak. In the nineteenth century, in the Tao-kuang reign, a censor wrote in his memorial: "Throughout the districts of Shou-chou (under the Feng-yang prefect), Po-chou, Meng-ch'eng (Ying-chou prefect), and Ho-fei (Lu-chou prefect), in Anhwei, the character of the people is so arrogant and tends so seriously toward inter-community strife that they are always seeking to undo the opposite side by summoning great numbers of assistants for armed battles."[43] The districts enumerated by the censor at that time were also the areas of growing Nien activity. According to the Fang-lüeh, the Nien "were fond of armed battles and gathered associates, with whom they swore to enjoy happiness and to endure calamities together."[44] In the early years of Hsien-feng (the 1850's), the inherited feuds between the rural communities of Po-chou, in Anhwei, and those of Kuei-te and Yung-ch'eng, in Honan, mounted to the climax. The greatest tension arose from an attack by Chang Lo-hsing led against the north out of vengeance. The story runs as follows:

> In 1852, when Chang Lo-hsing was absent from home, one of his nephews, who made an attempt to steal sheep in the district of Yung-ch'eng, was captured by the magistrate and put into jail together with his eighteen followers. Hearing this news when he came home, Chang Lo-hsing assembled Kung Te, his lieutenant, and a band of ten thousand men out of Kung's followers, and assailed Yung-ch'eng city, finally rescuing his nephew by storming the prison.[45]

The materials at hand do not directly connect this story with the subsequent fighting between the rural communities of Yung-ch'eng and those of Po-chou. But in view of the fact that Po-chou, south of the boundary line, was the center of the Nien "nest" and that after this episode the Nien leaders, especially Su T'ien-fu (蘇天福), took over direction of the communal battles against Kuei-te and Yung-ch'eng, Chang's assault on Yung-ch'eng marked the beginning of the following mutual slaughters between the two districts. In 1854 Su T'ien-fu and other Nien leaders gathered both Nien members and the civilian inhabitants, and plundered rival communities on the north of the boundary.[46] On the opposite side, the people of Kuei-te, under the leadership of the

_____

43. Hsüan-tsung Ch'eng-huang-ti sheng-hsün, 83/43.
44. Fang-lüeh, 320/4.
45. Wo-yang feng-t'u chi, 15/8.
46. Yüan Chia-san, Memorials, 5/19-20; Shantung chün-hsing chi-lüeh, 2A/1-2.

16

commissioner of local corps,[47] Chu K'ai (祝 懂), responded to the attack with more violence. Chu K'ai, on the pretext of fighting the Nien, surprised rival communities in the south and massacred the inhabitants, whether they belonged to the Nien or not.[48]

This ruthlessness of the northern communities in turn embittered the southern people, who became easy prey for the Nien Society. From 1854 on, Chang Lo-hsing, from his headquarters in the town of Chih-ho (雉河) (under the jurisdiction of Meng-ch'eng but near the border of Po-chou), organized four hundred communities into a defense unit against the north.[49] The same precaution was taken by the opposite camp. The people of Kuei-te, Yü-ch'eng, Yung-ch'eng, and Hsia-i, who had suffered from the Nien, commemorated their affliction by wearing mourning gowns and organized a resistance force of several tens of thousands of men.[50] The Nien also found it urgent to enlarge their bands and to widen their sphere of influence.

On the surface, it seemed to be the villagers of Po-chou who were utilizing the Nien to strengthen their position against the enemy from the north. But in actuality the situation was the other way around; that is, the Nien, as an unruly secret society, was exploiting the local feuds for its own purposes. In the vicious cycle of vengeance between Yung-ch'eng and Po-chou, the Nien Society was the only gainer; such Nien leaders as Chang Lo-hsing and Su T'ien-fu seized the leadership in some of the rural areas of Po-chou.

The local unrest was a striking feature reflecting the decay of the government's administrative and military organization. While the district magistrates and local military posts failed to make peace and order in the rural areas, secret societies like the Nien, the Fu, and the Eight Diagrams sect took over the leadership under the pretext of assisting in the villages' defense.[51] This

---

47. The local corps was not a new thing appearing in the fifties. For its origin, see the introduction to local corps in Ch'ing-ch'ao hsü-wen-hsien t'ung-k'ao, 215/9617. In our period, it was the unrest in Kwangsi at the end of the Tao-kuang reign that made the court issue an edict in 1850 to encourage the setting up of local corps by communities for self-defense against the rising bandits. Loc. cit. Franz Michael has a special treatment of this subject in his "Military Organization and Power Structure of China During the Taiping Period," Pacific Historical Review, vol. XVIII, no. 4 (November, 1949). Also see Part I, sec. 3, and Part II, sec. 3, of the present study.

48. Fang-lüeh, 7/7-8.

49. Shantung chün-hsing chi-lüeh, 2A/2.

50. Shantung chün-hsing chi-lüeh, 2A/7-8.

51. The same thing happened to the community factions in Shantung. The revolt of the Long Spear Society was not a result of the dispute between the Society and the government, but an outcome

can be considered as the starting point from which the Nien moved
to wrest from the Ch'ing officials the authority over the villages
upon which they were going to build their own domain. In consideration of the later Nien sway in Huai-pei, which was founded on the
union of the rural communities, the appearance of community
defensive and offensive organizations and their control by the Nien
were of great significance.

Thus, around 1853, the Nien, as a secret society, was providing leadership for the resurrection of the endemic peasant
unrest. However, an organization capable of leading the peasants
was not necessarily strong enough to raise an extensive rebellion.
The nature of the primary organization of the Nien then merits
scrutiny.

Before 1853, the primary organization of the Nien was that of
numerous bands, with which the leaders sought to satisfy their
followers' desires for material gain or for vengeance. Since
undertakings such as smuggling, robbery, and fighting between
communities were not pursued without interruption and were not
concentrated in a single area, the bands "pinched together" for
those purposes were bound to be dispersed in location. Any individual Nien member who, with a certain adventurous aim in mind,
was capable of "pinching" together a certain number into a band
could claim that he was in possession of a nien.[52] In conflicts
between communities, wherever the adversaries preferred to rely
on the Nien support, bands on the model of the Nien would be
formed. Since such hostilities were not peculiar to a definite area,
the Nien bands organized to serve that purpose would likewise be
scattered according to the location of the communities involved.
Therefore, the first characteristic of the original Nien units was
their geographical decentralization. Before 1853, one could hardly
point out a site which might be considered as their political or
military headquarters. As noted in the Introduction, the "bad
people" under the name of Nien were scattered along the frontiers
of five provinces. Some of the Honan Nien deliberately built their
strongholds in dangerous and secluded regions. For example,
Chio-tzu-shan was located at the intersection of the frontiers of
three districts of Honan and one of Hupeh. No means of access
other than tortuous paths led to the "nest" which was hidden deep
in the mountains.[53]

Secondly, the numerous bands were independent of one
another. This characteristic is revealed by the fact that each band

of the antagonism among the village communities themselves. The
rise of the Eight Diagrams sect was likewise the result of such
antagonism. (Shantung chün-hsing chi-lüeh, 11A/4-5.)

52. Fang-lüeh, 1/1-2,8,17-18.
53. Ibid., 1/10.

leader called himself t'ang-chu (堂主) or "lodge master."[54] The
term, t'ang-chu was obviously borrowed from the Society of
Heaven and Earth (T'ien-ti-hui 天地會) which prevailed in the
south.[55] The leader of each unit of the Society bestowed a fancy
name on his t'ang to hide its real name from the government. The
bandits relied on the residence of the t'ang-chu as a haven of
refuge, seeking shelter and food there. In return, the t'ang-chu
was entitled to a portion of the spoils.[56] Though there was a distinction between the Society of Heaven and Earth and the White
Lotus Society, the latter in the 1850's imitated not only the
former's terms, such as t'ang-chu or hsien-feng (先鋒), but its
practices as well.[57] The bandit leader of Tzu-ch'uan, Shantung,
Liu Te-p'ei (劉德培), was supported as a t'ang-chu by his followers.[58] The leader of the Eight Diagrams sect, Yen Hsiu-lun (顏秀
倫), erected a stronghold in Hsing-hsien, Shantung, where he
harbored "religious bandits" and collected tribute from them as
compensation.[59] Both the bandits in Tzu-ch'uan and those in Hsing-
hsien arose in Shantung, farther from the south than the Nien
centers, yet they were influenced by the Society of Heaven and
Earth in some terms and usages. The Nien, concentrated at the
borders of Shantung and Anhwei, would presumably have been
affected by the t'ang-chu system in the same way as their fellow
religious bandits in Shantung, an area further to the north.

   With the source of the term t'ang-chu clarified, it becomes
easy to recognize the effect of this decentralizing system on the
organization of the secret societies. The characteristic of the
units led by the t'ang-chu was that, in spite of their similarities
in organization, each one had an independent chu or "host," above
whom there was no central body for general leadership.[60] We have
seen that any Nien member, if he were capable enough to gather a

54. Shantung chün-hsing chi-lüeh, 2A/1. Literally the term
t'ang-chu should be translated as "hall (or lodge) masters";
however, the leaders of the variously designated t'ang or "halls"
headed small organizations which were at once independent of one
another and yet bound together by the fraternal ties of the whole
secret society.
55. Hirayama Amane has an explanation about shan-t'ang (山堂)
or "mountains and halls." Every unit of the Society of Brotherhood
(哥老會), a branch of the Society of Heaven and Earth, adopted the
name of a certain mountain as its fancy name. The name adopted did
not necessarily correspond to an actual mountain. There were also
various fancy names of "halls," derived from the Chung-i T'ang
(忠義堂) or the Hall of Loyalty and Righteousness in the novel,
Shui-hu chuan (水滸傳) (Hirayama Amane, pp. 81-82).
56. Kwangsi t'ung-chih chi-yao, T'ang-fei so-lu (堂匪瑣録),1/1.
57. Shantung chün-hsing chi-lüeh, 2A/1; Hirayama, p.39
58. Ibid., 20A/5.
59. Shantung t'ung-chih, 117/3347.
60. Hirayama, pp. 81-82.

19

number of followers, could announce that he had at his disposal a
nien. Thus the t'ang-chu system was a reflection of the indepen-
dence of leaders and the decentralization of the entire Nien
Society which existed before the t'ang-chu rallied to Chang Lo-
hsing's standard in 1853.

With such independent leaders, no coordinate action could be
taken. In a tiny area like the border of K'ai-chou in Chihli and
Kuei-te in Honan, the Nien were divided into twenty parts,[61] to say
nothing of the multiplicity of Nien units in the vast valley of the
Huai.

The third outstanding characteristic of the Nien's primary
bands was their elastic size. As noted above, a leader could claim
that he had one nien by assembling from three to several thousand
men. In the winter of 1852, at the eve of the rebellion, Chang Lo-
hsing gathered only a thousand men with the support of Feng Chin-
piao (馮金標), another Nien chief,[62] although the force Chang
led to storm the Yung-ch'eng prison to rescue his nephew a few
months earlier was said to have been composed of ten thousand
men. In 1853, the Nien in Po-chou combined fifty-eight small
nien into one nien;[63] simultaneously, the Nien who arose in Ying-
chou, a neighboring district of Po-chou, filled each of their bands
with from several hundred to several thousand men.[64] The Nien of
Ts'ao-chou, Shantung, was reported to comprise thirteen nien,
but the number of this combined force remained less than three
thousand until it incorporated some wandering bandits.[65] Since
these figures are mostly based on official estimates which are
challengeable, one may question their accuracy. Nevertheless,
the figures, even if only roughly correct, show the flexibility in
the size of the Nien bands.

To summarize, the Nien forces, as represented by such
scattered, incoherent, and irregular hordes, were local in nature.
No doubt they were capable of creating considerable disturbance
in their respective localities. But in the early fifties the Nien
were supposed to have embarked on a greater enterprise. They
found themselves in need of two weapons: a general leadership and
a tighter organization.

2. The Military Organization of the Nien

During the winter of 1852, the Nien not only began to realize
the necessity of a united leadership and a tighter organization but
also made initial attempts to bring the two into being. In that

61. Wang K'ai-yün, 14/1.
62. Anhwei t'ung-chih, 102/10.
63. Wo-yang feng-t'u chi, 15/8-9.
64. Anhwei t'ung-chih, 102/15; Fang-lüeh, 4/17.
65. Fang-lüeh, 6/3.

winter, the Nien leaders from Hsiao-hsien, Feng Chin-piao and
Chang Feng-shan, together with sixteen other Nien leaders, concentrated their bands in the Meng-ch'eng area, where they proclaimed Chang Lo-hsing, a Nien leader of the town of Chih-ho,
Meng-ch'eng, their "head" (shou 首).[66] In the first month of the
next year, the leaders assembled in a temple at Chih-ho and
started the rebellion with a sacrifice to a flag.[67] Indeed, the setting up of a leader and the sacrifice to a flag were natural steps,
common to other rebellions in their beginning stages. However,
this matter of formality symbolized something concrete in the
Nien organization. First, the concentration of bands in Meng-
ch'eng indicates that the Nien were trying to build a unified force
out of scattered and incoherent bands. Secondly, the acknowledg-
ment of Chang Lo-hsing as their head means that the leaders, who
had formerly been their own masters, were willing to delegate
their power, at least temporarily, to a general chief. The sacrifice to a flag implies not only that the disunited and disorganized
Nien had rallied under one standard, but that they were pledged to
a greater enterprise--rebellion; that is, they bade farewell to
such petty offenses as drinking, gambling, smuggling, local fighting, kidnapping, and robbing. While the combination of bands
enhanced the size and strength of the Nien forces, the shift in
emphasis to the new enterprise began to make evident the real
objectives of the Nien Society.

Obviously the steps taken at this time were still far from
bringing about any institutional innovation. The unification of the
numerous bands formerly led by eighteen leaders certainly marked
an improvement over the previously scattered forces. Yet this
coalition, though representing a higher degree of unity, did not
last, because it was not yet founded on an institutional reality.
Immediately after its formation, the combined force met a test
which resulted in disaster.

The prefect of Ying-chou, Mao Han-yü (毛含煜), could not
tolerate an organized revolt in the district under his jurisdiction
and launched an attack on Chih-ho. Before Mao's advancing troops,
the Nien forces dispersed. Leaders like Chang Lo-hsing and Feng
Chin-piao abandoned their base and surrendered to the local corps
commissioner, Chou T'ien-chüeh, in Su-chou.[68] There Chang was
granted the post, "the eye of the militia."[69] Chang's capitulation
may indicate that the defeat in Chih-ho broke his confidence in the

66. Anhwei t'ung-chih, 102/10.
67. Wo-yang feng-t'u chi, 15/8-9.
68. Wo-yang feng-t'u chi, 15/8-9 says that Chang surrendered to
Chou. Su-chou chih, 10/23 gives a different story: Chou refused
Chang's first offer of surrender in the second month, but summoned
Chang to his camp two months later.
69. "The eye of the militia" (勇目) was a general name for
lesser officers of the militia. The raising of militia by the pro-

21

prospects of rebellion or that he desired a breathing space for his
beaten forces. Whatever the reason, his service in Chou's camp
was short-lived, for financial deficiencies forced Chou to disband
the militia corps under the command of Chang and Feng.[70]

As far as the Nien organization is concerned, no obvious
change appears in the records for the period between the Chih-ho
setback and the autumn of 1855. This does not mean that the Nien
leaders neglected this problem. During these two and a half years
they continued to try to effect a union of the forces, a project
which they had cherished since the winter of 1852. The two and a
half years can be considered as a transitional interval leading to
the final phase of the Nien's organizational development.

In the tenth month of 1853, the Nien leaders in the Meng-
ch'eng and Po-chou area incorporated fifty-eight bands into one,
in addition to which, they pressed many villagers into service.[71]
There were on that occasion four leaders who called themselves
the Four Deva Kings (Ssu-ta-t'ien wang 四大天王). Five months
later (the third month of 1854), a Po-chou Nien leader, Chang
Chieh-san (張捷三), established his headquarters in the town of
I-men (義門), from which his influence expanded to Chih-ho and
Lin-hu-p'u (臨湖鋪).[72] In the second month of the next year,
Kung Te was upheld as "supreme leader" (tu-nien-t'ou 都捻頭)
of six thousand men.[73] These three cases illustrate the issue
which the Nien leaders at this time thought crucial. What they
really achieved, however, was not a unification but an expansion
of forces. This quantitative change proved no remedy for the situation. The accumulated forces under the Four Deva Kings and
those under Chang Chieh-san were destroyed by Yüan Chia-san,
the successor to Chou T'ien-chüeh. With their commanders slain,
their troops annihilated, and their "nests" rooted out, they had
met a greater disaster than in the Chih-ho battle of 1853.

These incidents also reveal that during this period Chang Lo-
hsing himself did not actively take part in the task of organization.
In the Anhwei t'ung-chih, there is a list naming the Four Deva
Kings and other lesser leaders who had attended the rally in the
tenth month of 1853. Chang Lo-hsing's name is not found there.
We have seen that Chang Chieh-san had extended his control to
Chih-ho, Lo-hsing's base; however, Lo-hsing was not counted
among Chieh-san's collaborators.[74] Kung Te had once been Lo-

vincial authorities also reflected the decay of the government
army. See Michael, "Military Organization and Power Structure of
China During the Taiping Period," Pacific Historical Review, XIII,
4 (Nov. 1949).
   70. Wo-yang feng-t'u chi, 15/10; Su-chou chih, 10/23.
   71. Fang-lüeh, 4/17; Anhwei t'ung-chih, 102/15.
   72. Anhwei t'ung-chih, 102/19.
   73. Yüan Chia-san, Memorials, 6/31.
   74. Anhwei t'ung-chih, 102/15, 19.

hsing's lieutenant; but his later action setting himself up as supreme leader of six thousand newly gathered men was apparently done independently of Lo-hsing. Besides the indications found in these reports, the passive role played by Chang in organizational work during this interval is also revealed by a memorial by Yüan Chia-san. As late as the tenth month of 1854, Yüan reported that Chang was continuing to occupy Chih-ho under the pretext of safe-guarding that town on behalf of the government. [75] The Wo-yang feng-t'u chi records that "for three years [1853-1855] Lo-hsing drifted between submission and revolt." [76] This explains why, in the third month of 1855, the Su-chou magistrate, Kuo Shih-heng (郭 士 亨), did not hesitate to offer Chang a pardon, expecting that Chang would once more come to the government's side. [77] Insofar as later events show that Chang possessed great organizing ability, his comparative inactivity may well have been one of the reasons for the stagnation in the Nien organization between the spring of 1853 and the autumn of 1855.

It was not until the first month of 1856 that a systematized military organization took form. [78] The Yü-chün chi-lüeh dates this event in the autumn of 1855. [79] The Fang-lüeh partially supports the Yü-chün chi-lüeh, for it tells us that in the autumn of 1855 the Nien formed five big bands out of a vast multitude of lesser units, that in the winter they united the five bands to invade Honan, and that the chiefs of the five bands were Chang Lo-hsing, Su T'ien-fu, Kung Te, Wang Kuan-san (王 貴 三), and Hou Shih (侯 實). [80] I see no contradiction in these records. In view of the experiments and failures of the previous two and a half years, one should not expect that the Nien could inaugurate a new military organization overnight. Thus, before its emergence in the first month of 1856, some preliminary steps must have been taken. The formation of the five bands in the autumn of 1855, recorded by the Fang-lüeh, could have been this step leading to the final phase a few months later. This speculation is also compatible with factual developments in 1855.

From the third month of 1855 on, there are signs which indicate Chang Lo-hsing's reappearance on the scene and the intensification of the Nien's military activities in Huai-pei. [81] Local

75. Anhwei t'ung-chih, p. 24.
76. Wo-yang feng-t'u chi, 15/10.
77. Ibid. The reasons for Chang's inactivity in this period have not yet been fully ascertained. It is likely that the defeat at Chih-ho in the first month of 1853 taught him to wait for a more suitable time to strike again.
78. Ibid., 15/11.
79. Yü-chün chi-lüeh, 7, Wan-fei 5/10.
80. Fang-lüeh, chüan 15 and 6. The Hsiang-chün chih follows the Fang-lüeh in dating the formation of the five bands in the autumn of 1855.
81. Anhwei t'ung-chih, 103/2-7.

23

campaigns fought by small bands gradually gave way to a grand
assault on the surrounding provinces by an enormous force which
reportedly covered an area of several ten li with its flags.[82] The
conflict, involving such a gigantic force, could not have been conducted without a tight organization. The establishment of the
banner system, described in the following passages, represented
merely a climax to this progress of organizational development.

In the first month of 1856 the Nien on the north side of the
Huai elected Chang Lo-hsing as "Lord of the Alliance" (meng-chu
盟主), with the title "Great Han Prince with the Heavenly
Mandate."[83] In principle, the entire force which gathered around
Chang was divided into five large banners, distinguished by five
colors, yellow, red, blue, white, and black. Each of the five
banners was in turn comprised of five small banners bordered by
the five colors. For example, the five small banners under the
yellow banner uniformly used yellow flags but bordered them with
the five colors which marked the five big ones.[84] The division of
banners, the distinction in colors, the commander of each unit,
and the location of each formation is summarized in the following
chart:[85]

82. Fang-lüeh, 9/20. The radical change in the military situation of Huai-pei following the spring of 1855 might have been due
to the departure of Yüan Chia-san in the third month of 1855;
Anhwei t'ung-chih attributes the Nien's revived seditiousness exclusively to the recall of Yüan by the Imperial government, because
Yüan was regarded as the most able official and was feared by the
Nien (103/2); and to the stabilization of the Taiping position
south of the Huai, which served the Nien in tying down the government main forces in that area. Perhaps internal changes in the
Nien camp were also responsible, but the materials available
provide no information on this.
83. Yü-chün chi-lüeh, 6, Wan-fei 2/13-18.
84. Yü-chün chi-lüeh, 7, Wan-fei 5/10; Anhwei t'ung-chih,
103/7; Hsü-hsin Meng-ch'eng hsien-chih, 6/5.
85. Unlike the Taipings the Nien left no records. Information
for this chart was drawn mainly from an illustration in the local
gazetteer of Wo-yang, Chih-ho, and also from a petition sent to
the Court by the gentry and common people of Kuei-te, whose
communities had suffered from the Nien. (Wo-yang feng-t'u chi,
15/10; Yü-chün chi-lüeh, 6, Wan-fei 2/13-18.) These sources must
be used with caution since the petition was prepared several hundred li outside the Nien area and its authors were presenting
grievances against the Nien. When the names of the bandit leaders
are mentioned, their real names and nicknames are often confounded.
Only the chiefs of the five big banners can definitely be recognized. The leaders like Sun Kuei-hsin, Liu T'ien-fu and Li Yün
were big figures in the Nien, but the sources do not tell us which
bordered banners they led and only vaguely indicate the names of
the big banners to which they belonged. The description of banners
is even less adequate. Some banners appear without leaders, while

Banner	Name	Location
YELLOW	Chang Lo-hsing	Chang-lao-chia (張老家), Chih-ho, Meng-ch'eng
	Chang Tsung-yü (succeeded Lo-hsing)	Chang-lao-chia, Chih-ho, Meng-ch'eng
	Chang Ch'eng-te (張慎德)	Ts'ao-shih (曹市)
Red border	Hu Yü-shan (胡玉山)	
White border	Yin Tzu-hsing (尹自興)	
Square yellow	Han Lao-wan (韓老萬)	
WHITE	Kung Te	Kung-chi-shih (宮記寺), Po-chou
	Chiang T'ai-lin (江太林)[86]	Chiang-lao-chia (江老家)
	Sun K'uei-hsin (孫葵心)	
	Ch'eng Ta-tao (程大道)	Chiang-lao-chia
Blue border	Sheng Chien-ju (盛見如)	
Black border	Wang Huai-yü (王懷玉)[87]	
RED	Hou Shih-wei (侯世偉)[88]	Hou-lao-ying-tzu (侯老營子)
White border	Li Ho-ling (李鶴嶺)	Niu-k'eng-li-chuang (牛坑李莊)
Yellow border	Chou Huai-lin (周懷林)	Chou-chia-lou (周家樓)
Black border	T'ien Hsien (田鱻)	Yung-ch'eng (永城)
Blue border	Wang Ta-wei (王大位)	

many leaders are not identified as to banners. Information on the native places of the Nien leaders is important because it helps to establish the location of the banner which they led. However, such information is even scarcer than that on the leaders and banners. Occasionally villages or towns are mentioned as residences but no reference is made to the district. In some cases, different records give different dwellings for the same person.

86. Fang-lüeh (157/23-24) attaches him to the red banner with white border, but Yü-chün chi-lüeh puts him in the white banner. The fact that he fought all the time together with the leaders of the white banner proves that he could not belong to the red banner. The only trouble is that the available data do not show which bordered banner under the big white one was under his command.

87. Fang-lüeh (157/23-24) puts him in the red banner with yellow border.

88. Yü-chün chi-lüeh puts him in the red banner with yellow border. But in Fang-lüeh there is a Hou Shih, leading the big red banner. In my judgment, Hou Shih-wei and Hou Shih are the same person.

Banner	Name	Location
BLACK	Wang Kuan-san (王貫三)	Wang-lou (王樓), San-kuan-chi (三官集), Hsia-i (夏邑)
	Lo K'e-yu (羅克有)	Ta-lo-chia (大羅家)
	Chao Hao-jan (趙浩然)	Chao-chuang (趙莊), Mai-t'ou (買頭), Yung-ch'eng
Red border	Teng Tso-jen (鄧作仁)	
White border	Li Ju-mei (李如梅)	
Square black	Chang Hsiao-ming (張小明)	
BLUE	Su T'ien-fu (蘇天福)[89]	Su-chia-chai (蘇家寨)
	Liu T'ien-fu (劉天福)[90]	Sun-ho (孫河)
Black border	Li Yün (李允)	Meng-ch'eng
	Ko Ch'un (葛春)	
White border	Yang Jui-ying (楊瑞英)	Kao-lu (高爐)
Yellow border	Chou Lao-ming (周老明)	
HUA		
Narrower	Lei Yen (雷彥)	Po-chou
Broader	Li T'ing -yen (李廷彥)	

Under Chang Lo-hsing, the chiefs of the banners proclaimed themselves "lords" (ch'i-chu 旗主) and "vice-lords" (fu-ch'i-chu 副旗主). Chiefs of the small banners were called "headmen" (nien-t'ou 捻頭). [91] These titles are at times confusing and tend to lead to some misunderstanding by indicating that the Nien had a

89. Yü-chün chi-lüeh does not tell what banner Su commanded. Nor does it give the name of the chief of the big blue banner. Wo-yang feng-t'u chi assigns the square black banner to him. Fang-lüeh says that he called himself "lord of the banner" and that in 1856 he led the blue banner on an expedition on an equal footing with the other four lords. The square and triangular banners were created in later periods, but Su was one of the big chiefs from the very beginning. Until I find other negative evidence, I shall follow Fang-lüeh; that is, I shall regard him as the chief of the big blue banner.

90. Shantung chün-hsing chi-lüeh says that Liu led the blue and black banner to invade Shantung several times (2A/14; 2B/4), but in another place in the same book, Liu is said to have led the red banner (3B/5).

91. Fang-lüeh, 24/11.

constitutional hierarchy identical with that of the Taipings. Certainly Chang Lo-hsing accepted from the Taipings the title of Prince of Wu (Wu-wang 沃王),[92] and most of the top figures of the Nien were made "princes" by the Taipings and honored with the titles, hou, yü, yen, fu, an, or i (侯 掾 燕 福 安 義);[93] but as far as the Nien organization was concerned, this tie with the Taipings was rather superficial. The Nien organization, as seen in the banner system, remained intact. If there was any imitation by either the Nien or the Taipings, it was by the Taiping remnants who copied the Nien's art of war and incorporated themselves into the Nien bands.[94]

Where then did the concept of this peculiar system come from? No answer comes directly from the Nien themselves, but comparable usages practiced by religious rebels in other regions provide a clear picture.

To the north, in Hsing-hsien and Ch'iu-hsien, in eastern Shantung, there were "religious bandits" whose sect was called the Eight Diagrams and was a branch of the White Lotus sect. This sect was composed of eight "mansions" (kung 宮), each of which took one of eight diagrams as its designation and associated itself with one of the five directions (including the center), the five elements, the five colors, and the ten heavenly stems.[95] For example, the northern mansion of this sect was denoted by the diagram k'an (坎) and was associated with the north. The "religious bandits" of Shantung observed these designations rigidly. The band which had taken the diagram k'an hoisted black banners[96] and named their camp Jen-kuei (壬癸), two of the ten heavenly stems.[97] The other four bands gave colors and names to their banners in the same fashion.[98] The eight diagrams, the five directions, the five colors, and the ten heavenly stems were combined as follows:

92. Ibid.
93. Chang Tsung-yü was granted the title Prince of Liang (Liang-wang 梁 王); Jen Chu (任柱) the title Prince of Lu (Lu-wang 魯 王). T'ai-p'ing t'ien-kuo shih-shih jih-chih, Appendix 32, pp. 63-80.
94. Lai Wen-kuang, Prince of Chün of the Taiping, changed his infantry into cavalry and incorporated them into the Nien in 1864. To this adaptation Lai owed his survival, while his comrades, Prince of Fu, Prince of Tuan, and Prince of Ch'i, perished. (See next chapter.) (Yü-chün chi-lüeh, 11, Wan-fei 17/1; Fang-lüeh, 216/67; Anhwei t'ung-chih, 108/26.)
95. P'ing-ting chiao-fei chi-lüeh, 26/24.
96. Shantung chün-hsing chi-lüeh, 12A/3-4.
97. Ibid., 12B/2.
98. The west mansion of the sect, denoted by Ch'ien-tui (乾兌), hoisted white banners; the east mansion, by Chen-hsün (震巽), green banners; the south mansion, by Li (離), red banners; the central mansion, by K'un-keng (坤艮), yellow banners.

27

```
                        South
                        Fire
                        Red
                        Ping-ting


     East              Center              West
     Wood              Earth               Metal
     Blue              Yellow              White
     Chia-i            Wu-chi              Keng-hsing


                        North
                        Water
                        Black
                        Jen-kuei
```

    The adoption by the Nien of colored banners, especially of the
five colors, was not accidental. They did not imitate the Taipings,
though the latter used colored banners, too. The Taipings reserved the yellow banners for the Prince of the East and the
Prince of the West.[99] Obviously this arrangement was the application of the ancient convention that the color yellow must be used
only by royalty. It had nothing to do with the cult of the five colors
which corresponded to the five elements and the five directions.
In my opinion, Nien military institutions should be traced back to
the tenets held by the White Lotus and its branches.[100] Before the
Nien banner system came into existence, in 1853 the government
troops had discovered among the war booty captured from the Nien
some flags bearing the eight diagrams.[101] After 1856, the Nien

    99. Chang Te-chien, Tsei-ch'ing Hui-tsuan, chüan 5, flags.
    100. Parallels can be drawn between nearly all aspects of the
Eight Diagrams and the Nien organization. In 1837, a censor sent a
memorial saying that three years prior to the formation of their
banners, the Eight Diagrams bandits "clandestinely appointed chiefs.
Each headman took charge of a banner with authority over a hundred
men, sometimes even over several hundred." (Hsüan-tsung Ch'eng-
huang-ti sheng-hsün, 85/13) The banners designated by the five
colors possibly originated in the White Lotus sect, the mother cult
of both the Nien and the Eight Diagrams. It was the directional
formula. (Wei Yüan, Sheng-wu-chi, 13/30) They called, for example,
a big band hao (虓) or "signal"; a band designated by white flags
was called pai hao or "white signal." Each hao was able to initiate
separate campaigns in various regions. It is likely that the model
set by the White Lotus of the 1790's became a common legacy shared
by the subsequent branches of that sect.
    101. Yüan Chia-san, Memorials, 2/32.

army used a number of terms such as "front outpost," "right brigade," and "left brigade" in order to distribute positions to the small banners.[102] This distribution, far from revealing a complete picture of the internal organization of the Nien banners, implied nothing more than the application of the idea of the five directions. The Nien also subdivided the banners into five units instead of four or six, because each was to be assigned to a fixed direction according to its color. Moreover, the government officials reported that besides Chang Lo-hsing, there were four marshals corresponding to the four directions -- east, south, west and north -- who commanded the whole Nien army.[103] The factor of directions, in this case, defined the distribution of banners. Because of this scheme of five directions, the large banners, like the small ones, were divided into five, and it is possible that each of the five large banners would, at least theoretically, hold position in its respective direction during maneuvers.

Apart from the conceptual influence, circumstantial necessity also led the Nien to adopt the banner system. Since it was very difficult for the Nien leaders to centralize tens of hundreds of independent bands thoroughly and abruptly, to systematize them into the banner system seemed the proper solution. The large banners brought under control the small ones, yet they themselves stood on an equal footing with the yellow banner chief, the Lord of the Alliance. This was not the first time poeple had worked out such a compromise. Before the Nien, the Manchus had followed the same pattern in evolving the Manchu banner system.

Likewise, the Nien leaders could not suddenly cast the loose bands in a rigid pattern. The irregularity which had prevailed in the previous organization did not fade away completely. In the Nien banner system, one may occasionally find that two persons who dwelled in different communities or fought in different provinces commanded an identical banner.[104] The fact that various chiefs separately commanded banners of the same color indicates that the whole army never rigorously limited itself to five major bands and that the subdivisions in each big unit must also have been more than five. Later, irregularity extended from the contents of the

---

102. Yü-chün chi-lüeh, 6, Wan-fei 2/13-18.

103. Fang-lüeh, 30/10.

104. The units bearing the yellow banners, which were supposed to be under the direct command of Chang Lo-hsing, were not concentrated in Chih-ho. A certain Chang Shen-te and his brother Chang Shen-ts'ung (張愼聰) shared the same color but encamped their troops in a different town, Ts'ao-shih. (Wo-yang feng-t'u chi, 15/ 12) The chart shows that Ch'eng Ta-tao, living in Chiang-lao-chia, commanded the white banner with blue border at the same time; Sheng Chien-ju, with his residence unidentified, was also the chief of the banner. The same thing was true of Ko Ch'un and Liu T'ien-t'ai in the blue banner.

banners to their colors and forms. As the Nien army expanded, a
banner with variegated colors was added to the original five with
their plain colors. To meet the needs of the steadily growing
bands, banners of a new type were designed. Whereas the original
flags were rectangular in form, variety was now added by creating
square and triangular banners for the newcomers.[105]

Just as the entire army was formed to comprise a certain
number of divisions and subdivisions, each of the small banners
was seemingly designed to contain from two to four thousand men,
including the mounted troops.[106] Thus the maximum size of a
large banner was fixed at twenty thousand men. But since the Nien
did not tend to limit the number of banners strictly, why should
they be expected to control the size of the individual banners?

When the banners were on the battlefield, it was not unusual
to find the Nien concentrating all five banners in one direction with
the intention of covering a vast area for plunder.[107] In ordinary
cases, however, only two or three banners were joined together.
Sometimes, while the white, blue and black banners were pillaging
Shantung, banners of the same colors could be discovered on the
banks of the Huai.[108] Even on the same battlefield, banners of the
same color appeared in various positions and fought various
lengths of time.[109]

In spite of these variations, the Nien military organization
was now an institution instead of a temporary gathering of independent bands. From this time on, the Nien ceased to call their
military unit a nien, a term symbolizing a decentralized organization. They renamed their military formations "banners." The banners furnished the Nien a military framework under a unified high
command. It is true that Chang Lo-hsing directly controlled only
one of the five banners, and his title, as acknowledged by the other
chiefs, was no more than "Lord of the Alliance." However, the
reservation of the color yellow for Chang's banner displayed his
supreme position.[110] According to the creed of the White Lotus,
yellow denoted the center of the five directions [111] and was therefore a sign of distinction. Moreover, the title, "Great Han Prince
with the Heavenly Mandate," had already given Chang supreme
rank in the Nien. In fact, though the chiefs of other banners occasionally took independent action, under usual circumstances most

105. Fang-lüeh, 157/23-24.
106. Ibid., 24/11; 127/16-19.
107. Ibid., 13/15; 15/6.
108. Shantung t'ung-chih, 117/3324-25; Fang-lüeh, 56/4-5.
109. Shantung chün-hsing chi-lüeh, 3A/12-15.
110. Anhwei t'ung-chih, 103/7; Yü-chün chi-lüeh, 6, Wan-fei
2/13-18.
111. The same situation arose in the Eight Diagrams sect: "The
leader of that sect, Chang Shan-chi, ascended to the post of
'general chief' (總頭目) and bore the yellow banner...The villagers

of the Nien force was subject to Chang's will. In 1858, the number
of men under Chang's command numbered one hundred thousand.[112]
The yellow banner alone could never have directed so huge a number.

No doubt the establishment of the Nien banner system was a
remarkable progress in organization, as compared to the aggre-
gate of numerous bands in the first month of 1853. Chang now faced
a test much more serious than that of 1853. Yüan Chia-san concentrated troops from three provinces, expecting to eliminate the
Nien once and for all.[113] In the same manner as in 1853, Chang Lo-
hsing was again driven out of Chih-ho. But events subsequent to the
defeat did not correspond with those of the previous defeat. Instead
of offering to surrender, Chang Lo-hsing within a few days regrouped a thousand men around the four hundred left from the Chih-
ho battle,[114] and within two years had subjugated almost the whole
of Huai-pei.[115]

Chang's survival and expansion prove that this improved organization was functioning. From 1856 on, the forces scattered
throughout various localities found in the banners a center to which
they could rally. The basis of Nien power was thus raised from a
lower organizational level to a higher one, from a local to a regional level. In the meantime, Chang's devotion to his undertaking
represented an increased desire among the Nien leaders for dignity, power, and material reward. His title of Great Han Prince
indicates that the Nien had the intention of overthrowing the existing non-Chinese dynasty.[116] It is regrettable that the pretentious
title does not provide us with a more exact understanding of the
Nien ideology.[117]

---

who joined the sect called their organization 'The Society of the
White Lotus' (白蓮社)." (Shantung chün-hsing chi-lüeh, 12B/2) At
that time, we find the band under Chang Shan-chi's direct control
entitled Chung-yang Wu-chi Tu or "Central Wu-chi Earth" (中央戊己土),
a combination of the direction, the heavenly stem, and the element
which yellow implied. (Shantung chün-hsing chi-lüeh, 12A/9-10) So
yellow which designated the center and the earth was particularly
reserved for the "general chief."

112. Fang-lüeh, 53/17-18.
113. Yüan Chia-san, Memorials, 8/30.
114. Fang-lüeh, 18/12.
115. Ibid., 47/23-24.
116. The Chinese usually called themselves the men of Han in
contrast to the surrounding less civilized peoples. This title thus
implies the Nien's national consciousness.
117. In 1853, two years before the appearance of the banner
system, Chang Mou (張茂), a Nien leader, had proclaimed himself
Prince of Hsi-huai. (Hsü-hsiu Lu-chou fu-chih, 22/4) A seal engraved with four characters 興國天子, meaning "the son of the
heaven who opens a new dynasty," was taken from the Nien by the
government troops in battle. (Yüan Chia-san, Memorials, 2/32)

31

3. The Earthwall Communities of the Nien

After 1855, the Nien confronted their adversaries with a unified force instead of with local mobs. This new military machine
was not established on flimsy foundations. It would not have lasted
long if its founders had not possessed a solid domain from which
they could draw manpower and other resources for its sustenance.
Corresponding to the advancement of the military setup, this basis
could no longer remain unorganized.

Earthwalls (yü 圩 , chai 寨) provided the Nien with the main
means to integrate and to consolidate their territories. The earthwalls, though not a Nien innovation, are associated with the Nien
history in a peculiar way, for the Nien were able to utilize them
and build their power base on them. The area north of the Huai, an
open plain on which flowed the tributaries of the Huai, had facilitated intercourse among districts within that area and with the outside world. The appearance of earthwalls altered the whole picture.
Innumerable strongholds replaced the easily accessible plain, and
the navigable rivers became natural barriers for those walls which
stood along their banks.[118] The provincial authorities of Anhwei,
even in peacetime, had always found this region, located at the
northwest corner, outside their tight control. Now this corner was
widely fortified. For nine years following 1856 it defied the rule of
the government.

The way in which the earthwalls were erected around the villages made it possible for the communities to become strongholds.
Ordinarily earth served as the chief material; later on bricks took
the place of earth.[119] At the top of the wall a row of parapets was
added, and outside it one or two ditches were dug. The height of
the wall usually surpassed one chang, while the ditches were two
chang wide.[120] Besides the numerous gun ports on the wall, there
were gun turrets attached to its inner side. Each wall was strong
enough to withstand independently any siege or attack from the
enemy. But under ordinary circumstances, three or four earthwall
communities were associated into a defensive union in which each
rendered assistance to the others. If one were attacked, the others
would raid the enemy's flanks or rear.[121] It was not rare for the
government armies to spend several months in achieving the
break-through of a single wall. But no sooner was one wall broken
than two or three more walls were built within the neighborhood.[122] As long as the defensive strength of these walls was

118. Fang-lüeh, 68/4-5.
119. Fang-lüeh, 208/26.
120. Yüan Chia-san, Memorials, 7/28.
121. Ibid.
122. Ibid., 13/51.

insurmountable, the Nien realm, in spite of its plains and rivers, remained impenetrable.

The arrival of the Taipings in Anhwei in 1853 was the direct cause for the building of earthwalls in many communities throughout the Huai Valley. After the fall of Anking, the provincial capital, the people throughout the province erected earthwalls in which they stored provisions and trained garrison forces for self-protection.[123] This measure obtained approval from I-liang,[124] the governor-general of Liang-Kiang, in 1855.[125] Under the encouragement of the highest authority of the province, the earthwalls sprang up like mushrooms.

The village communities on the north of the Huai which harbored the Nien elements exploited this opportunity. Walls of the same type appeared in their area. However, one cannot ascertain the exact date when the Nien first built them. The fact that government troops encountered resistance from earthwall fortifications when they reached Chih-ho in 1856 gives us some vague idea of their beginning.[126] It indicates that the inception of Nien wall construction could not be later than 1856, for at that time the invaders found not only walls encircling the villages and towns but ramparts stretching across the Wo River. A defensive system like this must have been finished long before the enemy arrived.

Yet the enemy came. The arrival of government forces indicates that by this time the "old nests" of the Nien, though capable of fortifying themselves, had not yet expanded to such an extent that they could stop attackers several hundred li from them. The Nien failed to do this in 1856, either because they had not yet absorbed the peripheral earthwall communities, or because the Nien communities still remained scattered, with hostile or neutral villages standing among them. To absorb the outlying communities and to liquidate the nearby ones required not only more conquests but more organization. This task took the Nien three years to accomplish. From 1856 to 1859 what drew the Nien's attention and represented their real success was not the expeditionary campaigns in distant areas but the work of stabilization in their homeland.

The table in the last section shows that the residences of Nien banner chiefs were concentrated on the two sides of the Wo basin. They covered the west of Meng-ch'eng, the east of Po-chou, the southwest of Su-chou and the southeast of Yung-ch'eng (see map).[127] These were the so-called "old nests." From them the Nien advanced to the Fei River and then to the Sha (沙) River on the west,

123. Fang-lüeh, 208/26.
124. 1791-1867. Hummel, pp. 389-390.
125. Fang-lüeh, 11/5.
126. Ibid., 17/16-17.
127. Yüan Chia-san, Letters, 1/34; Fang-lüeh, 129/18.

33

and to the Hui (⿰氵⿱穴⿱田) River on the east.[128] The Sha and the Hui can be considered as the boundaries. Between the two rivers lay the heart of the Nien domain, linked together by the earthwall communities which were all converted by the Nien. Beyond the two rivers, the Nien communities became more and more scattered. Still farther away lay targets for plundering.

By the summer of 1858 innumerable earthwalls of the Nien covered an area of approximately 45,000 square li, bounded by Su-chou to the north, Lin-huai to the south, Po-chou to the west, and Lin-pi to the east.[129] At the southern margin of this sphere, "Chang Lo-hsing and Kung Te maintain a hold on the cities of Feng-yang and Huai-yüan, commanding the whole Huai. Leading to Meng-ch'eng and Po-chou to the north, the Nien territory covers a thousand li from west to east, embracing three cities. The Nien chiefs turn the cities into fortified centers, around which a circle, of a radius of several hundred li, includes countless bandit nests. They are linked in such an organic way that when you touch the head, the tail will react."[130]

This statement is somewhat of an exaggeration. Since its writer, Yüan Chia-san, intended to exact more reinforcements and more money from the government, he contrasted the position of the Nien with his. The boundaries were only vaguely drawn, and the figures of the length used by him were uncertain. The Nien extension over such an immense area as described above was by no means a thorough subjugation of the whole of Huai-pei. Yüan himself admitted that in 1858 the villages at the intersection of Hsü-chou were still wavering between the government and the Nien.[131] The Nien "peeped" at and encroached upon Lin-pi and Szu-chou, that is, the districts to the west of Su-chou, but they never achieved permanent occupation there. Late in 1862, the dependable Nien nests hardly stretched beyond the southwest of Su-chou. In other words, on the east side of the Nien area, the Nien rule had scarcely crossed the Hui. In 1859, the governor of Anhwei, Weng T'ung-shu,[132] stated regretfully that to win over the people between the Fei and the Sha was hopeless, although he saw a chance of preventing the southern bank of the Sha from joining the Nien.[133] This indicates that the Sha stood for the western limit of the Nien domain. On the north side, Feng-hsien and P'ei-hsien in Kiangsu and Shan-hsien and Ts'ao-hsien in Shantung had suffered from Nien invasion every year since 1857, but these cities served the Nien only as paths leading to the rich area of south Shantung.[134]

128. Fang-lüeh, 68/4-5.
129. Yüan Chia-san, Memorials, 8/7.
130. Shantung chün-hsing chi-lüeh, 2C/1.
131. Yüan Chia-san, Memorials, 9/30.
132. d. 1865. Hummel, pp. 858-859.
133. Fang-lüeh, 68/4-5.
134. Yüan Chia-san, Memorials, 9/30.

In the south, the Huai was not wide enough to check the advance of the Nien as the government officials had supposed. The seizure of the three cities Huai-yüan, Feng-yang, and Ting-yüan on the south bank added numerous earthwall communities to the Nien realm.[135] But these newly conquered communities could be held only as long as the three cities remained in the Nien's hands. When the government army recovered Huai-yüan and Feng-yang in 1859 and Ting-yüan in 1861, the attached communities also changed hands.[136] To the west of Feng-yang, the Nien came face to face with Miao P'ei-lin, the chief of local corps of Shou-chou.[137] Any encroachment of the Nien in that direction was doomed to eventual failure.

The barriers met by Nien expansion on every side did not minimize the ascendancy of the Nien power in the northwest corner of Anhwei. On the contrary, these limitations offered the Nien an opportunity to entrench themselves more firmly in their bases between the Sha and the Hui. The work of cutting out this domain could not have been commenced earlier than 1855. By that time the government army under Yüan Chia-san controlled the whole Huai banks from San-ho-chien down to Ch'ing-chiang-p'u, extending its influence to Hsü-chou and Su-chou.[138] Troops sent out from Lin-huai, Yüan's headquarters, still found it no difficult matter to arrest the Nien leaders in their home communities between the Wo and the Hui. In 1856, the people within several hundred li of Chih-ho began to side with the Nien,[139] yet among them the government continued to find some loyal subjects.[140] One year later these remaining loyalists went over to the Nien. 1858 was the crucial year for strengthening the home base. In that year the Nien gained the upper hand along the Huai, and the position they occupied created the possibility of their uniting with the Taiping in the south. But their real achievement at that juncture was not a southward expansion; it was the internal consolidation. In this consolidation lies the significance of the Nien's occupation of the Huai cities. Their advance from the rural areas to the cities so shocked their enemy that they were blind to the Nien's real success in the rear. The Imperial Commissioner, Sheng-pao (勝 保),[141] concentrated his whole army on a siege of the cities from 1857 to 1859.[142] Thus for two years the Nien succeeded in tying down the government's main force on the Huai bank and provided their home communities with the leisure necessary for the task of stabilization.

---

135. Fang-lüeh, 72/18-19; Yüan Chia-san, Memorials, 11/11.
136. Yüan Chia-san, Memorials, 11/25; 16/32.
137. See Part II, section 1.
138. Yüan Chia-san, Memorials, 8/7.
139. Fang-lüeh, 16/23.
140. Shantung chün-hsing chi-lüeh, 2A/13-14.
141. d. 1863. Hummel, p. 508.
142. Fang-lüeh, 37/14-16; 47/23-24; 48/16-17; 49/10-11; 56/1-2.

In the summer of 1858, Chang Lo-hsing, leaving his army in the south to continue the battle with Sheng-pao, came home to Chih-ho. His return intensified and finally accomplished the work of knitting together the earthwall communities into a single fabric.[143] Chang started his work by purifying the south side of the Wo; he then turned his spearhead to the northwest and finally to the north.[144] In those regions he not only assured himself of the adherence of old comrades but enlisted new member communities. In the southeast, that is, the south side of the Hui, he ordered the secondary chiefs like Jen Ch'ien (任乾), Li Ta-hsi (李大喜) and Li Yün (李允), to stiffen their defenses and to clean up the paths leading south to Feng-yang and Huai-yüan. This made grain flow plentifully from the Hui communities to those two cities.[145] This supply prolonged the resistance of those cities to the besieging government army, and the long resistance in turn kept the government forces under Sheng-pao in the south (the Huai) and those under Yüan Chia-san in the north (Su-chou) from joining each other, and thus obtained more time for the task of settling the old nests. The Nien's success in this was astonishing. In 1857 there were some villages, like scattered islands in the sea of the Nien, which still remained neutral.[146] But in 1859 those islands were overwhelmed.[147] In that year the government officials re-entered the Huai cities, but they dared not touch the Nien's central territory until 1863.

The Nien sometimes integrated their domain by force; Chang Lo-hsing subdued persistent earthwall communities by raiding and breaking them.[148] But force was not the only means the Nien adopted. They won over most of the villages by organization. Usually people achieve their conquests by seizing territory first and then establishing garrison forces in order to hold it. In such cases the occupation can last only as long as the garrison force is able to hold out. The Nien kept the Huai cities in this way. But in following this practice, which was an imitation of the Taipings in central Anhwei, they soon failed. To the north of the Huai, the Nien behaved in their own peculiar way. They did not send out troops to effect any occupation. They merely used the strongholds on the south side of the Wo as the nucleus from which their domination radiated until it reached the margins of the enemies' military bases. Then how was this process accomplished? How did they incorporate the outlying earthwall communities into the whole? How did they assimilate the wavering "islands"?

143. Yüan Chia-san, Memorials, 8/24-26.
144. Ibid., pp. 26, 32-33.
145. Ibid., p. 46.
146. Ibid., 7/21; Fang-lüeh, 26/6.
147. Ibid., 9/15.
148. Yüan Chia-san, Memorials, 8/24-26.

In the prerebellion stage the Nien had induced individuals to join their secret society and in this way increased the number of their bands. But later membership enlistment was pursued in a quite different way and with quite different purposes. They enrolled the whole community instead of individuals; and their objective was not only to increase their bands but also to broaden their territory. The device which they employed to attract followers became something more than the mere promise of a portion of the spoils.

Under what circumstances would a whole community be driven over to the Nien? T'an T'ing-hsiang,[149] governor of Shantung, had an explanation: "In an earthwall community, in case a few people joined the bandits, the wicked ones followed first, and inevitably the good ones yielded to their threats. Then it appears that the whole community became a bandit nest, possessing several thousand armed defenders behind the barricades."[150] This observation is superficial. Unless a new factor is considered, any kind of explanation will be incomplete. This new factor, which rendered possible the conversion of a whole community to the Nien, was the setting up of the local corps. The local corps, like the earthwalls, were nothing new, and their appearance was not confined to the northwest corner of Anhwei. The relevant fact is that the organization of the local corps and the erection of earthwalls were two measures taken by the government authorities to cope with the new situation resulting from the arrival of the Taipings at Anhwei, and that the power of local corps chiefs over earthwall communities served the Nien's purpose.

Wang Ting-an gives a good description in this regard:

> After the Taipings occupied Anking, the people built earthwalls for self-defense, storing provisions and raising fighting forces. [The inhabitants] picked brave youths to learn the art of fighting, and over them they placed a commander, called lien-tsung (練總), [or the general chief of the corps]. Affairs concerning the whole earthwall community had to be referred to the chief for final decision. In case of emergency the chief would assume the duty of watching and guarding or assisting the government army in fighting the attacking bandits. Sometimes antagonism arose between neighboring communities and resulted in armed conflicts. In the harvest season the chief led his corps men to reap and divided the crops equally with the landowners, that is to say, the landowners could not exert an absolute property right over their lands....[151]

---

149. d. 1870. Hummel, p. 428.
150. Shantung chün-hsing chi-lüeh, 18B/7.
151. Wang Ting-an, Ch'iu-ch'üeh-chai ti-tzu chi, 15/1.

This shows that before the Nien expelled official power from their area, the local government had already relinquished its power. It also allowed the chiefs of the local corps to be the yü-chu (圩主), or the masters of the earthwall communities. Thus the chief was the commander in chief and also the top administrator of his community. To crown his power, it was ordered that the chief raise revenue for his own local corps. Some of the chiefs secured their funds from land tribute, that is, they collected tribute from landowners according to the size of their estates.[152] Some of them collected "supplementary land taxes" and left to the government the regular land taxes, but later on they also kept the regular land tax for themselves.[153] Frequently incompetent officials had met armed resistance throughout the rural communities in northwest Anhwei and south Shantung when they insisted on the payment of land tax.[154] The equal division of land yield between chief and landowners, as stated above, might be considered one of the methods of raising funds, or it might be considered the final de- velopment of the chief's financial power.

The power of some chiefs was not confined to the earthwall communities where they resided. The t'uan-tsung (圑總), or the corps chief, controlled three or four villages besides his own.[155] Above him, the lien-tsung had several t'uan-tsung at his command, and thus dominated several tens or even more than a hundred earthwall communities. On the other hand, the authority of the local government department was shrinking until its scope was limited to the city wall, which was always under the threat of out- lying earthwall communities. The rural people, in view of the waning government power, found in the t'uan-tsung or lien-tsung the sole and immediate disposer of life and property.[156]

Once the Nien decided to seize an earthwall community, they had to consider the role played by the chiefs of local corps behind those walls. They understood that the easiest way to acquire an earthwall community was to win over its chief. As long as the powerful chief's cooperation could be secured, the whole com- munity could do nothing but obey. All the Nien had to do was to distribute flags to that community as a sign of joining the Nien banners.[157] Occasionally some chiefs refused to yield to the Nien. In those cases violence was unavoidable. Chang Lo-hsing in 1855 and 1856 killed all chiefs who had assisted the government army in

---

152. Shantung chün-hsing chi-lüeh, 20C/5; 20B/6.
153. Ibid., 14C/5; 22A/6-10; 22C/4.
154. Shantung chün-hsing chi-lüeh, 22B/8-9.
155. Ibid., A, pp. 6-10; Fang-lüeh, 207/19; 208/19-20.
156. Wang K'ai-yün, 16/2; Fang-lüeh, 207/19; Shantung chün- hsing chi-lüeh, 22A/10.
157. Yüan Chia-san, Memorials, 9/15.

38

the surrounding areas of Chih-ho.[158] Advancing from there, he annihilated both the eastern and western local corps of Meng—ch'eng. Most of the local corps, however, went over to the Nien peacefully.[159] Part of the reason for their defection was their incapacity or unwillingness to maintain meaningless resistance to the overwhelming Nien forces. Moreover, in view of the development of their autonomous status which was in no circumstances compatible with the government's authority, they reckoned that collaboration with the Nien would be the best way to perpetuate their power.

The chiefs whom the Nien needed to win over, either by force or by consent, were those who were originally not Nien members. In the Nien realm, some of the Nien leaders had already seized the position of local corps chiefs. We have seen that, at the eve of the rebellion, Chang Lo-hsing and Su T'ien-fu had taken over the leadership of their native communities by availing themselves of the intercommunity hostility. In 1853, under the government's encouragement to organize local corps against the approaching Taipings, many Nien bands "wore the mask of local corps."[160] They were always ready to trap the government army. If the government trusted them and sought their help in a united attack on the Nien, the false local corps were in a position to paralyze the government forces. In 1857, the earthwall communities in the area bound by Po-chou, Meng-ch'eng and Ying-chou organized themselves into armed units under the pretext of resisting bandits.[161] The same method was practiced in Shantung. A certain official even attributed the source of trouble in that province to the setting up of a local corps, on the grounds that the bandit leaders turned it to their own purposes.[162] Even after leadership was seized by the Nien, the local corps continued to show a friendly attitude towards the government officials so as to evade hostility in unfavorable circumstances. But actually leadership of the local corps was exploited by the Nien since the formation of the corps entitled the Nien chief to draft male adults of the community, including both Nien members and the civilian population. Thus, the formation of local corps became the most convenient way for the Nien to secure control over earthwall communities. Once the control was fully assured, the so-called local corps dropped all their pretenses and openly responded to the call of Chang Lo-hsing, when he came home from the Huai in 1858. Yüan

---

158. Wo-yang feng-t'u chi, 15/10; Hsü-hsiu Meng-ch'eng hsien-chih, 6/5.
159. Yüan Chia-san, Memorials, 8/32-33; Shantung chün-hsing chi-lüeh, 2A/13-14.
160. Yüan Chia-san, Memorials, 2/38.
161. Ibid., 7/21. Fang-lüeh, 26/6.
162. Fang-lüeh, 172/31.

Chia-san had regretted, in 1857, that some local corps in the Nien area were timid and wavering.[163] But now, after an interval of only one year, his regret became irremediable grief. Those "timid and wavering" local corps were all gone; and the term "local corps" vanished from the central area of the Nien forever.[164]

In the meantime, the Nien directly appealed to the sympathy of the peasants. The needs of the people and the nature of the local magistrates explain why the Nien were accepted for reasons other than the desire for spoils. As mentioned elsewhere, the local magistrates and their subordinate officials had become very distasteful to the people and powerless against the insurgents. When the insurrections broke out, the officials were so powerless that the people's attitude towards their local authorities turned from hatred to contempt.[165] On the other hand, the bandits were not as atrocious as the people had presumed. As time went on they became more and more familiar with the bandits.[166] Then they asked themselves whether the bandits could rid them of those hateful officials. We also know that from 1853 to 1862 famine occurred in Anhwei almost every year. The peasants, being on the verge of starvation, were in despair because of the government's failure to come to their relief. In fact, the officials had already found it extremely difficult to feed their own soldiers and "volunteers." How could they spare grain to feed the peasants?[167]

The Nien were sagacious enough to meet these needs and hopes of the people. When they broke into a city, they seldom disturbed the civilian inhabitants, and the first thing they did was to open the prison.[168] If there remained some officials who had failed to escape earlier, humiliation in front of the people, or death, was their fate.[169] Sometimes the Nien helped the people gain vengeance on the local officials who had caused them so much suffering. For example, in Ying-chou two constable heads of that prefecture arrested a criminal from a village west of the city and put him to death after a trial by the magistrate. The punishment aroused the rumor that the kinsfolk of the criminal were planning revenge. The two constable heads and their troops then took the neighboring village by surprise and killed several hundred people indiscriminately. The furious people raised a Nien leader,Li Feng (李鳳) by name, as their chief,swearing to redress their grievance by assaulting Ying-chou.[170] This shows that the Nien policy was to

---

163. Yüan Chia-san, Memorials, 7/21.
164. Ibid., 8/32-33.
165. Shantung chün-hsing chi-lüeh, 14B/5.
166. Ibid.
167. Wo-yang feng-t'u chi, 20/8.
168. Ch'üeh-shan hsien chih, 20/7-8; Fang-lüeh, 3/12-13.
169. Fang-lüeh, 3/12-13.
170. Yüan Chia-san, Memorials, 2/25.

take advantage of every opportunity to assume leadership in the countryside and, in so doing, to isolate the cities. By 1858 all government power was swept from the Nien realm, which lay between the Sha and the Hui. Governor Chia Chen (賈臻) described the distress of Ying-chou, the temporary site of his governorship: "With one step outside the city wall, all the surrounding area becomes alien to me."[171] Other cities like Meng-ch'eng, Po-chou, and T'ai-ho, which were located within that area, were as isolated as Ying-chou.[172] If the cities still remained in government hands, it was not because the officials had performed their garrison duties, but because some chiefs of local corps, who had grievances against the Nien, felt that their own interests were promoted by the maintenance and defense of these cities.

The relief of the starving people was the key to gaining their loyalty. The Nien never failed to grasp this chance. They fed not only the destitute masses in their homeland but also those at the borders of Kiangsu and Shantung.[173] The enlistment of starving people on a large scale occurred in 1860, when the flood of the Wo and the Fei made hundreds of thousands of people homeless. Chang Ming-hsing, Lo-hsing's brother, seizing this opportunity, called over a hundred thousand people to his standard.[174] The officials accused the Nien of "compelling" or "threatening" the starving people to join them.[175] Ordinarily, however, it is not difficult for one to win a starving man to his side, if he can afford to succor him. He need not compel or threaten. This is why the officials, even while accusing the Nien of recruiting by force, had to admit that the people in the Nien areas responded to the Nien's call in great numbers.[176] But to carry on the task of relief would have been impossible if the Nien had not kept at their disposal plentiful supplies of grain. To plunder the convoy of government supply was one way to secure the grain, but plundering could not be relied on as a permanent source.[177] Therefore, it was natural for the Nien to emphasize the production of wheat and barley in their homeland.[178] A bad harvest not only would discourage new members but would paralyze the morale and loyalty of the old members as well. The government saw this. Hence struggle over harvests became an important item in the campaigns along the marginal areas of the

171. Ibid., Letters, 1/36-37.
172. Shantung chün-hsing chi-lüeh, 2A/2.
173. Fang-lüeh, 3/4, 10; 22/30, 32; 27/16.
174. Ibid., 83/2-3.
175. Ibid., 22/32; 27/16.
176. Yüan Chia-san, Memorials, 8/24-26.
177. Fang-lüeh, 3/4.
178. The grant of grain seems to indicate that the land was still in the hands of the original owners. If the Nien had taken any step towards land redistribution, they would have used land instead of grain to attract the people.

Nien.[179] Each year in harvest season, the Nien usually stayed at
home. Even though they were out on expeditionary campaigns, they
rarely neglected to send back detachments to protect the home
guards and to reap the crops. The government armies tried very
hard to destroy the Nien's food supply, either by burning their
granaries or by destroying their crops in the field. But whenever
the government invaders attempted this, they found themselves
ambushed from both sides -- by the Nien from behind the wall and
by the forces from their neighboring communities hidden outside
the wall.[180] If there were any combatants who were on the verge
of starvation, they were the government armies in Anhwei, not
the Nien. The Nien's policy of keeping ample foodstuffs to sustain
both their new and old members not only played a major part in
broadening and stabilizing their domain but decided the results of
their contest with the government before 1863.

By utilizing the local corps and by winning over the people's
sympathy, the Nien completed their territorial organization by
1858. But the significance of the earthwall communities was by no
means confined to the Nien's territorial expansion and consolidation. These communities also decided the character of the Nien's
dominion.

Under the pressure of circumstances the provincial government had encouraged the rural communities to build earthwalls
and to form local corps behind those walls. From the outset, the
chief of the earthwall community, who was at the same time the
chief of the local corps, had the right to draft manpower and to
raise funds for his force. Later local officials gave the chiefs
authority to collect land taxes and to oversee judicial suits.[181]
Finally all governmental authority was taken over by them. A
community encircled by an earthwall, within which military, administrative, and financial powers were concentrated in the chief,
stood like a fortified principality. The seizure of leadership by
the Nien never altered the position of the chiefs. From the beginning to the end, the Nien of the old nests never sent agents to supplant the powerful chiefs of the newly enlisted earthwall communities, to say nothing of the communities which were originally
ruled by the Nien. Each community remained autonomous under
its own chief, just as it was in the days when it was taking the
government's side.[182] The only difference was that now the chiefs

179. Yüan Chia-san, Memorials, 7/15.
180. Ibid., 7/23-24; 8/1-17.
181. Fang-lüeh, 208/19-20; Shantung chün-hsing chi-lüeh, 20A/
6-10.
182. The official documents often accused the Nien of compelling the chiefs of earthwall communities to join them, but never
mentioned that the Nien sent agents from any central organ to ad-
minister any community or to supplant its existing chief.

42

acknowledged Chang Lo-hsing as their Lord of the Alliance and mingled their forces with the Nien banners. In peacetime, the chiefs stayed in their respective villages without intimate inter-course with other fellow chiefs.[183] In view of the banner system of the Nien, one should not be surprised at the autonomy of the units which made up the Nien's dominion. In the banners, the chiefs retained considerable freedom of action. In fact, throughout the Nien area the chief of an administrative unit was concurrently the commander of a military unit. His position in the army and his autonomous status in the earthwall community express two aspects of one thing.

The banner system, no matter how loose it was, was a step forward in comparison with the earlier bands. In the same way the domain composed of a mass of earthwall communities, though not tightly organized under a central regime, was a step forward in comparison with the scattered villages. Each earthwall communi-ty was a part of an organic piece of territory; each fighting force behind the wall was a unit of the banner system.

The provincial armies of Honan and Shantung were fully occu-pied with the work of guarding their own borders which were exposed to invasion by the Nien.[184] In the south Sheng-pao was concentrating his main force for a siege of the Huai cities. The only army whose mission was supposed to deal expressly with the Nien was that of Yüan Chia-san. During 1856-1857, he had made several attempts to test the defensive strength of the marginal earthwall communities of the Nien.[185] But a counterattack from the Nien on Sui-hsi-k'ou (濉溪口), the outpost of Yüan's headquarters at Su-chou, brought to Yüan so disastrous a defeat that from then on he banished every vision of "rooting out the Nien's nests."[186] He turned to a defensive measure on the ground that the Nien's central nests were too far away from his base at Su-chou, and that an offensive was too much for his tiny army.[187] Indeed his army was too weak to initiate any offensive, because both the infantry and cavalry at his disposal in 1856-1859 were only one-third the size of the combined forces from three provinces which had advanced to Chih-ho in 1854-1855.[188]

Nevertheless, military strength alone does not account for the whole situation. Yüan admitted that in the later period the whole face of the Nien area had changed, but he failed to see in this fact the crux of the matter. Even if he had had sufficient forces to

183. Fang-lüeh, 127/16-19.
184. Yüan Chia-san, Memorials, 13/51.
185. Ibid., p. 17.
186. Ibid., 9/23.
187. Ibid., Letters, 1/6. At that time the utmost Yüan could plan was to "press the Nien back to their nests." (Ibid., p. 9)
188. Ibid., Memorials, 8/51.

challenge the Nien nests, he would have met a rebuff more catastrophic than the battle of Sui-hsi-k'ou, for, after three years' efforts, the Nien had succeeded in consolidating the region between the Sha and the Hui into a hard core.[189] Within the boundaries of this hard core, the sympathy of all the people was on the Nien side.[190] The people lent full and active support to the Nien's war endeavors and boycotted the government armies whenever the latter dared to penetrate their lines. Thus the earthwall communities, though not an innovation of the Nien, were used by them in a radically new way.

It is a mistake to assume that the Nien were roaming bandits. They settled within fortified nests, which they strove to safeguard at any price. Their wandering in Shantung and Honan in the earlier period was the result of a desire to enrich their nests by plundering those provinces. Their wandering throughout eight provinces after 1863 was forced on them by the steady pursuit of Seng-ko-lin-ch'in (僧格林沁) which deprived them of any chance of rest, and later by Tseng Kuo-fan's (曾國藩) shrewd policy which barred them from their homeland. (See next part.) Their routes during those years prove that they made incessant efforts to return home before they eventually perished in the blockade circle between the Yellow River and the Grand Canal.

4. Components of the Nien Organization

In the Nien rebellion, the role played by the leaders was of special importance. Throughout the documents concerning the Nien the term "Nien-head" (Nien-shou) is emphasized in every aspect of the Nien's activities. In fact, the Nien's political and military organizations were less mature than those of the Taipings, and most of their activities depended on the initiative of

---

189. Li Hsü-i, governor of Anhwei, said that the number of the earthwall communities under the Nien's domination amounted to two thousand (Fang-lüeh, 147/29-30). These, of course, included the earthwall communities outside the central area and varied in number from time to time. The earthwall communities around Feng-yang, which had submitted to the Nien, turned back to the government in 1859 when the city was recovered by the government army (Yüan Chia-san, Memorials, 11/25), while those around Ting-yüan followed suit in 1861 (Ibid., 16/32). So far as the hard core was concerned, the available materials show that in the rural area of Meng-ch'eng, Po-chou, and Ying-chou there were less than a hundred earthwall communities (Po-chou chih, 亳 州 志 8/34); on the south side of the Hui there were over a hundred (Ibid., 8/7, 24-26; 18/33-35); and along the Wo and the Fei there were several hundred (Fang-lüeh, 83/2-3). In general the earthwall communities inside the hard core were far less than two thousand.

190. Fang-lüeh, 48/22.

an individual leader rather than on management through a mature system. Besides, the heads of various posts were taken by one man. In a Nien band, there was a leader; in a banner, a lord (ch'i-chu); in a local corps, a chief (t'uan-tsung); in an earthwall community, a master (yü-chu).

To form a band, to lead a local corps, or to rule an earthwall community required popularity and influence. In a little town or village, who possessed popularity and influence? Who furnished leadership? In many villages big clans held the commanding position. Some villages were composed of only one or two clans. In such cases the dominant clan's surname represented the whole village. Most of the Nien leaders came from villages of this type (see Table 1).[191] It is not the influence of the big clans which draws our attention, however, because it prevailed throughout the rural area of the whole country. What surprises us is that the big clans provided the Nien with a tremendous number of leaders. Analogies cannot be found in other contemporary rebellious groups. The Shantung chün-hsing chi-lüeh, in describing the peculiar traits of the Nien, particularly points out the fact that "brothers, fathers, and sons pursued banditry one after another."[192] Li Hung-chang (李鴻章)[193] shared the same view-point: "The Nien were different from the Taipings. The latter, who devoted themselves to the occupation of cities, would collapse in the event the commander was slain. On the other hand, the Nien were expert in mobile warfare. The leaders, who were from Meng-ch'eng, Po-chou, Ts'ao-chou and Yung-ch'eng, very frequently took both male and female kinsfolk along on their wanderings. Continued military life welded them into a strong army. In the case of the death of father or elder brothers, sons or younger brothers would take their places. Their behavior in this respect seemed to follow an established family rule."[194]

A family rule alone could not have driven tens of hundreds of clansmen throughout northwest Anhwei to risk banditry generation after generation. Insofar as the Nien was a secret society, collective association of the whole clan with the organization should be taken into account. In other branches of the White Lotus, the same custom was followed by Chang Shan-chi and Yen Hsiu-lun, top leaders of the Eight Diagrams sect in south Shantung.[195] Wang San-lo (王三樂), a leader of the Boxers, confessed that most of his

191. Wo-yang feng-t'u chi, 15/10; Yü-chün chi-lüeh, 6, Wan-fei 2/13-18.
192. Shantung chün-hsing chi-lüeh, 2A/1.
193. 1823-1901, Hummel, pp. 464-471.
194. Li Hung-chang, Li Wen-chung-kung ch'üan-chi, Letters to Friends and Colleagues, 7/29.
195. Shantung chün-hsing chi-lüeh, 13A/9-10; Shantung t'ung-chih, 117/3344.

Table 1

Nien Leaders Who Came from Villages
Dominated by their Clans

Names	Villages
Chang Lo-hsing (張樂行)	Chang-lao-chia (張老家)
Chiang T'ai-lin (江太林)	Chiang-lao-chia (江老家)
Sun K'uei-hsin (孫葵心)	Sun-lao-chia (孫老家)
Kung Te (宮得)	Kung-chi-shih (宮記寺)
Chang Shen-chiang (張慎江)	Chang-tan-lou (張單樓)
Lo K'e-yu (羅克有)	Ta-lo-chia (大羅家)
Chao Feng-chu (趙鳳珠)	Ta-chao-chuang (大趙莊)
Li Ho-ling (李鶴嶺)	Niu-k'eng-li-chuang (牛坑李莊)
Chou Huai-lin (周懷林)	Chou-chia-lou (周家樓)
Hsü Hua-te (徐化德)	Hsü-hai-tzu (徐海子)
Hou Shih-wei (侯實偉)	Hou-lao-ying-tzu (侯老營子)
Ch'en Chia-hai (陳架海)	Ch'en-ta-chuang (陳大莊)
Yen Hsi-ch'un (閻錫純)	Yen-chi (閻集)
Wang Lao-p'u (王老僕)	Ta-wang-chuang (大王莊)
Liu Chuang (劉莊)	Liu-nai-nai-miao (劉奶奶廟)
Li Hsiao-ch'e (李小徹)	Li-chia-chi (李家集)
Li Chung-fa (李重法)	Li-chia-chi
Li Kuang-yu (李廣友)	Li-chia-chi
Sun Kung (孫拱)	Sun-lao-chia (孫老家)
Yüan To (袁鐸)	Yüan-lou (袁樓)
Yen Ming (閻明)	Yen-chia-chi (閻家集)
Wang Kuan-san (王貫三)	Wang-lou (王樓)
Wei Hei (魏黑)	Wei-lu-k'ou (魏路口)
Chang Kuang (張廣)	Chang-chi-fang-chuang (張機坊莊)
Chang Hsing (張興)	Chang-chi-fang-chuang
Liu Yün-ch'ang (劉運昌)	Liu-t'i-ch'üan (劉提圈)
Li Lao-tsung-ho (李老總河)	Li-lou (李樓)
Hou Huang-lo (侯黃樂)	Hou-miao (侯廟)
Li Tung-ch'uan (李東川)	Li-hua-yüan (李花園)
Li Hei-kou (李黑狗)	Li-lou (李樓)
Li K'un-san (李琨三)	Li-lou
Li Sung (李松)	Li-lou
Li Erh-mai (李二麥)	Li-lou
Chang Hsiao-pao (張小保)	Ta-chang-ko (大張閣)
Sun Pa (孫八)	Sun-lou (孫樓)
Yüan Chu-ssu (袁朱四)	Yüan-p'ai-fang (袁牌坊)
Liu Teng (劉鄧)	Liu-nai-nai-miao (劉奶奶廟)
Chang Ch'uan-chung (張傳忠)	Chang-san-tso-lou (張三座樓)

46

Names	Villages
Chang Che-kuang (張澤廣)	Chang-san-tso-lou
Chang San (張 三)	Chang-san-tso-lou
Chiao Hsiang (焦 香)	Chiao-lou (焦 樓)
Ts'ao Sung-hsien (曹 松 先)	Ts'ao-lou (曹 樓)
Ts'ao Sung-t'ang (曹 松 堂)	Ts'ao-lou
Wei Shu-te (魏 書 德)	Ta-wei-chuang (大 魏 莊)
Wei Wen-shan (魏 文 山)	Ta-wei-chuang
Ting Hsien-k'ao (丁 獻 考)	Ting-lou (丁 樓)
Ting San-yüan (丁 三 元)	Ting-lou
Hsieh Hai (解 海)	Hsieh-lou (解 樓)
Hsieh Teng (解 登)	Hsieh-lou
Hsü Ke-shan (徐 革 山)	Hsü-lao-chia (徐 老 家)
Han Hei (韓 黑)	Han-ko (韓 閣)
T'ien Ch'un (田 春)	T'ien-ta-chuang (田 大 莊)
Su T'ien-fu (蘇 天 福)	Su-chia-chai (蘇 家 寨)
Yang An (楊 安)	Yang-lou (楊 樓)
Chao Hao-jan (趙 浩 然)	Chao-chuang (趙 莊)

clansmen were arrested on the charge of preaching heterodoxy and that his family had done this for generations, travelling widely over various provinces with the mission to convert people.[196] The Nien were no exception. A leader, nicknamed Hsieh Szü-lao-hu (謝 四 老 虎), headed a clan composed of a thousand families. He also harbored numerous brigands and allied his village with more than ten neighboring villages.[197] This took place before the ascendancy of Chang Lo-hsing. By Chang's time the collective adherence of a family or a clan to the Nien Society had become a custom followed by him and many other leaders[198](see Table 2).[199] They shared leadership with their brothers and nephews and drew two to three hundred followers from their respective clans.

Some clans joined the Nien before the rebellion, some after. Seniority, however, did not affect their position in the community. What mattered was the clan's influence, not its seniority. For example, Chang Lo-hsing's name did not appear until 1851, yet he

---

196. I-ho-ch'üan chiao-men yüan-liu k'ao, collected in Ch'üan-lüan san-chung, pp.5-6.

197. Fang-lüeh, 3/15.

198. Ibid., VI, p. 15, 26; Yüan Chia-san, Memorials, 2/46.

199. Wo-yang feng-t'u chi, 15/10; Yü-ch'ün chi-lüeh, 6, Wan-fei 2/13-18; 8, Wan-fei 7/8; Shantung ch'ün-hsing chi-lüeh, 3C/8.

was the number one leader after the rebellion started. He gained
his commanding position in part because of his membership in a
prominent clan. "He lived in Chang-lao-chia, twelve li east of
Chih-ho, and had two brothers, Wen-hsing (問 行) and Ming-hsing.
Wen-hsing, the oldest one, died early. Tsung-yü [the general chief
of the West Nien in the sixties] was his second cousin (族 侄).
His family enjoyed several hundred mou of fertile land. His
character was fierce and violent. [Such a huge property and
character made his ruthless behavior] analogous to the insurrection organized by the prominent clans in the late Han dynasty."[200]
This narrative, presented by the local gazetteer of Chang's native
town, can be regarded as a short biography. The judgment passed
by the gazetteer on his character is not beyond argument, but the
comparison between the Chang family and the late Han clans is
justifiable. Similarly Jen Chu (任 柱), chief general of the East
Nien in the sixties, was brought up in a well-to-do family. In the
case of Chang and Jen, it was their wealth and influence which
paved the road to leadership, not leadership which made them
wealthy and influential.

A wealthy and influential family, supported by other branches
of its clan, doubtless commanded the community in which it lived.
Especially after the emergence of earthwalls and local corps, a
man who could call together only a few followers was hardly
qualified to direct a community. The head of a big clan, on the
other hand, could draw two or three hundred arms-bearers from
his clan alone. Outside the clan his popularity could evoke loyalty
from many people. Furthermore, it was easy and convenient for
the commander to draft his own relatives, than whom no followers
were more reliable. Loyalty or reliability provided the Nien with
a moral force, with which they succeeded in binding their loose
organization. In 1853, when the growth of the Nien force was still
far from maturity, it was this family bond which made the Nien of
Chih-ho smear their mouths with their victims' blood and swear
to resist the approaching government troops.[201] In spite of their
unpreparedness, they rallied several thousand men in a short
time.

So the exigency of circumstances, together with the clans'
established position, entitled the heads of large clans to leadership. The post of leader was not only a career for a Nien member
but also an inheritable estate for a clansman. Chang Tsung-yü
succeeded Chang Lo-hsing, and about ten of his kinsmen continued
commanding various lesser banners under the yellow banner. The
revival of the Nien power under Tsung-yü's standard taught the
government officials a great lesson.

---

200. Wo-yang feng-t'u chi, chüan 15.
201. Fang-lüeh, 4/22.

48

Table 2

Groups of Nien Leaders Coming from the Same Family

Surnames	Given names
Chang (張)	Lo-hsing (樂行)
	Ming-hsing (敏行)
	Tsung-yü (宗禹)
	Tsung-tao (宗道)
	Tsung-hsien (宗先)
	Ch'ing (清)
	Kuang (廣)
	Yün (雲)
	San-piao (三彪)
	Wu-hai (五孩)
Chang (張)	Shen-te (慎德)
	Shen-ts'ung (慎聰)
Liu (劉)	T'ien-fu (天福)
	T'ien-hsiang (天祥)
Li (李)	Hsiao-ch'e (小徹)
	Chung-fa (重法)
	Kuang-yu (廣友)
Sung (宗)	Hsi-yüan (喜元)
	Hsi-chu (喜柱)
Li (李)	Hei-kou (黑狗)
	K'un-shan (琨山)
	Sung (松)
	Erh-mai (二麥)
Chang (張)	Ch'uan-chung (傳忠)
	Che-kuang (澤廣)
	San (三)
	and 300 clansmen
Ts'ao (曹)	Sung-hsien (松先)
	Sung-t'ang (松堂)
Su (蘇)	T'ien-fu (天福)
	T'ien-yu (天祐)
	T'ien-cheng (天正)
Chao (趙)	Hao-jan (浩然)
	Hsin-jan (欣然)
	Kou (狗)
	K'e-tuan (克端)
Hou (侯)	Huang-lo (黃樂)
	and more than 200 clansmen

49

Surnames	Given names
Ch'eng (程)	Ta-lao-k'an (大老坎)
	Erh-lao-k'an (二老坎)
	San-lao-k'an (三老坎)
Liu (劉)	Ta-lao-yüan (大老淵)
	Erh-lao-yüan (二老淵)
Yen (閻)	Hsi-ch'un (錫純)
	Ming (明)
	Hsiao-ch'ien-sui (小千歲)

The low degree holders of the gentry played a no less important part than the big clans,[202] although most of the Nien leaders
held no degrees. (At least, the obtainable sources do not mention
that the first-ranked chiefs like Chang Lo-hsing and others
acquired any kind of degree.) Of course, some gentry also belonged to big clans. Tables 1 and 2 show that Yen Hsi-ch'un was a
prominent clan head in his village Yen-chi and was at the same
time a wu-chü (武舉), or provincial military graduate.[203] But the
majority of the gentry in the Nien held, or in some cases were
dismissed holders of, petty degrees like chien-sheng, kung-sheng,
or sheng-yüan. Apparently their prospects for advancement were
not as promising as those of their fellow gentry with higher
degrees. It was likely that, in their calculation, to join the rebels
was a shortcut to the realization of their aspirations.

202. The "low degree holders" refers to all those who had under-
gone a series of preliminary examinations before qualifying for
entrance to the provincial examination: the licentiates (sheng-yüan
生 員), the salaried licentiates (ling-shan-sheng 廩 膳 生), the
senior licentiates (kung-sheng 貢 生), and the students of the
Imperial Academy (chien-sheng 監 生). As for the role played by
the scholar-gentry on the government side and for other information,
see Chang Chung-li, The Chinese Gentry, Studies on Their Role in
Nineteenth-Century Chinese Society, University of Washington Press,
1954.
203. Yü-chün chi-lüeh, 6, Wan-fei 2/17. The same clan could
include both gentry and commoners. I particularly pick them out
because a clan head could easily form a fighting force simply by
mobilizing his own clansmen. A man without a clan behind him,
whether he was gentry or commoner, could not raise a band in the
same way. Maybe this is why the big clans usually provided leadership for the Nien.

Some of them did not join the Nien personally but sympathized with the Nien simply because their relatives belonged.[204] For example, in Ju-nin, Honan, two Nien members who plotted to guide their comrades into the city were discovered by the prefect in the house of a prefect candidate.[205] Or again, a Nien earthwall community under the jurisdiction of Shen-ch'iu, Honan, was once besieged by a government force. Among the besieged Nien there were over a hundred men belonging to the clan of a <u>chien-sheng</u>. Fearing that a slaughter after the break-through would involve his clansmen, this <u>chien-sheng</u> pleaded with the officials to ease the attack so that he could go in and persuade the Nien to surrender.[206] The story of Chang Lo-hsing shows the gentry playing the same sympathetic role, for he was once under the protection of the Chih-ho gentry. In 1853, Yüan Chia-san, reaching Chih-ho, demanded the delivery of Chang. The gentry of that town came out and presented to Yüan a guarantee that Chang would never conspire in association with the Nien against the government.[207] But no sooner had Yüan turned his back than Chang revolted again. The sympathy given by the gentry resulted in several such tragedies as that in which Ch'ung-an (崇安), a government brigade general, killed all the gentry who came forth to welcome his army. A considerable number of gentry and elders in Po-chou and Meng-ch'eng areas suffered from his ruthlessness.[208]

Passive help existed only in the prerebellion or early period. Later on most of the gentry in Nien areas formally took part in the Nien activities. To their associates they contributed something which could not be expected from uneducated people. The <u>Wo-yang feng-t'u chi</u> gives the reason for their participation:

> When the seditious vapor of the Taiping was growing, people were inclined to take adventurous courses. The intellectual class in particular saw in rebellious leaders "rare commodities." They either helped uphold the general chief, or offered him far-reaching projects for political aims. In the first month of 1856, Li Shih-hsien (李士銘) and Cheng Ching-hua (鄭景華), <u>kung-sheng</u> of Meng-ch'eng, after consulting other Nien members, initiated the election of Chang Lo-hsing as Lord of Alliance. They put Lo-hsing in a sedan chair and pressed on in a crowd toward the town of Chih-ho. There the group held ceremony by sacrificing to heaven and earth. They

204. Yüan Chia-san, Memorials, 2/40.
205. Fang-lüeh, 117/4-5.
206. Ibid., 104/1.
207. Yüan Chia-san, Memorials, 5/19.
208. Wo-yang feng-t'u chi, 15/11.

announced regulations which everybody had to obey, and then set up the banner system with five colors. . . . [209]

These members of the scholar-gentry decided upon the title "Lord of Alliance" to fit the primary form of the Nien, they directed an impressive ceremony to dignify the lord, they drew up regulations, and they founded the banner system. These activities indicate the decisive role played by the gentry in the Nien organization. As pointed out before, the banner system changed the character of the organization. Now it should be noted that the participation of the gentry helped bring about this change. Not only did their intellect, resulting from long years of academic training, contribute to the design of certain institutions, but also their participation itself transformed the quality of the organization. The gentry members resided in local communities, and some of them belonged to large clans, but their influence extended much further. Their personal contacts were not confined to their respective localities. The identity of their interest was almost nationwide, and they were keenly aware of their interest. Whereas the Nien Society's White Lotus heritage had provided a distinguishing consciousness, setting the Nien apart from ordinary bandits, the participation of the gentry gave to the Nien's incipient agitation broader political consciousness and organizing power, which made a true rebellion of it.

What really changed the Nien organization was not the term "banner," because the command of the newly formed banners still remained in the hands of the old chiefs. The significant change occurred when the two kung-sheng, Li Shih-hsien and Cheng Ching-hua, set up a lord of alliance at the head of the banners, and established regulations[210] which made the banners an organic entity. Of course, the gentry's intellect contributed to these devices, but it was the extensive nature of their foundation as a social force which made natural this development.

More examples may be cited to show the leading part played by the gentry. In 1848, five years before the rebellion, Tung Wen-chai (董文齋), a ling-sheng of Chü-yeh, Shantung, planned and initiated the insurrection of the Nien in that area.[211] At first, the appearance of these "high society bandits" (i-kuan-tao-tsei 衣冠盜賊) shocked the government officials; later such bandits grew in number and no longer appeared so surprising. During the

---

209. Ibid., 15/11.
210. Unfortunately the above-quoted sketch does not tell us the political ideas with which the two kung-sheng inspired Chang Lo-hsing, nor the details of the regulations announced on that occasion.
211. Hsüan-tsung Ch'eng-huang-ti sheng-hsün, 81/35-36.

rebellion period, Miao P'ei-lin was said to have conducted the
planning in Chang Lo-hsing's headquarters. There his reputation
grew so high that everybody in Chang's army called him "Miao
Hsien-sheng" (苗 先 生).[212] In the marginal Nien areas like Fei-
hsien, Shantung, the government officials, after having broken an
earthwall community, captured a ling-sheng who was supposed to
be the chief adviser in that area.[213] In the same fashion, the Fu-
fei entrusted their planning to a ling-sheng, Li Tsung-t'ang (李宗棠)
and a degraded official, Liu Shu-yü(劉淑愚).[214] Further to the
north, Tung Ch'ien-ju (董乾儒), a chü-jen, devoted himself to the
construction of earthwalls on seven strategic spots and to the enlistment of civilians into the Eight Diagrams sect.[215] Certain
"sheng-yüan and chien-sheng without the means of livelihood" (wu-
lai sheng chien 無賴生監) participated in the Eight Diagrams sect
as "flag bearers," a kind of branch leader, as early as 1837.[216]

Available materials tell us that the following degree holders
served as chiefs of armed legions in the Nien camp.[217]

Chien-sheng:	Liu Han-hsing (劉漢興)
	Teng Pao-shan (鄧保山)
Dismissed sheng-yüan:	Ch'ien Lo-wen (錢洛文)
	Yao Lo-kuang (姚洛廣)
	Han Lo-hsing (韓洛興)
	Lo Ch'ing-hsün (羅青訓)
	Chao Ho-sheng (趙合生)
Wu-sheng:	Kuo Ch'an (郭燦)
Kung-sheng:	Yüan An-yü (袁安愚)
	Fan Shao-hsing (樊紹薪)
	Kao Ch'eng-hsün (高承勳)
Ling-sheng:	Yang Fang-hen (楊方恒)
	Chang Hsüeh-yüan (張學源)
Wu-chü:	Hu Hao-shan (胡浩善)
	Yen Hsi-ch'un (閻錫純)

Among these, Hu Hao-shan, a chü-jen of Su-chou, raised a force
of several thousand men in support of the Nien's blue banner.[218]

---

212. Wo-yang feng-t'u chi, 15/12. Ch'ing-pai-lei-ch'ao tells a
different story. When Chang Lo-hsing invaded Hsia-tsai in the first
month of 1856, Miao avoided Chang by fleeing to Shou-chou. (7/158)
213. Fang-lüeh, 182/24.
214. Shantung chün-hsing chi-lüeh, 18B/7.
215. Ibid., 19B/2.
216. Hsüan-tsung Ch'eng-huang-ti sheng-hsün, 85/13.
217. Yin Chia-ping, Cheng-chiao chi-lüeh, 2/5; Shantung chün-
hsing chi-lüeh, 2A/7; Yü-chün chi-lüeh, Wan-fei 1/9-10; 2/17; Fang-
lüeh, 104/1; 150/18.
218. Shantung chün-hsing chi-lüeh, 2A/7.

53

Such cases, however, were rather rare.

Since the Nien organization was a patchwork rather than a highly centralized machine, a member of the gentry had to possess an armed force of his own before he tried to play a leading part in the Nien. By what means could he raise that force? He could not rely on his gentry position alone. A great part of the gentry listed above attained their power through another channel, namely, the formation of local corps.

The gentry usually held the commanding authority in the organization of local corps. They did this in obedience to the Imperial ordinance, because the Emperor felt that only their class could supply him influential and reliable servants for local affairs.[219] To the disappointment of the government, however, what the gentry did under the mask of local corps in the border areas between Anhwei and Shantung was contrary to the government's wishes.

In the beginning the gentry used the local corps as a source of profit. Since raising funds for the local corps was their major business, exacting "corps fees" (t'uan-fei 團 費) from the people became their legal right.[220] Treating the funds like spoils, they divided them with the local officials according to a ratio agreed upon by both sides.[221] At this stage they were still acting as agents of the local government, and their activities did not go beyond misappropriation. Once their military power was affirmed, however, their appetites grew larger. It was not difficult for a wu-sheng, whose degree was not too high, to mobilize the local corps of several districts, amounting to several thousand men.[222] No one was able to prevent the gentry of this type from entitling themselves t'ang-chu or chai-chu (寨 主).[223] As the struggle between the government and the Nien dragged on, these chai-chu became a third force, strong enough to affect the balance of power between the two adversaries.

That this third force laid its weight on the side of the Nien is understandable. As stated before, the forces on the local level began to grow more powerful when the central government's power was declining. The growth of local forces was thus at the expense of the government's authority, and was by nature incompatible with the regeneration of Imperial power. At the same time, the local forces could easily identify their cause with that of the

219. Ch'ing-ch'ao hsü-wen-hsien t'ung-k'ao, 215/9617; Fang-lüeh, 14/1-3.
220. Shantung chün-hsing chi-lüeh, 24A/16.
221. Ibid., 22A/6-10.
222. Ibid., 22B/6.
223. Ibid., 11B/2.

rebels, who likewise sprang from the localities.[224] Before they formally joined the Nien or other bandits, the local corps under gentry command pursued brigandage in defiance of the law.[225] From the beginning some gentry had utilized their privilege of close contact with the officials to negotiate terms of pardon for bandits.[226]

To the Nien the big clans and the gentry supplied leadership. Sometimes clan membership and the examination degree were combined in one person; sometimes gentry accepted leadership besides offering counsel. When earthwalls and local corps came into the picture, the positions of yü-chu and t'ang-chu could not go to people other than the clan heads who commanded the majority of their fellow villagers or to the members of the gentry who possessed social influence.

The third and basic element was, of course, the peasants. Yüan Chia-san explained why a huge number of commoners joined the Nien:

> The Nien assembled more and more members, not less than several hundred thousand... The gangsters, envious of the Nien's gains from plunder, eagerly took part with them. The loyal followed, because now they were nothing but homeless paupers and found no other way of living. Therefore, whenever the Nien's plunder-ing bands started to move, hundreds of thousands of commoners followed.... [227]

Obviously this is a misinterpretation. The last section has shown us by what methods the Nien induced the people to join them. Yet Yüan's remark is sufficient to show what an immense number of followers the Nien had drawn from the common people. Another official reported that in 1862, out of the whole of north Anhwei, only the magistrate of T'ai-ho succeeded in keeping his people from joining the Nien.[228]

Most of the commoners were peasants. They composed the larger part of the earthwall inhabitants. According to Governor Li Hsü-i's (李 績 宜) estimate, the population of each earthwall

---

224. A number of gentry, though declining to support the Nien cause, still did not show loyalty to the government. When their local corps swelled to their full height, they hoisted rebellious flags of their own. Miao P'ei-lin of Anhwei, Liu Te-p'ei of Shantung (Shantung chün-hsing chi-lüeh, 21A/1), and Li Chan (李 晴) of Honan (Fang-lüeh, 148/10-11) are examples of such action.

225. Shantung chün-hsing chi-lüeh, 11B/2; 22B/4.

226. Ibid., 13A/11.

227. Yüan Chia-san, Memorials, 9/51-52.

228. Fang-lüeh, 110/23.

community numbered from a thousand to three thousand.[229] To the west of Lin-huai-kuan, there were three large earthwall communities, each of which had only slightly more than a thousand inhabitants.[230] Wang-yü (王 圩), a big earthwall community on the south of the Hui where the Nien's main force was concentrated, provided shelter to approximately two thousand people.[231] Some of the people were native inhabitants; some of them were brought in by the Nien. The Nien's spoils included not only grain, cattle, and horses, but also human captives--men and women, adults and children.[232] When government forces broke through any earthwall community, they always reported that they found a multitude of refugees and released them from the bandits.[233] These so-called refugees were none other than the people whom the Nien had transferred from other places.

The chief source of the Nien's power was the male adult peasants. The Nien depended upon them as recruits for the army and as producers of provisions. During the intervals between expeditionary campaigns, the farmers lived in their own communities, pursuing their daily agricultural duties. In the event of mobilization, the chiefs held conferences to decide the number of men each earthwall community was to offer and to fix a date and place for their assemblage.[234]

Runaways and deserters from the government militia also formed a part of the Nien forces. The militia, well known as "volunteers," cannot be described here.[235] Its organization was intended to make up for the deficiency of the decadent regular army.[236] In general, the volunteers in north Anhwei and south Shantung were so weak, inexperienced, and undisciplined that the Nien found it easy to capture them on the battlefield or to induce them to desert their camps.[237] Frequent mutinies or defection in

229. Ibid., 147/29-30.
230. Ibid., 127/16-19.
231. Fang-lüeh, 77/18-19. The last section tells us that Miao P'ei-lin drove many people into his earthwall. In Shantung, a chief of the Eight Diagrams sect, called Yen Hsiu-lun, extended his earthwall to the size of a city and induced about thirty thousand people to move in there (Shantung chün-hsing chi-lüeh, 13B/5). But earthwall communities on Miao's and Yen's model were very rare.
232. Yü-chün chi-lüeh, 6, Wan-fei 2/13.
233. Yüan Chia-san, Memorials, 7/25.
234. Fang-lüeh, 127/16-19.
235. For detailed story about the "volunteers," see Franz Michael, "Military Organization and Power Structure of China in the Nineteenth Century" (unpublished manuscript).
236. Yüan Chia-san, Memorials, 3/51; 9/19.
237. Fang-lüeh, 273/4. Yen Ching-ming (閻敬銘), governor of Shantung, compared the Hunan volunteers and the volunteers of the northern provinces: "Hu (Lin-i), Tseng (Kuo-fan), and Tso (Tseng-t'ang) initiated [the formation of volunteers] in their native

consequence of financial difficulty produced more and more
"roaming volunteers" (yu-yung 游勇). For these the Nien nest was
an ideal hide-out.[238] Some disbanded volunteers, even though they
had gone home and resumed farm work, finally joined the Nien
when the latter's influence reached their villages.[239] Sometimes
the Nien, without waiting for mutiny or dissolution, enticed the
volunteers away from their commanders with promises of gain.[240]
The volunteers came to the Nien by different ways but they all
brought the same gift. First, the volunteers could introduce to the
Nien whatever military knowledge they had gained from the government army.[241] Secondly, since they were aware of the strength
and weaknesses of the government forces, they could supply the
Nien with ample information about the enemy.[242] These special
contributions constituted the main difference between volunteers
and ordinary peasants, though both belonged to the same class. In
the Nien organization the volunteers were fewer in number but
they offered greater service.

The salt smugglers, the old collaborators of the Nien, made
up one of the earliest elements of the Nien bands. After 1853,
records about their activities in Huai-pei became rare. It is, however, unlikely that they suddenly withdrew from Huai-pei, for
most of them were natives of that area. It is more reasonable to
suppose that they gave up the contraband trade to pursue a bigger
enterprise, namely, activity in the Nien Rebellion. When the West
Nien reached Tientsin in 1868, the salt smugglers in that region
joined the Nien and induced them to invade the Tientsin suburbs.[243]

On their looting raids, the Nien frequently incorporated into
their bands the local bandits in Honan and Hupeh.[244] Near P'u-
chou and Fan-hsien, where the Yellow River changed its course in
1855, several thousands of dislocated people banded into armed
forces.[245] In the spring of 1865, they joined the Nien and thus
increased the latter's forces to such a degree that they could anni-

---

districts, emphasizing the education of talented and able persons
...[Therefore] purposeful men responded to their call enthusiastically... Now to call volunteers becomes a resounding measure
throughout the northern areas. In fact, only gangsters assemble
[in response to the call]. These people know nothing about loyalty
to their sovereign, allegiance to their superiors, and the art of
fighting their enemy...." (Shantung chün-hsing chi-lüeh, 4A/7)
  238. Su-chou chih, 10/23; Yüan Chia-san, Memorials, 2/49.
  239. Shantung chün-hsing chi-lüeh, 17B/6.
  240. Shantung chün-hsing chi-lüeh, 20A/7.
  241. Fang-lüeh, 8/17.
  242. Ibid., 279/6-9.
  243. Ibid., 309/10.
  244. Fang-lüeh, 3/18; 38/2.
  245. Shantung chün-hsing chi-lüeh, 11B/9.

hilate Prince Seng's army.[246] In Huai-pei itself, the disappearance
of the local bandits can also be regarded as a result of incorporation into the Nien.[247]

The Nien army, basically composed of the peasants under the
command of the big clans in their respective communities, was
not a professional army. When they attacked, the Nien commanders hurled hordes of their native villagers on the enemy to com-
pensate for their inferiority in weapons. In defense of a home
community, all the inhabitants behind the wall devoted their lives
to safeguarding it.[248] When the battle was over and they went back
to their ploughs, they appeared to be ordinary farmers. The Nien
leaders, unlike the Imperial officials, had no trouble in raising
military funds as long as the looting expeditions and agricultural
production were not disrupted. Nor did the Nien leaders need to
keep a watchful eye on their soldiers to guard against defection or
mutiny.[249] Between the Nien commanders and soldiers, family
and communal ties coexisted with comradeship. It was this
relationship which bound several thousand Meng-ch'eng and Po-
chou peasants to their leaders in the darkest year, 1864.[250] In the
battles of 1868, the same devotion drove the kinsmen of the top

---

246. Yü-chün chi-lüeh, 11, Wan-fei 18/1; Fang-lüeh, 230/20.

247. Yüan Chia-san's memorials show that the government forces
in Huai-pei were also challenged by the local bandits, but after
1854, records like this disappeared. (Yüan Tuan-min-kung chi,
Memorials, 5/18)

248. See section 6.

249. We have seen that volunteers who deserted from the government militia joined the Nien. After their joining, they proved as
reliable as the other elements in the Nien camp. The reason for
their reliability is simple. Those whom they served now were influential men of their own native communities, instead of officials
from other lands. Furthermore, the Nien leaders could promise them
more benefits than the officials who could not afford adequate and
regular payment. (Complaints about deficiency of revenue and about
the miserable conditions of the army can be found in almost every
official memorial.)

250. Following the capture of Chang Lo-hsing in 1863, the
Taiping capital, Nanking, fell in 1864. The Taiping remnants under
Lai Wen-kuang, Ch'en Te-ts'ai (陳得才), Ma Jung-ho (馬融和), and
Liang Ch'eng-fu (梁成富), with whom the Nien had been cooperating
since 1863, perished in the battle at the Hupeh-Anhwei border.
Thanks to their cavalry, the Nien survived the Taiping remnants but
encountered the pursuing government forces on every side. At this
critical moment, the Nien under Chang Tsung-yü, Jen Chu, Niu Hung-
sheng (牛宏升) and Li Yün-t'ai (李蘊泰) swore to continue the
fighting, with the full support of the Meng-ch'eng-Po-chou followers. (T'ai-p'ing t'ien-kuo shih-wen ch'ao, 2/99) For the story, see
Part II, section 2.

Nien leaders to fight to the bitter end.[251]

5. The Cavalry of the Nien

The Nien's construction of earthwalls does not mean that they were content with the resources of a small area or with a limited range of activities. The strongholds between the Wo and the Hui furnished bases and retreats, but they represented only the stationary and defensive aspect of the Nien's military structure.

The government officials' attempts to destroy Nien granaries and crops in the fields indicate that the Nien never abandoned agriculture. Tseng Kuo-fan admitted that, while the Nien leveled the farmhouses of outlying districts to the ground, they continued to enjoy the shelter and agricultural harvests of their nests in Meng-ch'eng and Po-chou.[252] The continuance of farm work in the Nien areas, however, does not mean that the Nien area was economically self-sufficient. Famine played a large part in driving the Nien to take arms, and during the rebellion, famine continued to haunt north Anhwei almost every year.[253] In addition to natural calamities, war disrupted the Huai Valley. Grain production diminished, but at the same time the Nien increased their numbers by enrolling more and more starving people. It was impossible to keep the Nien quiet in their destitute area while neighboring provinces remained fairly prosperous and wealthy. Shantung, farther from the threat of the Taipings and free from Nien plundering in early Hsien-feng years, had ample stores of grain.[254] Because of the irrigation system and the flourishing of salt fields, Ch'ing-chiang-p'u and Huai-an, in north Kiangsu, still had plentiful supplies of grain and salt. Chou-chia-k'ou, in Honan, located at the junction of the Ying and the Chia-lu rivers, was a center of trade.[255] Shantung, Ch'ing-chiang-p'u and Chou-chia-k'ou, then, became the objects of Nien plundering.[256]

---

251. See Part II, section 4, where the limitation of this family and communal loyalty is also discussed.
252. Shantung chün-hsing chi-lüeh, 4C/10.
253. Yüan Chia-san, Memorials, 7/32; Fang-lüeh, 83/2-3; Yu-chün chi-lüeh, 6, Wan-fei 3/19-20.
254. Fang-lüeh, 49/13.
255. Yüan Chia-san, Memorials, 9/39; Letters, 1/6.
256. From 1859 on, the Nien pillaged Shantung every year. The campaigns in 1860 lasted four months and covered more than twenty districts. (Shantung chün-hsing chi-lüeh, 3A/4) On their way home, the Nien's caravan of spoils extended several hundred li, and included a tremendous amount of grain and several thousand cattle and horses. Honan suffered more frequently and more seriously than Shantung. (Yu-chün chi-lüeh, 6, Wan-fei 2/13; Fang-lüeh, 4/2) Located immediately to the east of Anhwei, it not only was the first

The Nien went on expeditions year after year for the purpose of looting. But they did not use their irresistible advance in the neighboring three provinces as a step to the occupation of cities. In other words, they never attempted to use their military triumphs to expand their territory. They were even reluctant to take the cities south of the Huai, to say nothing about the districts of other provinces.[257] The Nien never remained in the areas they plundered, no matter how wealthy, but brought their spoils back home. Generally the Nien gave government officials the impression that the difference between themselves and the Taipings was that the former focused their attention on plunder, the latter on the seizure of cities.[258] The Shantung chün-hsing chi-lüeh gives an interesting description of the Nien expeditions:

> Usually [the Nien] hoisted flags and massed troops
> in spring and autumn. They pillaged near and far areas.
> Following the wagons heavily loaded with spoils, [the
> victors] feasted and sang on the way home. After the
> grain thus collected was consumed, [they] came out again.
> [The regularity of going and coming] resembled that of
> traders.[259]

Thus the Nien behaved like traders, going back and forth between their nests and adjacent provinces.

The means enabling the Nien to move back and forth freely, frequently, and swiftly was their formidable cavalry. South of the Huai, paths between rice fields interlocked; on the northern side, a plain extended to Yen-chou in Shantung, to K'ai-feng in Honan, and to Hai-chou in Kiangsu. This plain provided ample space on which ten thousand horses could gallop.[260] While economic conditions compelled the Nien to seek provisions in distant areas, geographical circumstances facilitated a high degree of mobility. Chang Mou (張 茂), a Nien leader, employed four hundred horsemen for vanguard duty early in 1853.[261] Four years later, even the small town of Liu-kou (柳 溝), a Nien earthwall community,

province to be invaded but also became the center from which the Nien made thrusts into other provinces, and the main route of returning Nien forces, still anxious for plunder. (Hu Lin-i, Hu Wen-chung-kung ch'üan-chi, Memorials, 1/339; 2/919; Fang-lüeh, 246/14-18) On each expedition the Nien succeeded in acquiring immeasurable war booty. The Nien also aimed at the huge store of provisions in Ch'ing-chiang-p'u. (Fang-lüeh, 75/15; 76/21)

257. Yüan Chia-san, Memorials, 13/29.
258. Fang-lüeh, 146/5; 149/6.
259. Shantung chün-hsing chi-lüeh, 2A/1.
260. Yüan Chia-san, Memorials, 8/32; Shantung chün-hsing chi-lüeh, 2C/1.
261. Yüan Chia-san, Memorials, 3/7.

maneuvered a mounted troop of four thousand men; Han-yü (韓圩), another earthwall community, possessed a thousand horses, ten times more than the attacking enemy.[262] In the succeeding year, the T'ai-ho Nien had eight hundred horsemen in their band of ten thousand men, and the Po-chou Nien had six hundred in their band of three thousand.[263] In Hui-ts'un (回村), an earthwall community, one-fourth of the band was mounted.[264] The Meng-ch'eng - Po-chou area as a whole was able to bring up three thousand horses to the front lines to deal with the enemy; these were in addition to those kept at home and those used on the Huai bank.[265] In 1860, the number of Nien horses reached twenty thousand.[266] Thereafter, until their suppression, the Nien always maintained a cavalry of this size.

By means of this gigantic cavalry, the Nien were able to over-run eight provinces for fifteen years. Mastery of cavalry was one of the Nien characteristics. Like the banner system and the collective adherence of a whole clan to the secret society, the adoption of mounted troops was a usage shared by the Nien and the Eight Diagrams sect. Wherever the Eight Diagrams bandits arrived, they first sought out the horses.[267] Like the Eight Diagrams, the Nien collected horses first from their native places. According to Yüan Chia-san, however, the area around Hsü-chou was not a place where horses were raised.[268] This statement seems to present a contradiction, but Yüan meant that the Hsü-chou area did not specialize in raising horses as did the grasslands outside the Great Wall. For the purpose of securing horses from Manchuria and Inner Mongolia, Yüan contrasted these two regions with the areas around his own headquarters. Yüan also mentioned that he had trained less than a thousand mounted volunteers.[269] If it had been difficult to obtain horses in north Kiangsu and north Anhwei, the training of mounted volunteers would have been equally difficult. Mounted volunteers, however, were far inferior to regular cavalry transferred from Manchuria. The governor of Honan, Cheng Yüan-shan (鄭元善), though he agreed to the drafting of natives as mounted volunteers, still insisted on buying horses from outside the Great Wall.[270] In Yüan Chia-san's estimation, a thousand cavalrymen from outside

262. Fang-lüeh, 27/2; 31/3.
263. Ibid., 40/14-15.
264. Yüan Chia-san, Memorials, 8/46.
265. Ibid., 8/32-33, 50.
266. Ibid., Letters, 1/25.
267. Shantung chün-hsing chi-lüeh, 12A/23-24; 13B/8; Fang-lüeh, 174/24-27.
268. Fang-lüeh, 45/23.
269. Ibid., 44/3; 45/23.
270. Fang-lüeh, 159/6-7.

the Great Wall could match four thousand Nien cavalry.[271] Financial conditions made the government armies in the Huai Valley
prefer a cavalry small in number but good in quality. The fact
that the government officials did not organize as vast a cavalry in
the Huai region as did the Nien, and that they kept asking for
horses from Manchuria, does not imply that large numbers of
horses were unavailable in that region. From the outset, the Nien
were able to support several hundred horsemen in each large band,
and the term "mounted bandits" appeared in official reports.[272] In
Szu-chou (泗 州), the Nien forced their captives to give horses
instead of money as ransom.[273] This is a good example of the Nien
method of procuring horses in Huai-pei. The early Nien cavalry
was not striking in number but, in proportion to their whole army,
the cavalry's size was considerable. Before 1855, the range of the
Anhwei Nien's plunder had not yet gone too far beyond the frontiers
of that province. It is unlikely that they got horses from places
other than their home area.

The Nien's homeland certainly supplied some horses, but the
horses gathered there can be considered only as the core of the
Nien cavalry. The Nien cavalry in the later period procured its
horses elsewhere. Plunder of the neighboring provinces was the
Nien's second method for procuring horses. After 1856, the Nien
invaded Honan every year. Luck was on the side of the Nien from
the very beginning. The first attempt resulted in a huge acquisition of goods, captives, cattle, mules, donkeys and horses; the
cargo of spoils covered a length of two hundred li.[274] In 1863,
when Chang Tsung-yü was rebuilding the Nien's main force after
the fall of Chih-ho, he regarded Honan as the major source for the
procurement of horses. When he passed Hsiang-ch'eng (項城), he
captured many people who were ransomed by payment in horses.[275] Consequently, the market rate for horses in that district
climbed.

Shantung supplied the Nien with more horses than did Honan.
Early in 1861, the rising Eight Diagrams bandits in both Hsing-
hsien and Ts'ao-hsien startled their enemy by maneuvering a large
cavalry force.[276] A single earthwall community, P'u-t'ou (鋪頭),
southwest of Lin-ch'eng, sent a cavalry force of two thousand men
to deal with Sheng-pao.[277] Sung Chin-shih (宋景詩), Yang P'eng-lin
(楊鵬嶺) and other Eight Diagrams leaders, after surrendering
to Sheng-pao, were appointed officers of mounted militia, which

271. Yüan Chia-san, Letters, 1/25; 2/24.
272. Wang K'ai-yün, 14/1; Yüan Chia-san, Memorials, 2/32.
273. Anhwei t'ung-chih, 246/29.
274. Yü-chün chi-lüeh, 6, Wan-fei 2/13.
275. Hsiang-ch'eng hsien-chih, 31/15-16.
276. Shantung chün-hsing chi-lüeh, 12A/4.
277. Ibid., 12B/4.

were nothing more than the original mounted bands at their command. When Sung Chin-shih rebelled again, he led over a thousand mounted militia, galloping from Shensi through Shansi and Chihli back to Shantung, sweeping aside all resistance from the garrisons in those provinces.[278] After Sung's forces returned home, they expanded their mounted bands by drawing in more horses from their native districts.[279] All these facts indicate that, though Shantung was not so famous in producing strong horses as the provinces outside the Great Wall, it could easily provide the rebels with several thousand horses. The Nien in north Anhwei were unable to increase their mounted troops to five thousand men until 1855, when the shift of the Yellow River made the southern border of Shantung accessible to them.[280] It has been said that after 1859 the Nien considered Shantung as a defenseless pool from which to draw spoils, and the districts around Hsü-chou as familiar routes leading to Shantung. The invaders "included the blue, white, and red banners, of which cavalry had already composed the main part. Now in addition to the original cavalry, the Nien sought for horses wherever they looted. Their horses thus increased steadily."[281] The amount of spoils taken can be shown by an episode in the eighth month of 1861. At that time the Nien's looting raids covered five to six hundred li, and the main objectives were grain, cattle, and horses.[282] When Prince Seng-ko-lin-ch'in overtook the looters, he compelled them to abandon their spoils; it took the Prince several days to transport the Nien spoils to his headquarters.[283] Besides horses, the Nien acquired camels from Shantung. Near Szu-chou, east of the Nien area, a group of twenty thousand Nien from Su-chou had several thousand horses and nearly a hundred camels.[284] In 1861 ten thousand Nien approached Shou-chou. The ex-governor, Weng T'ung-shu (翁同書), on seeing from the city wall more than a thousand horses and about twenty camels led by men with long hair, immediately convinced himself that these must be the Nien returning from Shantung.[285] The flood of the Wo and Fei rivers in the summer of 1860 overwhelmed the Nien nests. The Nien leaders, Chiang T'ai-lin, Wang Huai-i, Ch'eng Ta-wei (程大偉), and Liu Kou (劉 狗), "emptied their nests" to invade Shantung with over a hundred

278. Shansi t'ung-chih, 78/37.
279. Shantung chün-hsing chi-lüeh, 15B/1; 16A/3; Fang-lüeh, 183/10.
280. Fang-lüeh, 9/9; Shantung chün-hsing chi-lüeh, 1A/2-3.
281. Yüan Chia-san, Letters, 1/9.
282. Shantung chün-hsing chi-lüeh, 3A/5.
283. Ibid., 3A/17.
284. Yüan Chia-san, Memorials, 14/29-30.
285. Ibid., 14/31.

thousand men.[286] The fact that the number of the Nien's horses suddenly increased to twenty thousand in 1861 suggests that the expedition of the preceding year was planned principally for the procurement of horses.

The Nien also obtained horses by purchase. For example, Sun Kuei-hsin, a leader of the Nien's white banner, had at his command a cavalry of four thousand horses.[287] Not content with what he already had, he offered to pay high prices for additional horses.[288] A record of Yüan Chia-san shows that a black market for horses existed in north Anhwei:

> The Nien are using high prices to induce treacherous people to transport horses to their support. Recently I heard that Ch'in Chan-ao (秦占鰲), sergeant of the local military post of Szu-chou, and Chao Chin-tou (趙金斗), a local corps chief, allowed some horse traders to pass after taking bribes from them... A Moslem of Ting-yüan, Wang T'ung-t'ien (王通天), and others, have twice secretly transported thirty to forty horses to sell to the Nien in Ting-yüan for heavy profits. [Ch'in and Chao] should have arrested and sent them to my headquarters. But Wang T'ung-t'ien and others promised to pay money. The bribe obtained in the first instance amounted to a hundred and fifty liang of silver. In the second case the shortage of money made them use horses as substitutes...[Besides this case] there is a cavalry officer, Ch'i-k'e-chin-a (奇克 金阿) by name, who on the 29th of the fifth month entrusted a man of Wang-chia-yü, called T'ang Hua-chün, through his groom, Hsüeh Ming, to sell some horses for him.[289]

The case of Wang T'ung-t'ien was no doubt not the first instance of this kind in the Nien area; but unlike their predecessors, Wang and his companions were not lucky enough to avoid notice. A local underofficer and a local corps chief were also involved in Wang's trading. Even worse, a government cavalry officer attempted to profit from selling horses. The high price offered by the Nien was so attractive that it influenced not only traders but government officers as well. The evidence then shows that the Nien obtained their horses not only from their homeland in north Anhwei but also from Honan and especially from Shantung; and not only by looting but also through purchase.

---

286. Shantung chün-hsing chi-lüeh, 2C/15.
287. Yüan Chia-san, Memorials, 8/50.
288. Ibid., Letters, 1/5.
289. Ibid., Memorials, 13/4-5.

A fourth source of horses for the Nien was the remnants of Prince Seng-ko-lin-ch'in's Manchurian and Mongolian cavalry.[290] Tseng Kuo-fan said in a letter to Li Hung-chang: "Originally the Nien were not important bandits. Since they acquired many horses from Prince Seng's cavalry, ...they have presumably become a strong enemy."[291] In another letter he said: "After the defeat of Miao P'ei-lin, the Nien force was declining. As a result of Prince Seng's disaster, the bandits seized five thousand horses from his cavalry. From then on the Nien business becomes unmanageable. Now with their horses surpassing ten thousand, they are undoubtedly our equal in strength."[292] Both Tseng and the <u>Shantung chün-hsing chi-lüeh</u> estimated that Prince Seng lost five thousand horses to the Nien.[293] But the memorial forwarded by Kuo-jui (國 瑞), Prince Seng's first assistant, stated that at the time of the Prince's death, steady losses had already reduced his horses to two thousand.[294] Even if the Nien had captured all Seng's horses, the number could not have been so large as five thousand. Moreover, the Nien's success in reviving their force after 1863 was not entirely due to the gains from Prince Seng's cavalry. Tseng's remark, however, indicates how seriously government officials regarded Prince Seng's losses. The reason is very simple. We have referred to the fact that the horses from Manchuria and Inner Mongolia were far stronger than those from the south and were consequently preferred by the government officials. It is no wonder that government officials shed tears over the loss of these excellent horses. Besides, the riders of these horses also went over to the Nien. Unlike the ordinary horsemen, they had been picked from the veteran Manchurian and Inner Mongolian cavalries. Their surrender gave birth to a new mounted corps in the Nien army, called "the North Corps."[295] This new force rendered to the Nien a marvellous service in the campaigns of 1865-66.[296]

The fifth source from which the Nien obtained their horses was the areas in Shensi, Shansi, and Chihli which were looted by Chang Tsung-yü after he had diverted his force to the west. In 1866, when Chang Tsung-yü entered Shensi from Honan, his force numbered eight to nine thousand, including both infantry and cavalry; but after a startling victory over the government army at

290. See Part II, section 2.
291. Tseng Kuo-fan, <u>Tseng Wen-cheng-kung shu-cha</u>, 25/19.
292. <u>Ibid.</u>, 25/27.
293. <u>Shantung chün-hsing chi-lüeh</u>, 9A/9-10.
294. <u>Fang-lüeh</u>, 232/21.
295. <u>Ibid.</u>, 273/4.
296. Tseng Kuo-fan, <u>Tseng Wen-cheng-kung shu-cha</u>, 26/5.

Pa-ch'iao (灞橋), another eight to nine thousand men, most of whom were mounted, were added to the original force.[297] Thus, in the winter of 1866 the total number of Chang's force was six-teen to eighteen thousand. Te-hsing-a (德興阿),[298] a government commander in Shensi, made this estimate. But in the later part of the same memorial, he reported that Chang demonstrated his force along a road of several dozen li. The local gazetteer of Hu-hsien (鄠縣) even presents so vast a figure as four hundred thousand to magnify Chang's triumphant position after Pa-ch'iao.[299] Even though one prefers Te-hsing-a's conservative estimate of sixteen to eighteen thousand, he will see that Chang's cavalry could not be less than ten thousand, because a great part of Chang's force was mounted. In the winter of 1867, Chang Tsung-yü, crossing the Yellow River to Shansi, returned to the East again.[300] When he arrived at Chihli, his horses increased to such a degree that he changed all his infantry into cavalry, with one man sometimes leading several horses.[301] According to Tso Tsung-t'ang (左宗棠),[302] these horses were gained from plunder-ing along Chang's route from Shansi and Honan to Chihli.[303] Li Hung-chang agreed with Tso on this point. He said: "In recent years the Nien have wandered throughout the northern provinces. The most they gained from looting those regions was horses. On the vast plain they cross a hundred li quick as a wink."[304] Li reckoned that the total number of Chang's horses was forty to fifty thousand.[305]

Both the East Nien and West Nien held fast to their horses to the last moment. After their suppression, the cavalry of the East Nien captured by the government forces in 1867 numbered about ten thousand,[306] while those of the West Nien captured in 1868 numbered more than twenty-five thousand.[307]

---

297. Fang-lüeh, 274/20.
298. d. 1867. Hummel, pp. 762-767.
299. Hu-hsien hsiang-t'u-chih, A, p. 10.
300. Shansi t'ung-chih, 128/37-38.
301. Fang-lüeh, 306/7-8.
302. 1812-1885. Hummel, pp. 711-712.
303. Fang-lüeh, 306/7-8.
304. Ibid., 309/11-12.
305. Li Hung-chang, Li Wen-chung-kung ch'üan-chi, Letters to Friends and Colleagues, 8/3,
306. Shantung chün-hsing chi-lüeh, 7C/3-5.
307. Ibid., 9A/9-11; 9B3-8; Fang-lüeh, 316/5. These figures are fairly reliable. They were derived not from a general estimate but from the reports forwarded by various commanders. These com-manders had no reason to exaggerate, because the horses thus captured had to be delivered to their respective superiors' head-quarters.

Evidently it was only during the three years (1865-1868) following Seng-ko-lin-ch'in's death that the Nien increased their cavalry forces greatly. 1868 was also the year of the Nien's suppression in Shantung. Thus the expansion of their cavalry in the last three years did not regain for them their lost homeland, where the conditions essential for their survival prevailed. Yet the closer the Nien drew towards their fate, the more ferociously they fought. This increased ferocity resulted mainly from the enlarged Nien cavalry. Along with the size of their cavalry forces, the Nien's skill in deploying cavalry also astonished the officials. Li Hung-chang praised Jen Chu, the chief of the East Nien, as "the best cavalry commander in the whole country."[308] If the Nien cavalry in the closing years did not save the Nien, it at least dismayed the loyalists and kept the armies of six provinces, in addition to the Hsiang and Huai armies, constantly mobilized and engaged.

6. The Tactics of the Nien

The function of the Nien's earthwalls and cavalry was manifested in their tactics. Corresponding to these two phases of the Nien's military structure, their tactics were also two-fold. Seng-ko-lin-ch'in summarized them thus:

> [The Nien] capture civilians for recruits in their army. By virtue of doing so, their cavalry and infantry increase rapidly to several thousand, extending a hundred li, while the government forces are far inferior in number. If we hope to root out their nests, we have to bring provisions and water over one or two hundred li, because the areas around the Nien area have previously been laid waste. When we withdraw, we will likely be ambushed from every side. This is the main reason the government armies cannot risk a decisive battle with the Nien for ten years.[309]

The Nien did not always recruit their army by capturing civilian people. As noted above, the Nien employed various methods to induce people to join them. With the people's full support, the earthwall communities maintained a solid defense at home. On the other hand, the cavalry led mobile thrusts abroad. Since the service of the people was indispensable, both in defending the homeland and in assailing the outside targets, the people's

---

308. Li Hung-chang, Letters to Friends and Colleagues, 7/29.
309. Wang K'ai-yün, 14/4.

activities also had two phases. "The inhabitants in the district of Po-chou, most of whom are countryfolk of the Nien leaders, act as fellow bandits when they follow the leaders outside their native villages and become civilian people again when they return and pick up their plows."[310]

Let us take a look at the stationary aspect, that is, the defensive work performed by the earthwalls. The Nien's defensive network, knit together by earthwall communities, gradually took shape during the years 1857-1859. In other words, the earthwalls did not start to function as a defensive system until 1857. Before that time the Nien had not yet made use of earthwalls on a large scale. Yüan Chia-san presented this point concisely: "Several years ago the Nien were not aware of the reliability of trenches and earthworks. At one time they emphasized open field warfare. From Hsien-feng seventh year on, all of them learned the usefulness of deep trenches and high breastworks. This change made the Nien place equal emphasis on defensive warfare."[311] The Nien, however, had learned the usefulness of trenches and earthworks before 1857. What Yüan said here was not close to the fact. In 1856 when Yüan arrived at Chih-ho, he found earthworks standing across the Wo River.[312] Perhaps Yüan's remark signifies that the Nien did not use earthwalls systematically until 1857; this would conform to the development of the Nien's central area. Yüan repeated on another occasion: "The Nien of former days considered open field warfare their special skill. Recently they have erected earthwalls, garrisoned them, and provisioned them. The bandits' earthwalls stand like the forests."[313] This change of tactics on the part of the Nien was the first thing which annoyed Yüan, because this new defense measure drove Yüan's army from the whole Nien area and compelled him to set up his headquarters outside its boundaries after 1857.

The withdrawal of Yüan's army raises some significant questions. What drove the government forces from the area? And how did the earthwall communities function as units of defense?

The construction of earthwalls had previously been under government sponsorship and encouragement. Its objective was to store all the villages' agricultural products behind a guarded wall so as to leave only an empty field for the plundering bandits.[314] There was a particular term for this measure: "to solidify the wall and to clear up the fields." Now the Nien had turned the earthwalls to their own purpose. The function of earthwalls re-

---

310. Fang-lüeh, 14/6.
311. Yüan Chia-san, Letters, 1/25.
312. Fang-lüeh, 17/16-17.
313. Ibid., Memorials, 13/51.
314. Fang-lüeh, 11/5; 58/3.

mained the same, but now the system was directed against the government officials. After 1856 the Nien pursued a scorched-earth policy within a radius of two hundred li outside their central area.[315] By 1857, the Nien had completed the denudation of the Anhwei-Honan borderland.[316] Between Po-chou and east Honan extended an area three hundred li wide and two hundred li long which contained no trace of human habitation. Within that no man's land, no grain was left in the field, and every well was filled up. If any government troops ventured into this area without carrying provisions and water, they would starve and suffer from thirst.[317] When they reached the Nien area, they found that the entire landscape, except for earthwalls standing here and there, was as barren as the outlying area, for the Nien had cleared the fields of their products and stored them inside the walls. Each wall stood like a fortress, behind which the inhabitants were concealed. If the government forces remained to test the strength of those fortresses, they would find that all the male adults rallied under their yü-chu to resist and that the youngsters and women backed the defenders by stirring up dust with rakes.[318] When the food the attackers carried along with them was exhausted, the only alternative left was to retreat. Retreat was usually disastrous as the once empty land would become filled with raiders who assailed the weary and fleeing invaders on every side. This was the lesson the Nien taught the Honan army at the end of 1856. During the next year, 1857, the Nien considered the earthworks and trenches as the best means of defense and extended their construction over wider and wider territories. In the face of such a defensive network, the Honan army dared not risk further penetration. On the east side, Yüan Chia-san made some attempts, but in vain. The Nien not only repulsed his offensive but hurled back counterblows.[319]

Of course, such a method of defense depended on the wholehearted allegiance of the people. Lacking it, the Nien could not have carried out the policy of "solidifying the wall and clearing up the fields." Popular support of the Nien was aided by poor discipline among government armies which embittered the people. According to Tseng Kuo-fan, the civilian earthwall communities in Shantung and Honan, as well as those in north Anhwei, "hated the government soldiers as death foes."[320] In Honan, the civilian

315. Ibid., 14/6; 88/13.
316. Yü-chün chi-lüeh, 6, Wan-fei 2/13-15.
317. Fang-lüeh, 16/23.
318. Shantung chün-hsing chi-lüeh, 14B/5.
319. Yüan Chia-san, Memorials, 9/23.
320. Tseng Kuo-fan, Tseng Wen-cheng-kung ch'üan-chi, Comments to Reports, 3/58.

earthwall communities closed their doors to government armies, who thus found no place to buy foodstuffs. In some places, soldiers left behind by their company were stripped by the hostile people of clothing and weapons; some of them were buried alive.[321]

The use of earthwalls as an effective instrument to ward off the attacking enemy was not confined to the Nien's home sphere. They used the walls wherever they wanted to halt the pursuing enemy. When Chang Lo-hsing entered the Ssu-chou area, he captured a civilian earthwall and built a new one to the northwest as a flank of the front.[322] In Honan, in order to evade the government armies, the Nien seized civilian earthwall communities and turned them into fortresses.[323] The Nien even extended this principle to city defense. In the years 1857-1860, as noted before, the Nien held successively the Huai cities: Feng-yang, Huai-yüan, Lin-huai-kuan, and Ting-yüan. Around the suburbs of these cities the Nien erected over ten earthworks in front of the besieging armies.[324] Apart from this purely defensive use, earthworks were often raised at key transport spots for the purpose of safeguarding the Nien supply lines and, at the same time, of severing those of the enemy. In 1858, along the Hui there occurred a series of battles to establish footholds. Yüan Chia-san ordered the local corps under Miao P'ei-lin to build five earthworks on the north bank of the Hui in order to "cut the throats of the bandits."[325] In view of the threat, the Nien built eleven earthworks overnight around the enemy works as a countermeasure. Henceforth, all the key posts, by which the provisions of the government forces had to pass, were held by the newly erected Nien earthworks.[326] At that time, the Hui Basin was already considered a completely Nien territory. It was because he had no confidence in his own ability to pierce the Nien nests that Yüan turned to Miao for aid. But the fact that the Nien were more expert in using earthwalls paralyzed Yüan's efforts.

Nien tactics had their mobile aspect. In the previous section it was stated that every year, in spring and autumn, the Nien launched expeditions. Before they set out, they had to call up the banners. For this step, they had a special term -- "to form contingents for the banners" (chuang-ch'i 裝 旗). Before they equipped the banners, they staged operas.[327] Along their way they dispatched patrol horsemen to set fire to the villages they passed. For the patrol horsemen they also had a special term, "scouting

---

321. T'ing-chün chi-lüeh, 10/16.
322. Fang-lüeh, 56/18.
323. Fang-lüeh, 87/19.
324. Yüan Chia-san, Memorials, 13/1.
325. Ibid., 9/61.
326. Ibid., 9/33.
327. Fang-lüeh, 127/16-17.

horses" (pien-ma 邊馬). The main job of these scouting horses
was to determine whether or not there were any strong government forces around a contemplated target.[328] The Nien knew how
to evade a superior enemy and how to raid a weak point. Their
way of battering their opponents was at variance with that of the
Taipings. Between the two, Seng-ko-lin-ch'in made this comparison:

> The Nien nests are located near our essential land.
> They possess numerous horses, all swift in moving.
> Occasionally the banners dash in the various directions,
> but usually they are combined. Plunder in neighboring
> provinces does not lead them too far from their nests.
> They are always ready to run back to the nest in the
> event that the government armies' pursuit is steady. Un-
> less one retains them in battle for several hours in hand-
> to-hand combat, he will not win decisively. All this I
> have witnessed in Anhwei where I was engaged with Chang
> Lo-hsing. As for the wandering Taipings, they are cut off
> from their nests, with the wide Yangtze standing in the
> way. To go back to Nanking is not easy for them. Most
> of their components joined temporarily, and they are
> short of horses. Their speed is only equal to our infantry.
> On the battlefield, once our troops rush at them their
> battle array collapses. This I see in the present campaigns
> with the Taipings.[329]

Both Tseng Kuo-fan and Tso Tsung-t'ang held the same viewpoint.
They believed that to handle the Nien was far more difficult than
to deal with the Taipings.[330]
    While their earthwalls enabled them to stick to their nests in
defiance of furious assault, their cavalry enabled them to slide
away from stronger foes and to take weaker ones by surprise.
Therefore elusiveness was the first characteristic of the Nien
cavalry. It struck government leaders as the main difference
between the Nien and the Taipings. The above quotation shows
that the government leaders did not fear the Nien but regretted
that the Nien did not give them a chance to join in decisive battle.
Liu Ch'ang-yu (劉長佑),[331] governor-general of Chihli, made this
point very clear: "The bandits never fight to the death, nor do they
linger on the battlefield. As soon as we definitely locate their

328. Wang Ting-an, Ch'iu-ch'üeh-chai ti-tzu chi, 11/1.
329. Fang-lüeh, 214/33-34.
330. Tseng Kuo-fan, Tseng Wen-cheng-kung shu-cha, 25/6; 26/56;
Fang-lüeh, 273/4.
331. 1818-1887. Hummel, p. 515.

traces, they dash off or melt away to either side.[332] The Nien employed this method very early. In 1855 Chang Lo-hsing and Kung Te made a feint at Ying-chou, and when they succeeded in drawing the government armies in that direction, they diverted their bands southward to storm Meng-ch'eng and Huai-yüan.[333] In the sixties, when they were driven from their nests, they became ten times more elusive, for they found no way to avoid the pursuing enemy but to confuse them by fleeing in every direction. Along the Hupeh-Honan-Anhwei border, the military situation changed several times in a single day.[334] During this period the Nien held to the principle of not engaging the government army, but rather enticing it on until it was fatigued. The campaigns against Seng-ko-lin-ch'in from 1864 to 1865 were typical of this method. In the spring of 1865, the Nien moved between Hupeh and Honan, with Seng-ko-lin-ch'in's cavalry always at their rear. Then suddenly they dashed from west Honan through east Honan, toward Shantung, and in less than ten days they appeared in Shantung. From there they thrust southeast to Kiangsu and then turned back to Shantung. Within one month they had driven through four provinces.[335]

To strike as swiftly as lightning throughout several provinces was not intended merely to wear down the government pursuers. Wang Ting-an gives an explanation of the Nien tactics of elusiveness:

> On hearing from their spies that the arrival of the government forces was imminent, the Nien flew away hurriedly. After several days' and nights' pursuit by the government mounted troops, they reversed their banners to fight the pursuers furiously. They outflanked our army with two strong detachments of cavalry. With their fighting spirit mounting to its height, both horses and men moved as fast as wind and rain. Usually the government armies fell in their trap. [336]

The Nien never fled without purpose. Like mad beasts they kept running until circumstances allowed them to turn back to bite the exhausted hunters. One mounted man was usually accompanied by one or two footmen. All of them held long-handled spears with which they rushed at the enemy like a torrent. Meanwhile they extended their flanks to encircle the enemy, wave upon wave.[337]

332. Fang-lüeh, 183/23.
333. Fang-lüeh, 24/13-20.
334. Ibid., 222/15.
335. Wang Ting-an, Hsiang-chün chi, 16/6-7.
336. Wang Ting-an, Ch'iu-ch'üeh-chai ti-tzu-chi, 11/1.
337. Yüan Chia-san, Memorials, 8/37.

These were the tactics the Nien employed to trap Seng-ko-lin-ch'in in 1865. Previously, Prince Seng's leading lieutenants, Heng-ling (恒齡), Shu-t'ung-o (舒通額), and Su-Ko-chin (蘇克金), had been slain in this manner.[338] Their loss, instead of teaching their commander in chief a lesson, enraged the prince. He determined to redeem his humiliation by desperate pursuit. Turning a deaf ear to every warning from the Court,[339] he proceeded about two hundred li a day, neglecting food and sleep.[340] After the reins had blistered his hands, he tied the string around his neck and continued the chase. The forces he carried along with him were more fatigued than he. The Nien, deeming the time ripe, turned around. First they annihilated his main force, and then they besieged the prince in an empty earthwall fifteen li south of Ts'ao-chou. After nightfall an attempted sortie brought him within reach of ambushers in the woods outside an abandoned earthwall. There he was killed.[341]

This smashing victory heightened the Nien's morale, strengthened their force, and affirmed their confidence in using mobile and elusive tactics. Tseng Kuo-fan, Imperial Commissioner succeeding Seng-ko-lin-ch'in, suffered from the same trick that had troubled his predecessor. He complained to Li Hung-chang: "The Nien are at the peak of their power. They are skillful in fighting but are very prudent in employing their 'strong points.' Unless the government troops press them to fight, they never provoke a battle. But in action they struggle so vigorously that they will not be satisfied until they have succeeded in encircling the government forces with their infantry and cavalry. In any contact they are so cautious that a slight withdrawal may cause retreat as rapidly as lightning."[342] Then he warned Li: "The cavalry of the Huai-Hsiang armies is far inferior to that of the Nien. We have to do our utmost in its training. The whole country concentrates hope and expectation on both of us. When the existing situation flits across my mind, I am tormented to the extreme."[343]

338. Hsüeh Fu-ch'eng, Yung-an pi-chi, 4/1; Wang K'ai-yün, 14/8.
339. Fang-lüeh, 207/2.
340. Hsüeh Fu-ch'eng, 4/1; Wang Ting-an, Ch'iu-ch'üeh-chai ti-tzu-chi, 11/1.
341. Hsüeh Fu-ch'eng, 4/2; Wang Ting-an, Hsiang-chün chi, 14/8.
342. Tseng Kuo-fan, Tseng Wen-cheng-kung shu-cha, 26/15. Tseng Kuo-ch'üan, governor of Hupeh in 1865, was annoyed in the same way, and warned his troops to hold to their positions so as to avoid being demolished by the onrushing Nien cavalry. He also restrained them from pursuing the Nien on the ground that an ambush would cause an irremediable disaster. (Tseng Kuo-ch'üan, Tseng-chung-hsiang-kung shu-cha, collected in Tseng chung-hsiang-kung ch'üan chi, 9/29)
343. Tseng Kuo-fan, Tseng Wen-cheng-kung shu-cha, 26/15.

The Nien's swift mobility exposed Tseng's slowness, which in turn disappointed and disquieted the Court. The criticism that the conqueror of the Taipings had become helpless in the face of the Nien caused Tseng's resignation.

Tseng's successor, Li Hung-chang, had no bright prospect for success. A few months after Li came to the front, the Nien defeated his number-one lieutenant, Liu Ming-ch'uan, and all but annihilated his entire force.[344] Four months before their suppression, the East Nien were still continuing their old tactics. Under favorable geographical conditions, they would outflank the enemy forces or take them by surprise; otherwise, they would slide away like a "gale," leaving their new and inexperienced followers to satisfy the enemy and to slow down the pursuit.[345] Later, when the West Nien returned to south Chihli, Chang Tsung-yü laughed and declared that Jen Chu had become blunt. He attributed the suppression of the East Nien to their failure to practice the evasive tactics in the right manner.[346] Chang was convinced that the government armies should not be met directly, and that all the Nien ought to do was to wear out the enemy. He observed this rule strictly. When he entered Shantung, he wandered over a thousand li within half a month. The government armies of about two hundred thousand men under five commanders in chief pursued the Nien at a speed of a hundred and thirty li a day without ever gaining an opportunity to engage them.[347]

The government armies were forced to learn that the best way to cope with the stubborn earthwalls was to prevent the Nien from returning to their nests; that the way to subdue the sweeping cavalry was to hinder its mobility. The cavalry problem was secondary, but the earthwalls involved the basic nature of the Nien organization. The government armies could not bar the Nien from their nests unless they could maintain a hold on the nests themselves. This could be achieved only by winning over the people. The government commissioners in north Anhwei before 1865 were not able to comprehend the nature of the Nien organization. How could one expect them to take any effective action? The answer to this involves a study of the struggle between the Nien and the Loyalists.

---

344. Ch'ing shih-kao, Biographies, 196/9.
345. Fang-lüeh, 283/20.
346. Li Hung-chang, Letters to Friends and Colleagues, 8/5.
347. Ting Pao-cheng, Ting Wen-ch'eng-kung chou-kao, 2/30.

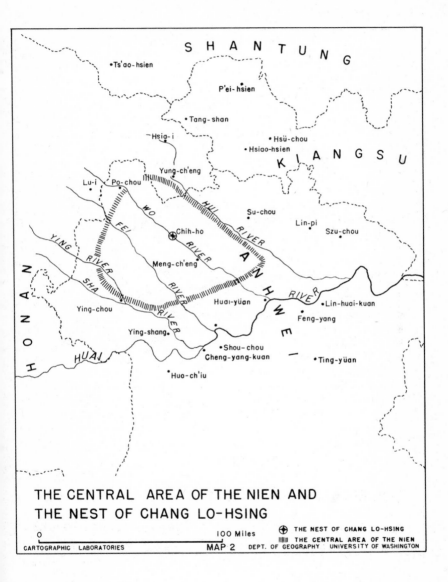

THE CENTRAL AREA OF THE NIEN AND
THE NEST OF CHANG LO-HSING

0 ——————————————————— 100 Miles

CARTOGRAPHIC LABORATORIES
MAP 2

⊕ THE NEST OF CHANG LO-HSING
|||||| THE CENTRAL AREA OF THE NIEN
DEPT. OF GEOGRAPHY   UNIVERSITY OF WASHINGTON

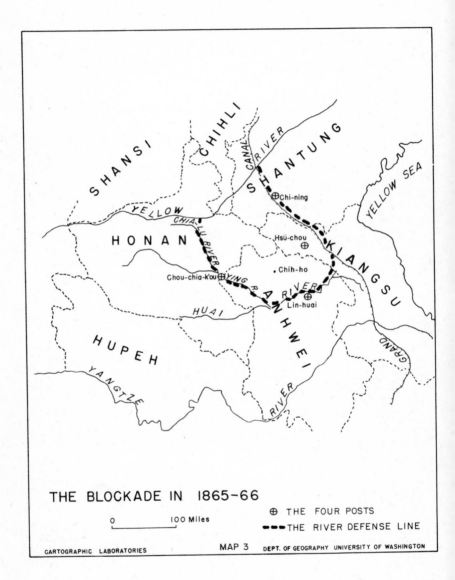

SHANSI

CHIHLI

SHANTUNG

CANAL

RIVER

⊕ Chi-ning

YELLOW

CHIA-LU RIVER

HONAN

Hsü-chou ⊕

KIANGSU

YELLOW SEA

· Chih-ho

Chou-chia-k'ou ⊕ YING RIVER

RIVER

HUAI

Lin-huai ⊕

ANHWEI

HUPEH

YANGTZE

RIVER

GRAND

THE BLOCKADE IN 1865-66

0 ___ 100 Miles

⊕ THE FOUR POSTS

●●● THE RIVER DEFENSE LINE

CARTOGRAPHIC LABORATORIES   MAP 3   DEPT. OF GEOGRAPHY UNIVERSITY OF WASHINGTON

PART II. THE STRUGGLE BETWEEN THE NIEN
AND THE LOYALISTS

1. The Failure of the Loyalists on the Military Front
Before 1865

In the 1850's Chang Lo-hsing succeeded in integrating the
Huai-pei local forces into a regional army directed against the
declining Manchu dynasty. Yet, as previously stated, the Nien was
not the only force springing up at that time. Besides the Nien,
there were numerous "turbulent forces" which were hostile to the
government as well as to the Nien. In 1862, the government called
some elements of the Hsiang Army to the Huai-pei theater.[1] Thus
the government made the struggle in Huai-pei more complicated
by adding a regional force to the Nien, the "turbulent forces," and
the Imperial forces which were already there. There was fighting
between the Nien and the forces which took the government's side,
conflict between the loyalists and the "turbulent forces," rivalry
among the "turbulent forces" themselves, and friction between the
Imperial forces and the regional forces. This was the hodgepodge
in Huai-pei before 1865.

From 1858 to 1865 it was the Imperial armies which undertook
the main part of the campaign against the Nien. The Emperor had
sent officials like Lü Hsien-chi (呂 賢 基) and Yüan Chia-san back
to their native regions to mobilize local forces to aid the government.[2] Yet, as will be shown later, this measure did not bear
fruit. After 1862, though the influence of the Hsiang Army penetrated Huai-pei, the main force which faced the Nien was the
cavalry under Seng-ko-lin-ch'in. Throughout this period, no
regional force was organized in Huai-pei. The regional forces
appearing in other spheres were busy containing the Taipings.

---

1. Wang Ting-an, Hsiang-chün chi, 7/9, 11. The collapse of
Kiang-nan Ta-ying (江 南 大 營) (the Imperial army corps outside the
city of Nanking which was dealing with the Taipings) in the third
month of 1860 compelled the Hsien-feng emperor to appoint Tseng
Kuo-fan, the commander in chief of the Hsiang Army, as governor-
general of Liang-Kiang. This signified that the dynasty accepted
the regional force as a lesser evil. In 1861-2, the pacification of
Huai-nan made Huai-pei accessible to the Hsiang Army. Tseng dispatched a corps of his army to Huai-pei, which established its
headquarters at Lin-huai.
2. See Part II, section 3.

But were the Imperial forces capable of routing the Nien? Along with the other parts of the Imperial ruling machine, both the Banner Armies and the Green Standard Army had deteriorated before the rise of the rebels.[3] With such forces shouldering the burden, the government could not win out in the struggle during this period.

The deficiency of the regular army first manifested itself in the execution of the policy of "rooting out the nests," the policy which the officials had worked out to deal with the stubborn Nien earthwalls. From the official viewpoint, this strategy was the correct one, and it was not altered by subsequent commanders who succeeded in suppressing the Nien in 1867-1868. Before 1865, however, the impotence of the regular armies made the execution of this policy impossible.

Chih-ho was the major target the officials intended to "root out."[4] The town was located at the border of three provinces. The garrison forces in the border areas of Honan and Kiangsu did not think it wise to interfere with another province's business. Especially in view of the Nien's elusive movements, the garrison officers dared not divert their forces to a neighboring province and expose their own posts to Nien raids. The location of Chih-ho would doom any offensive action to failure unless government officials could carry it out by joint action. Ying-kuei (英桂), governor of Honan, presented this case to the Throne and got the

---

3. The Banner Armies comprised the eight Manchu, eight Mongolian, and eight Chinese banners. They were the backbone of the Imperial military power. The Green Standard Army was the regular Chinese Army, parallel to the Banner Armies. Both of them, regardless of whether they were stationed in the capital or in the provinces, were centrally controlled. See Michael, "Military Organization and Power Structure of China in the Nineteenth Century," unpublished manuscript.

4. The appearance of numerous Nien bands in Chih-ho in 1853 and their resistance to the government forces in the spring of that year, brought that town to the officials' attention. (Yüan Chia-san, Memorials, 2/38) Yet during the two years subsequent to this episode, the local government troops passed back and forth freely. (Ibid., 5/19-20) According to Sheng-pao, "by the seventh month of 1855, the Nien's force had not surpassed one or two thousand men. In consequence of [government officials'] mismanagement, places like Pai-lung-wang-miao (白龍王廟) and Hui-ting-yü (惠定圩) suffered from plundering bands. Henceforth, the town of Chih-ho was held as an old nest from which [the Nien] made trouble in three provinces." Half a year later the five Nien banners were formally hoisted in Chih-ho. Since then, except for two moments of temporary occupation by government forces, the town remained the center of the Nien sphere until 1864 and the main object of the officials' policy of "rooting out nests."

Emperor's permission to appoint Wu-lung-o (武隆額) commander
of the troops from three provinces (Honan, Anhwei, and Kiangsu)
with the title of t'i-tu, or provincial commander in chief.[5] Before
the plan for joint action had been put to a test, the Nien took the
initiative. While Wu-lung-o was arguing with the Court over the
fact that he had only five thousand men, the Nien struck the new
commander a knockout blow.[6] Wu fled before the Nien and lost
five districts within ten days (the eleventh month of 1855).[7] This
disaster put an end to the first plan of cooperation. Infuriated by
the timidity of Wu-lung-o, the government shifted the joint com-
mandership to Ying-kuei, governor of Honan, assisted by Yüan
Chia-san.[8] Wu-lung-o alone should not be held responsible. It was
the troops drawn from the three provinces that frustrated the
first experiment.

In the fifth month of 1856, the troops from the three provinces
forced their way to Chih-ho and succeeded in capturing it.[9] Yüan
entrusted the occupation to a cavalry of four thousand men under
Hsi-ling-a (西凌阿). Hsi-ling-a, a Manchu, just as impotent as the
other Manchu soldiers, evacuated Chih-ho in front of a returning
Nien band whose size was smaller than that of his cavalry.[10] In
the same year the Honan army made another effort, penetrating
as far as Lin-huai. Ch'ung-an, a Manchu brigade general in
Anhwei, instead of pressing forward to meet the Honan army,
fled back to the city of Po-chou, with only about twenty men left.[11]
The flight of Ch'ung-an was caused by a raid by a Nien band of
only several hundred men.

Depressed by the timid and uncooperative armies in Anhwei,
Ying-kuei restrained his army from crossing the border in spite
of Imperial orders directing him to hasten the advance.[12] He
ascribed his failures to the tardiness of the forces of the other
two provinces, for the most part made up of regulars.[13] Fu-chi,
governor of Anhwei, asserted that as long as the provincial
forces of Anhwei itself were tied down in Lu-chou by the Taipings,
the Honan provincial authorities should consider it their duty to

---

5. Fang-lüeh, 9/22. (See table.)
6. Yü-chün chi-lüeh, 6, Wan-fei 2/13-15; Fang-lüeh, 10/13; 20/
21, 28-29.
7. Yü-chün chi-lüeh, 6, Wan-fei 2/13-15.
8. Fang-lüeh, 11/23; 13/20. Ying-kuei's Honan Green Standard
Army was reinforced by the regulars from Chihli, Shensi, and Shansi
(Ibid., 13/20-22).
9. Ibid., 23/13-18.
10. Fang-lüeh, 23/18; 20/2-3.
11. Ibid., 23/17-18.
12. Ibid., 20/21-26.
13. Yü-chün chi-lüeh, 6, Wan-fei 2/19-20; Fang-lüeh, 14/21-23.

Table 3

Prominent Officials Commissioned to Deal with the Nien[*]

Temporary Duty	Name	Duration	Permanent Office	Head-quarters
Assistant commissioner of the Anhwei local corps	Chou T'ien-chüeh	1853, 2-10	Title of vice-president of the Board of War	North Anhwei
Assistant commissioner of the Anhwei local corps	Yüan Chia-san	1853, 3-1855, 4	Supervising censor	North Anhwei
Commander of the armies from three provinces	Wu-lung-o	1855, 10-12	Provincial commander in chief	North Anhwei
Director of the pacifying campaigns of three provinces	Ying-kuei	1856, 1-1858, 9	Governor of Honan	Kuei-te
Director of military affairs at the Honan-Anhwei border	Yüan Chia-san	1856, 8-1858, 2	Candidate for director of the Courts with the third rank	Po-chou
Imperial commissioner for Anhwei military affairs	Sheng-pao	1858, 8-1860, 1	Lieutenant general of the Mongol Bordered Yellow Banner	Feng-yang
Director of the pacifying affairs of three provinces	Yüan Chia-san	1858, 8-1859, 2	Director of the Court of the Imperial Stud	Hsü-chou

* This table is a digest from the table in Kuo T'ing-i, T'ai-p'ing t'ien-kuo shih-shih jih-chih, Appendix, pp. 153-154.

Temporary Duty	Name	Duration	Permanent Office	Head-quarters
Director of pacifying affairs of three provinces	Fu Chen-pang	1859, 2-1861, 1	Brigade general of the Hsü-chou post	Hsü-chou
Imperial commissioner for Anhwei military affairs	Yüan Chia-san	1859, 10-1862, 8	Acting director-general of Imperial grain tributes	Lin-huai
Director of pacifying affairs in Honan	Sheng-pao	1860, 1-6	Mongol lieutenant general	
Imperial commissioner for military affairs dealing with the Nien	Seng-ko-lin-ch'in	1860, 11-1862, 8	Prince of Korchin	Shantung North Anhwei
Director of pacifying affairs in the Hsü-chou and Su-chou area	T'ien Tsai-t'ien (田在田)	1861, 1	Brigade general of the T'ai-yüan post	Hsü-chou
Imperial commissioner for pacifying affairs of three provinces	Sheng-pao	1861, 4-8	Candidate for director of the Courts with third rank	Shantung
Imperial commissioner for pacifying affairs in Anhwei and Honan	Sheng-pao	1861, 8-1862, 8		North Anhwei

Table 3, Concluded

Temporary Duty	Name	Duration	Permanent Office	Head-quarters
Imperial commissioner for pacifying affairs on the Chihli-Shantung-Honan border	Seng-ko-lin-ch'in	1862, 8-1865, 5		Shantung Honan Hupeh

pacify the Anhwei bandits whose nests bordered east Honan.[14] However, the Honan governor argued that, lacking the coopera- tion of the other two provinces, he was unable to enforce the plan of joint invasion alone. So, in addition to feebleness, division of command was a defect of the regular armies.

Sheng-pao was the successor of Ying-kuei in dealing with the Nien, but his main function was to recover cities along the Huai. The person who actually took command of the troops of the three provinces was Yüan Chia-san.[15] After the campaign of Liu-an, Yüan proceeded eastward to Hsü-chou, leading only a thousand men, to wipe out the Nien nests.[16] The situation which had em- barrassed Ying-kuei did not change for the better. Though Yüan was promised a company of a thousand men from Hsü-chou, less than a hundred arrived at his camp. Shantung sent him not more than a hundred and fifty men. Honan not only stopped sending reinforcements but detained a Shensi army of a thousand men who were moving from Honan to Hsü-chou. The proposed army from the three provinces was out of the question.[17] Yüan then revised his plan in the winter of 1858. Instead of requesting Shantung and Honan to put their respective troops at his disposal, he urged the

14. Fang-lüeh, 14/1.
15. Fang-lüeh, 46/31. Sheng-pao recruited his troops from the Shensi-Kansu armies. Of his eight thousand men, three thousand were regulars. (Ibid., 38/8; 53/8-9; 63/3-4)
16. Ibid., 44/3. In 1857 Yüan led a thousand men of which eight hundred came from the Honan and Hsü-chou regular armies. (Ibid., 5/6) After the Liu-an campaign, when he turned eastward to the Hsü-chou and Su-chou area, he was reinforced by a thousand Shansi-Kansu regulars under Ying-kuei, twelve hundred Shansi-Kansu regulars under Sheng-pao, and some fragments left by the regulars from Shantung, Chihli, Hunan, and Szechwan. (Ibid., 44/3-5; 53/1; 8/12; 9/2; Yüan Chia-san, Memorials, 8/3, 11, 33-34; 13/51)
17. Yüan Chia-san, Memorials, 8/19-20.

governors of those two provinces to give him coordinated support by responding from the west to his advance from the east.[18] To this request, the two provinces answered that they could not send their troops too deep into Nien territories while their own frontiers were exposed to the cunning enemy.[19]

While the officials in north Anhwei were avoiding the frank admission of their inability to attack, the Emperor made a decision. In the first month of 1860, he transferred Sheng-pao to Honan, charging him with the military affairs of that province; placed Yüan Chia-san in command of the Anhwei campaigns; and assigned the areas around Hsü-chou and Su-chou to Fu Chen-pang. Each commander had his own garrison line, and each was to be responsible for any penetration of it by the Nien.[20] Obviously this was a passive policy, a reversal of the former unrealistic policy of using three uncoordinated armies to crush the Nien nests.

The weaknesses of the Imperial armies also paralyzed the measures adopted to cope with the Nien cavalry, the Nien's second weapon. After 1859 the total number of the Nien's horses, according to Yüan Chia-san's observation, was "not less than twenty thousand. Though their ranks are uneven in comparison with those of the government cavalry, their skill is superior and their number is immense. The number of government horses hardly reaches forty per cent of the Nien's. They are always under the threat of an encirclement by the enemy."[21] As two liang of silver were required for each mounted soldier every month, the officials needed 40,000 liang monthly to maintain an equal force of twenty thousand horses.[22] Therefore, the officials concluded that, whereas the Nien were proud of the quantity of their horses, the government armies should emphasize quality, and that five to six thousand excellent horses would be sufficient to handle the whole Nien affair.[23] The officials' desire for horses of good quality made the acquisition of horses from outside the Great Wall their first concern. The following table will give a general idea of the number and frequency of Court responses to these requests for horses.[24]

Date	Number of horses	From	To
10, 1855		Kirin	Anhwei
8, 1856	2000	Chahar	Honan
10, 1856	500		Anhwei
12, 1856	500	Chahar	Hsü-chou

18. Fang-lüeh, 54/23.
19. Shantung chün-hsing chi-lüeh, 3C/2.
20. Fang-lüeh, 73/1-2.
21. Yüan Chia-san, Letters, 1/25.
22. Hsiao I-shan, pp. 393-394.
23. Yüan Chia-san, Letters, 1/25.
24. Fang-lüeh, 9/30; 19/33; 21/10-11, 33; 22/9, 29, 37; 23/3-4; 26/1; 28/9; 29/30-31; 45/14-15, 30; 55/13, 21; 60/2-3; 65/4-5.

Date	Number	Source	Destination
12, 1856	500	Kirin	Anhwei
3, 1857	500	Chihli	Anhwei
5, 1857	400		Anhwei
6, 1858	3000-4000	Chahar	Hsü-chou
6, 1858	4000-5000	Chahar	Anhwei
12, 1858	250	Heilungkiang	Honan
5, 1859	500	Heilungkiang	Hsü-chou
5, 1859	500	Heilungkiang	Anhwei
1, 1862	1000		Honan-Anhwei border
1, 1862	522	Sian	Honan-Anhwei border

This table includes only the horses sent by the central government to reinforce the armies dealing with the Nien. It excludes those originally possessed by the commanders before 1855, those obtained from other sources, and those in Seng-ko-lin-ch'in's army and the subsequent Hsiang-Huai armies. However, such a picture, though drawn from incomplete materials, still clearly shows that the central government continued to send mounted troops and horses several times a year to the three provinces and that the total number amounted to more than fifteen thousand. This figure disproves the contention that a picked cavalry of five to six thousand horses could have handled the whole thing. Moreover, the Imperial cavalry shared the weaknesses of the infantry. The reinforcements were not assigned to a unified command, and the Manchu generals who received the reinforcements, such as Ch'ung-an, Hsi-ling-a, and Te-leng-o (德楞領), proved inadequate as commanders.[25] The quality of the cavalry itself was not entirely excellent. The officials always complained about the weakness of the recruits from Suiyuan.[26]

If the sending of mounted reinforcements and horses produced any result, it was the increase of the dissension among commanders in the Nien area. Usually the horses sent from the north to Anhwei had to pass through Honan. Honan provincial authorities, taking advantage of their position, detained cavalry detachments destined for other provinces.[27] This irritated the governor of Anhwei, and the resulting disputes widened the gulf between the provinces. When cavalry forces were sent by Anhwei

25. Most of the government cavalry in north Anhwei, north Kiangsu, east Honan, and south Shantung was directed by Manchu generals. Ch'ung-an, Te-leng-o and Hsi-ling-a have been mentioned. Te-leng-o's story is found in Fang-lüeh, 87/4-5.

26. Fang-lüeh, 72/3.

27. Ibid., 21/10-11; 28/30-31.

to cooperate with Honan in checking the Nien's invasion of that
province, they were detained there; the governor of Anhwei considered this intolerable.[28] Finally this cavalry was released by
Honan, but when it passed Hsü-chou on its way to Huai-yüan, the
garrison authorities in Hsü-chou detained it again.[29] Since Hsü-
chou was north of Anhwei, on the route which reinforcements had
to travel, disputes between Hsü-chou and Anhwei frequently
occurred.[30] Discounting other factors, the quarrels over horses
alone could have kept apart the three provinces which were supposed to drive jointly against the Nien domain.

The same shortcomings also dominated the cavalry under
Seng-ko-lin-ch'in, the Mongolian prince. In 1860, the prince
assumed the responsibility of pacifying the bandits in the Shantung-
Anhwei border in response to the requests from Ying-ch'i (漢榮),
governor of Honan,[31] and from Yüan Chia-san.[32] Ying-ch'i pointed
out that the appointment of Seng-ko-lin-ch'in would provide the best
hope for breaking the deadlock in the Huai area, because the ten
thousand Manchurian and Mongolian horsemen under Seng-ko-lin-
ch'in were all first-class fighters. Yüan assured the Emperor that
the small Nien cavalry was no match for the gallant prince. Yüan
then proposed that officials from governors-general down to
brigade generals should obey Seng-ko-lin-ch'in, and that Chihli,
Shantung, and Honan should collectively raise two hundred thousand liang of silver to support him.[33] It seemed to Ying-ch'i and
Yüan that the emergence of Seng-ko-lin-ch'in would make up for
all the deficiencies they had complained about for five years.

Indeed, the strength of Seng-ko-lin-ch'in's army was the
greatest of any the government had ever sent to handle the
Shantung-Anhwei bandits. At the outset Seng-ko-lin-ch'in's expeditionary army included 2,000 Manchu infantrymen, 5,000 Green
Standard infantrymen of Chihli, and 4,000 men of the Shensi-
Kansu armies.[34] The strength of this army lay in the 1,000
horsemen drawn from the Heilungkiang cavalry, the 500 from the
Cherim league, and the 800 from the Chao Uda league. In addition
to these, Seng-ko-lin-ch'in sent for 1,000 horses from Chahar and
later a cavalry of 500 men from Tumet.[35] Reinforcements from
Manchuria and Inner Mongolia constantly maintained between
4,000 and 5,000 horsemen under his command until 1864.[36] As

28. Ibid., 22/9, 15.   29. Ibid., 22/37.
30. Ibid., 21/33; 110/2-3; 65/4-5.
31. Yü-chün chi-lüeh, 8, Wan-fei 7/19-20.
32. Hsiang-ch'eng hsien-chih, 22/16. What Yüan referred to here
was the clash between Seng-ko-lin-ch'in and the Anglo-French war-
ships in 1859.
33. Yüan Chia-san, Memorials, 10/41.
34. Fang-lüeh, 87/10.   35. Fang-lüeh, 89/3; 98/8.
36. Ibid., 88/25. After defeats in 1864 Seng had only 2,000
horsemen left. (Ibid., 232/21)

for his 100,000 liang of silver per month, the Court ordered the Chihli provincial treasury to provide the major part, with some contributions from Shansi.[37] Later on, as Prince Seng pushed to the south, he drew 50,000 liang from Shantung, 30,000 from Honan, and 20,000 from Shansi, together with the subsidies from the Liang-Huai salt likin.[38] Fearing that these funds would be delayed, special Imperial edicts warned the said provinces against dilatoriness. A tremendous cavalry sustained by abundant revenue had been an unattainable ideal of the Huai area commanders. Now this ideal seemed to have been realized in Prince Seng's force.

As indicated by Yüan's utterance, the first thing the southern commanders expected from Seng-ko-lin-ch'in was a supreme command, capable of coordinating the divided armies throughout several provinces. But here they were disappointed. On hearing of Seng-ko-lin-ch'in's arrival in south Shantung, Yüan Chia-san sent a special messenger to inform him of the geographical conditions and the general situation in regard to the bandits. Seng-ko-lin-ch'in, influenced by the advice of I-hsing-o (伊興額), a Manchu cavalry commander in south Shantung, refused to receive Yüan's messenger.[39] Since he lacked sufficient information, Seng-ko-lin-ch'in's first drive on the Nien resulted in a catastrophe.[40] His inability to use the Chinese language prevented him from answering communications from various headquarters and made him an easy prey to his interpreters' "ill-counsels."[41] Furthermore, his overconfidence in his own cavalry lost him the sympathy of other armies. The dissension among the Huai commanders continued unabated. Indeed, the entry of Seng-ko-lin-ch'in did not basically alter the government's melancholy position in the Huai theater.[42]

---

37. Ibid., 87/10.   38. Ibid., 233/13.
39. Fang-lüeh, 112/10-11.   40. Ibid.
41. Yüan Chia-san, Memorials, 15/12.
42. Fang-lüeh, 162/10-11. Seng-ko-lin-ch'in did not enter Huai-pei until the autumn of 1862. Between the twelfth month of 1860 and the eighth month of 1862, he concerned himself with the religious bandits in Shantung. There he had engagements with the Nien only when the latter invaded that province. Early in 1863, he succeeded in occupying Huai-pei and in capturing Chang Lo-hsing. (See next section.) However, before he could enjoy the fruits of victory in Huai-pei, the revival of Shantung religious bandits diverted him to the north again, leaving the Nien's substantial force intact. As soon as he had pacified the Shantung bandits, the Imperial officials, distressed by Miao P'ei-lin's second rebellion, urged him to return to Huai-pei. Seng-ko-lin-ch'in's entanglement with various rebels in 1863 thus gave Chang Tsung-yü an opportunity to accomplish the regrouping of the Nien. It was this refreshed force which harassed Seng-ko-lin-ch'in in 1864 and finally ended his career early in 1865.

Nor was the cavalry itself really invincible, especially when it met unfavorable geographical conditions. In the first half of 1864, the Nien roamed for five months in the Honan-Hupeh border area, where mountains and rice fields made the topography different from that in the Honan-Shantung-Anhwei intersection.[43] There Seng-ko-lin-ch'in's horses found little space for free action.[44] It was in such unfavorable circumstances that the Nien dealt him a crushing blow in the battle of Lo-shan in the eighth month of 1864.[45] Twelve of his principal lieutenants perished in this battle, which marked the beginning of the end for Seng-ko-lin-ch'in's enterprise. The prince then found infantry more useful and enrolled twenty thousand men out of the dissolved Shensi militia.[46] This resort to infantry signifies that Seng-ko-lin-ch'in himself formally admitted his cavalry's ineffectiveness.

Like other Imperial armies, Seng-ko-lin-ch'in's army was characterized by its general lack of discipline. Most of his under-officers were ruthless and corrupt.[47] Complaints that his soldiers "made trouble for the people" flowed from the oppressed people, but found a deaf ear in Seng-ko-lin-ch'in. Everywhere the civilian earthwalls closed their doors to him; some cities in south Shantung, under the direction of their magistrates, boycotted him.[48]

Another of Seng-ko-lin-ch'in's defects was his contemptuous regard for the enemy. His initial success during 1861-1863 had fostered this attitude. 1864 was the year in which the Taiping remnants under Lai Wen-kuang joined the Nien. (Lai's camps were close to those of Chang Tsung-yü, and Chang had fought shoulder to shoulder with the Taipings since the preceding year.[49]) Other Taiping remnants under Ch'en Te-ts'ai, Ma Jung-ho, and Liang Ch'eng-fu were decisively defeated by Seng-ko-lin-ch'in's cavalry at the Anhwei-Hupeh frontier in the tenth month. There several thousand men were slaughtered and over a hundred thousand men laid down their arms.[50] But Seng did not gain the same success against the Nien. The incorporation of Lai Wen-kuang's forces into the Nien strengthened the latter to a considerable extent.[51] Seng-ko-lin-ch'in was never aware of this. Excited by the unprecedented victory over the Taipings, he believed that the Nien under Chang Tsung-yü comprised less than six thousand men, even

---

43. Fang-lüeh, 213/19.   44. Ibid., 217/11.
45. Ibid., 219/24-25.
46. Ibid.
47. Wang K'ai-yün, 14/17
48. Fang-lüeh, 187/24; 209/3.
49. Yü-ch'ün chi-lüeh, 11, Wan-fei 17/1.
50. Anhwei t'ung-chih, 108/26; Fang-lüeh, 222/20.
51. Anhwei t'ung-chih, 108/26; Wang K'ai-yün, 14/7.

though they had combined with the forces of Ch'en Ta-hsi (陳大喜), the Honan Nien leader.[52] It was merely one month after he made this estimate that the despised Nien knocked him out in the district of Teng-chou (鄧州), Honan.[53]

A few months after the battles of Lo-shan and Teng-chou, the Nien killed Seng-ko-lin-ch'in near Ts'ao-chou, Shantung (the fourth month of 1865).[54] His army was the last regular force which could undertake an independent campaign against the Nien. It was also the last powerful force the central government could cull from the Banner and Green Standard contingents. Its annihilation closed the first phase of the Ch'ing-Nien struggle.

2. The Failures of the Loyalists on the Political Front Before 1865

The collapse of the Imperial administrative apparatus in Huai-pei represented another aspect of the general decay of the dynasty. Upon its ruin, the Nien built up their own ruling machine which commanded the loyalty of their fellow villagers. In the fifties, the officials incessantly attempted to force their way back to that lost territory. The policy of rooting out the Nien nests crystallized this intention. But at this time popular support was on the Nien's side. Even though the officials could occasionally secure military occupation of the Nien nests, the villagers regarded them as aliens or enemies. Their presence antagonized not only the seditious leaders but the rural populace in general. This was the crux of the Ch'ing-Nien struggle on the political front.

Of this fact the officials seemed not quite aware. The officials, to be sure, noticed that the dwellers behind the earth-walls, including women and youngsters, lent passionate support to the Nien garrisons, but they failed to recognize this as the key to the Nien's ascendancy. They complained that, even though the government forces could seize the Nien nests, once the occupying troops withdrew, the rebellious wave rolled back again. But they failed to inquire why they could not retain the nests. The failure to discover the Nien's appeal caused government officials to neglect the important work of regaining the people's support and of stopping further defection. They failed because they did not understand the problem--not because the problem was insoluble.

Li Hung-chang wrote critically in this connection:

---

52. Fang-lüeh, 223/4. In actuality, Chang had accomplished the regrouping of a formidable cavalry. See Part I, section 6.

53. Yü-chün chi-lüeh, 11, Wan-fei 17/4; Hsin-hsiu Nan-yang hsien-chih, 8/21.

54. See Part I, section 6.

The Nien rose up in Huai-pei in the sixth or seventh year of Hsien-feng. In a short time they were able to mass several tens of thousands of men, some with rods and some even unarmed, all incapable of formal battle. Commanders in chief like Sheng-pao and Yüan Chia-san wavered between the policy of suppression and pardon. They never devoted their efforts to any basic work. Prince Seng overran the bandits with the powerful cavalry from Manchuria and Inner Mongolia, eliminated several groups, and frightened off the rest. But the surrendered Nien had not been treated in a proper way, and therefore suspicion drove Chang Tsung-yü and Jen Chu to flee to the west.[55]

When Seng-ko-lin-ch'in entered the Nien nests, Chang and Jen were absent. To say that suspicion made them run away would not be correct. But Li's criticism of his predecessors' improper treatment of the problem is accurate. Yüan Chia-san himself made a confession when he retired:

> The destitute livelihood of the people requires relief and reconstruction. The bandits capitulate not because they have changed their minds or because they want to turn to a higher mode of life. For a long time they have regarded laws as naught and magistrates as of no consequence. Along with the work of invigoration, respect for law should be taught. The only thing I fear is the revival of the suppressed forces. In the years i and ping [1855-1856], my plan of pacification had succeeded in clearing up the north of the Huai. Simply because I removed my occupying forces too soon and left the task of rehabilitation undone, the dead ashes consequently rekindled and injuries are felt to the present time.[56]

Finally Yüan awakened, but too late. Here he admitted that what was really regrettable was not the failure to hold Nien nests but the failure to supplement occupation with reconstructive measures.

After 1856, the government forces were not able to occupy Chih-ho until Prince Seng's conquest of Huai-pei at the beginning of 1863. On that occasion the government forces subdued hundreds of earthwall communities along the Wo and the Huai and captured about ten first-ranking Nien leaders, among whom was Chang Lo-hsing.[57] Aside from military triumph, however, the officials

55. Li Hung-chang, Letters to Friends and Colleagues, 7/1.
56. Yüan Chia-san, Letters, 2/36.
57. Po-chou chih, 8/34; Fang-lüeh, 164/24-25; 178/1-5.

accomplished no more than had Yüan Chia-san. The victory of
1863, like that of 1856, failed to destroy the basis of Nien power.

Four months after this episode, Yüan Pao-hen (袁保恆), Chia-
san's son, drew up a program of rehabilitation and submitted it in
a memorial. Its essential points can be summarized: (1) Seng-ko-
lin-ch'in should stay in the Nien area until the agitation caused by
long years of disorder was over; (2) the government should select
able and honest personnel for local administration so as to restore
the dignity and authority lost during the rebellion; (3) more local
administrative units should be created in order to tighten controls;
(4) more public educational institutes should be set up to convert
the arrogant temperament of the Huai people; (5) plenty of barren
land resulting from devastation should be distributed to special
garrison forces for cultivation; and (6) the Liang-Huai salt administration should be reformed as a financial foundation for these
garrisons.[58] The main thing this program emphasized was the
tightening of government control over Huai-pei. The point of adding more administrative units to the old ones found particular
support among the provincial authorities like Tseng Kuo-fan,
governor-general of Liang-Kiang, and T'ang Hsün-fang (唐訓方),
governor of Anhwei.[59] The establishment of the districts of Wo-
yang and Feng-t'ai in Chih-ho, the Nien's old retreat, and in Hsia-
ts'ai, Miao P'ei-lin's old headquarters, and the creation of a
battalion post at Lung-shan might be considered as the net result
of the execution of this program. Besides this the Anhwei
officials achieved very little in the business of rehabilitation.

The result was that in the third month of 1863, one month
after the capture of Chang Lo-hsing, while the main government
forces were occupied in Shantung, Miao P'ei-lin revolted again.
Wherever Miao extended his sphere of influence, the earthwall
communities, which had once been considered as subdued and
pardoned by the officials, rose up enthusiastically in response to
his call.[60]

Meanwhile, Chang Tsung-yü came home. In the twelfth month
of 1862, in obedience to Chang Lo-hsing's order, Chang Tsung-yü
had left his nest to go to Ch'en Ta-hsi's assistance.[61] Therefore
the capture of Lo-hsing in the next spring did not involve Tsung-yü.
When Miao revolted, Tsung-yü sped homeward.[62] In the meantime,
earthwall communities along the Wo regrouped their bands under
the pretext of self-defense against Miao.[63] On arriving from the

58. Yüan Chia-san, Memorials, 1/1-7.
59. Po-chou chih, 8/34; Fang-lüeh, 180/19; 232/2.
60. Yüan Chia-san, Letters, 2/29.
61. Yü-ch'ün chi-lüeh, 9, Wan-fei 13/6.
62. Fang-lüeh, 190/2.
63. Ibid., 189/11.

south of the Huai, Chang found that his former associates, who had submitted to the government several months before, now welcomed him, and that the surrendered Nien to the west of Fou-yang also flocked to his banner.[64] They held him up to succeed Chang Lo-hsing as the Lord of Alliance.[65] Chang Lo-hsing's brother, Ming-hsing, also returned to Chih-ho; with the support of the two neighboring towns, Hsi-yang and Kao-lu, he sacked the granaries left by the government army.[66] The temporary quiet along the two banks of the Wo was thus broken.

After they recovered their home, the Nien did not lie idle there. One month after his return, Chang Tsung-yü led an expedition against Honan.[67] This time his absence from home saved him again, for in the eleventh month of 1863 Prince Seng suppressed Miao and cleaned up the Nien area for the second time.[68] In the third month of the next year, Chang cooperated with the Taiping forces which moved out from Han-chuang (韓 莊), Shensi, until the latter collapsed at the Hupeh-Anhwei border seven months later.[69] Then the Nien thrust into four provinces with Seng-ko-lin-ch'in at their backs. After Seng-ko-lin-ch'in's death, they continued to wander about in south Shantung, with the sole purpose of returning home.[70] Finally they succeeded. It was not long before they again built up their earthwall communities. According to official descriptions the earthwall communities, extending along the Wo banks for several li, were "like bees and ants."[71] The government garrison at Chih-ho held that town only because rescuing forces dispatched from the Huai Army arrived just in time.[72] That the Nien were able to return to their nests twice, each time to receive a favorable response from their countryfolk, implies that the officials had done little reconstruction work after ultimately gaining access to the Nien nests.

The officials neglected the basic work mainly because they

---

64. Wo-yang feng-t'u chi, 15/17; Yüan Chia-san, Letters, 2/32; Fang-lüeh, 190/12.

65. Yüan Chia-san, Memorials, 20/27.

66. Hsü-hsiu Meng-ch'eng hsien-chih, 6/16.

67. Yü-ch'un chi-lüeh, 10, Wan-fei 14/1. In this source, the author holds that because Mao Ch'ang-hsi, the local corps commissioner, encamped in Kuei-te, Chang Tsung-yü, feeling threatened, abandoned his nests. I do not agree with this. Mao had stayed in Kuei-te for about ten years, during which time the Nien went back and forth through his range of defense. Why should the Nien suddenly fear such a helpless garrison at a small post?

68. Ibid., Wan-fei 15/4.

69. Ibid., Wan-fei 16/8; Fang-lüeh, 213/7; 216/17. See Part I, sections 5, 6.

70. Fang-lüeh, 235/25; 239/5.

71. Ibid., 240/6-7.

72. Hsü-hsiu Meng-ch'eng hsien-chih, 6/23.

focused attention on the Nien's stubborn earthwalls. They let the outward features of the Nien organization blind them to the essential strength. They assumed that the destruction of those fortifications and occupation of the nests meant the recovery of control. They failed to see that wrecking the Nien fortress merely achieved half of the task. Even Prince Seng's sweeping victory in Huai-pei could not restore that area to the government.

Of course, to restore the officials' political position was as difficult as to restore their military position. But after the officials had succeeded in re-entering the Nien area, the regaining of the people's sympathy by intensified efforts was not an impossible undertaking.

3. The Contest over Local Support

The officials thus lost the battle to root out the Nien nests, to quell the Nien cavalry, and to gain the people's sympathy in the Nien homeland. Outside the Nien land, there were still vast local forces which had never gone over to the Nien. It should have been comparatively easy for the officials to enroll these wavering forces in their camp. As noted before, not all of the growing forces identified their cause with the overthrow of the existing rulers. Some of them, under the name of self-defense, assumed a neutral attitude; some even fought on the Imperial side when such fighting served their own interests. Some able gentry even formed powerful armies out of local contingents. The Hsiang (湘) Army initiated by Chiang Chung-yüan (江忠源), Lo Tse-nan (羅澤南), Li Hsü-pin (李續賓), and Tseng Kuo-fan in their native province, Hunan, belonged to this type.[73] Hence the local corps became an object attractive to both the rebels and the loyalists. Yet, insofar as the self-growing forces were independent of, if not hostile to, the existing rulers, the loyalists, with or without official titles and ranks, could seldom command their whole-hearted support unless the loyalists themselves sprang from the

---

73. Hsiang, the name of a river in Hunan, is used as an abbreviation for Hunan Province. The army, because it was recruited with Hunan volunteers, was called the Hsiang Army.

The study of the creation of the Hsiang Army is a tremendous subject. Immense amounts of material, primary and secondary, are available for it. Some works which deal particularly with this subject are: Wang K'ai-yün, Hsiang-chün chih; Wang Ting-an, Hsiang-chün-chi; and Lo Erh-kang, Hsiang-chün hsin-chih. For the struggle for the support of the local forces and the significance of the emergence of the Hsiang Army, see Michael, "Military Organization and Power Structure of China in the Nineteenth Century," unpublished manuscript. Lo Che-nan, 1808-1856, Hummel, pp. 450-451; Li Hsü-ping, d. 1858, Hummel, p. 463; Chiang Chung-yüan, 1812-1854, Hummel, p. 163.

same origin and maintained a personal tie with them.

In the Huai Basin, the local forces within the Nien area had served the Nien as the foundation of their power. Almost all the villages surrounding the Nien area had organized themselves into local corps and fortified their villages with earthwalls and trenches. Once the officials talked of winning over the local forces, they could not help but count on the local corps. The trouble with the officials was that they were appointed from above and thus lacked the necessary personal ties.

Sheng-pao had attempted several times to gain the assistance of the local corps. In 1858, the contrast between the long defense lines on the Huai and his small army reminded him of the usefulness of the local corps along the north bank. He ordered a chief to take over some posts which his army could not cover.[74] In the next year Sheng-pao reorganized the local corps between the Hui and the Huai; each t'uan comprised ten earthwall communities and contributed 120 men to guard ferry posts and 300 men to patrol.[75] One year later he worked out another measure--to draft from the local corps "strong adults," to whom intensified training would be given in peacetime and over whom a unified command would be provided in battle.[76] In the former two cases, since the part played by local corps was temporary in time and auxiliary in nature, Sheng-pao did not encounter obstruction from the local communities. But when Sheng-pao applied the latter measure to Kuei-te, Ch'en-chou and Kuang-chou in Honan, and Ts'ao-hsien and Shan-hsien in Shantung, objection came from the local corps chiefs. They argued that the local forces should be charged with the garrison duty of their own native places only, and that the peasants could not abandon their farm work for the sake of special training or campaigns in distant areas.[77] Since Sheng-pao expected the local communities to undertake the financial burden for these picked adults,[78] the local corps chiefs found another excuse for killing Sheng-pao's plan. They announced that, since the people of the communities had contributed a great deal to the existing local corps, they were incapable of subsidizing the trained corps.[79]

Sheng-pao's moves toward the creation of a fresh army followed the pattern of the Hsiang Army, but as described above, it met a different response. The local corps chiefs' argument that the trained force based on the local corps could not fight a

74. Fang-lüeh, 39/20.   75. Ibid., 65/24-25.
76. Fang-lüeh, 76/10; 77/7-8.
77. Yü-chün chi-lüeh, 8, Wan-fei 8/11; Fang-lüeh, 83/13;
Shantung chün-hsing chi-lüeh, 2C/14-15.
78. Fang-lüeh, 76/10; 127/7-8; 83/6.
79. Yü-chün chi-lüeh, 8, Wan-fei 8/11.

distant campaign was not realistic. In the Hsiang Army, recruits drawn from Hunan fought everywhere but in their native province. The essence of the problem was the local corps' unwillingness to submit to the leadership of Sheng-pao. Moreover, Sheng-pao, as an official appointed from above, could only exert the Imperial authority, an authority which had already faded.

Sheng-pao also favored the "policy of pardon" (fu-i 撫議). In the official sense, this policy meant to win over the "turbulent" forces, including the dissenters in the rebels' camp and the afore-mentioned "third force." In Sheng-pao's opinion, the Nien's expansion by absorbing the surrounding neutral forces did not rule out the possibility that the loyalists might augment their strength in the same way and at the same time isolate the Nien. Yet, before the officials tried to put the policy of pardon into practice, they should have recognized the fact that all the turbulent forces were, like the Nien, deeply rooted in their native communities. Unless they could directly appeal to the allegiance of these communities, the officials could not really bring them into submission. The officials did not see this. When they designed the policy of pardon, they merely concerned themselves with the problem of whether or not the chiefs would accept the titles granted by the government. To the officials, the chiefs' consent to change the flags of their forces meant the success of the policy. Though the policy of pardon was devised neither to pierce the Nien earthwalls nor to contain the Nien cavalry, it was similarly dominated by the officials' superficial understanding of the rebels' organization.

The first man who accepted Sheng-pao's pardon was Li Chao-shou (李昭壽), the Huai-nan Nien leader.[80] Though Li seldom cooperated with the Huai-pei Nien, the foundation of his strength was of the same nature, that is, it rested on local support. Before he came to terms with Sheng-pao in the summer of 1858, Li had extended his sway to the cities: Ch'u-chou, Lai-an, Ch'üan-chiao, Wu-ho, and T'ien-ch'ang, all in east Anhwei. After his submission, Li continued to occupy these cities. The number of his soldiers remained about thirty thousand, though the figure in formal reports was only fifteen thousand. So Li's submission was actually a change in name only, for he changed his name from

---

80. Except in taking the name Nien, Li was in no way attached to the factions north of the Huai. Li was born in Ku-shih, Honan, and he raised his bands in Huo-ch'iu, across the border to Anhwei, 300 li from the nests of the Nien under Chang Lo-hsing in Huai-pei. (Wang Ting-an, Ch'iu-ch'üeh-chai ti-tzu chi, 14/1-3) After 1853, Li drafted recruits, fought campaigns, concluded peace, and revolted again--all entirely on his own. There is no hint that Li cooperated with Chang Lo-hsing. Li once raided Chang's boats, loaded with spoils, as they were passing Wu-ho. (Ibid., 14/2-3; Fang-lüeh, 46/25-26)

Li Chao-shou to Li Shih-chung (李世忠). Two years later (the fifth month of 1860), when the government made him provincial commander in chief of Kiangnan, Li increased his troops to sixty thousand men. Within his sphere of control he set up custom offices to collect likin. In addition, Li took the liberty of transporting and selling the Huai-pei salt in defiance of all restrictions imposed by the government's licensing and tax system.[81] With his original armed forces and territory remaining intact, Li's submission brought him a high position and independent financial resources. He then became a thorn to the authorities in north Kiangsu and north Anhwei; there was friction from time to time between his soldiers and those of the Hsiang Army to the south.[82] The officials in the Kiangsu-Huai area were satisfied with Li's negative contribution, namely his service as a wedge between the Nien and the Taipings on the eastern flank; they never asked him to contribute positive support. His nominal commanders, Yüan Chia-san and, after 1861, Tseng Kuo-fan, exhausted every means to appease him, with the hope that he would not imitate Miao P'ei-lin.[83] Tseng deliberately refrained from using Li's forces so as to minimize his importance.[84] After the recovery of Chiu-fu-chou (九袱洲), near Nanking, and the suppression of Miao P'ei-lin, Li's position became unimportant. Tseng immediately brought the dissolution of Li's army into discussion with the Court and breathed with relief when this was accomplished in the first month of 1864.[85]

This was the achievement of Sheng-pao's policy of pardon. Yet one may argue that Li Chao-shou's submission had directly weakened the rebels' front and point out that Li never revolted again following his surrender in 1858.[86] In the case of Miao P'ei-lin,

81. Wang Ting-an, Ch'iu-ch'üeh-chai ti-tzu chi, 14/6.
82. Ibid., 14/10, 13.
83. Ibid., 14/17; Yüan Pao-heng, Yüan Wen-ch'eng-kung chi, collected in Yüan-shih chia-chi, Memorials, 1/8; Yüan Chia-san, Memorials, 11/45.
84. Wang Ting-an, Ch'iu-ch'üeh-chai ti-tzu chi, 14/6.
85. Ch'ing shih-kao, Biographies, 212/2; Wang Ting-an, Ch'iu-ch'üeh-chai ti-tzu chi, 14/17.
86. Li remained turbulent after his submission. But his relationship with the Huai-pei Nien was not harmonious, and he was antagonistic to Miao P'ei-lin, too. Furthermore, Li accepted the command of Yüan and Tseng after Sheng-pao was transferred to other theaters. Miao, on the other hand, relied on Sheng-pao as his only superior in opposition to Yüan and Tseng. After Sheng-pao's departure from the Huai area, Miao always felt uneasy in the presence of Yüan and, later, of the new Anhwei governor, T'ang Hsün-fang, a commander of the Hsiang Army. Perhaps these are the reasons why Li Chao-shou did not follow Miao P'ei-lin's footsteps. (The triangular relationship among Miao, Sheng-pao, and the Hsiang Army is too long a story to be related here.)

however, the policy of pardon resulted in tragedy.

The development of Miao's power was typical of the uncontrollable local forces. As a sheng-yüan of Feng-t'ai, Miao's prestige in his native town entitled him to lead a local corps. In 1857 he erected earthwalls in Hsia-ts'ai (下蔡), a town north of Shou-chou, and ordered the surrounding inhabitants to move within the walls. Meanwhile he strove to dominate the neighboring local corps. From Hsia-ts'ai his influence radiated to the southeast of Su-chou, east of Huai-yüan and Feng-yang, and into the districts near the upper sector of the Huai, an area containing over three thousand earthwall communities.[87]

Before his submission to Sheng-pao in the eighth month of 1858, Miao had brought the city of Meng-ch'eng under his control, had driven out the magistrate, and had levied land taxes.[88] This capitulation merely legalized his authority.[89] In addition to the land tax, he set up his own likin offices along the eastern sector of the Huai,[90] while his local corps bureaus in Meng-ch'eng, Ying-shang, and Su-chou took over the administrative power of those cities.[91] Shou-chou alone was an exception because the governor who chose that city as his temporary site was seized as a puppet by Miao's rival local corps chiefs.[92] In the first month of 1861, Miao, under the pretext of avenging his seven lieutenants who had been killed by local corps chiefs in Shou-chou, laid siege to that city; Shou-chou finally fell ten months later.[93] During this period, Miao conquered the Huai cities from Huo-ch'iu to Huai-yüan, extended his control to Su-chou and Meng-ch'eng, allied with the Nien to the north, and accepted from the Taipings the title of "Prince Ch'in" (Ch'in-wang 秦王).[94] In the spring of 1862, with Sheng-pao's reappearance in Anhwei, Miao bowed to his master.[95] But this submission was only an interval before his second revolt the following spring.[96]

Though circumstances in the fifties favored Miao, his ascendancy was due to a great extent to his natural gifts. In addition to his organizing ability, he was shrewd enough to exploit the antagonism existing between diverse factions of the

87. Hsü-hsiu Meng-ch'eng hsien-chih, 6/7; Fang-lüeh, 147/29-30.
88. Fang-lüeh, 31/11-12; Anhwei t'ung-chih, 54/9.
89. Wen-hsien ts'ung-p'ien, 22/5.
90. Ch'ing shih-kao, Biographies, 205/3; Yü-chün chi-lüeh, 9, Wan-fei 9/1; Fang-lüeh, 90/19-20; 109/20; 171/14.
91. Fang-lüeh, 92/18.
92. Ch'ing-pai-lei-ch'ao, 7/159-163.
93. Ibid.
94. Hsü-hsiu Meng-ch'eng hsien-chih, 6/8, 12; Su-chou chih, 10/30, 33; Yüan Chia-san, Memorials, 14/22; Letters, 2/19.
95. Since the interview between Sheng-pao and Miao in 1857, the latter regarded himself the former's pupil.
96. Hsü-hsiu Meng-ch'eng hsien-chih, 6/15.

government armies. Miao not only found a position for himself in the gulf between the hostile officials, but advanced this position by playing them off against one another. Profiting from his intimate relationship with Sheng-pao and the conflict between Sheng-pao and Yüan Chia-san, Miao set out to take over the customs offices along the Huai, to rob Yüan's provision boats, and finally to confine Yüan's authority to an isolated city, Lin-huai.[97] In 1863, after his second surrender to Sheng-pao, Miao found the advancing Hsiang Army under Li Hsü-i, newly appointed governor of Anhwei, dangerous to his security. Miao, taking advantage of the ill feeling between the Imperial forces represented by Sheng-pao and the regional forces represented by the Hsiang Army, tried by every possible method to bar the Hsiang Army from his sphere of influence.[98] When these attempts failed, Miao turned to a higher dignitary, Seng-ko-lin-ch'in, to whom the Hsiang Army as a regional force was also distasteful.[99] Seng-ko-lin-ch'in presented Miao's case directly to Tseng Kuo-fan, the commander in chief of the Hsiang Army, and insisted on the Hsiang Army's withdrawal from Shou-chou and Cheng-yang. The cautious commander in chief yielded in order to save Seng-ko-lin-ch'in's prestige and to avoid unnecessary friction with the prince.[100]

The policy of pardon thus produced results contrary to the expectations of its designer. New foes arose to threaten the government forces from the rear, while the Nien continued to be a threat on the front. Furthermore, enforcement of this policy widened the gulf which already existed between the Imperial forces and the regional forces. The treatment of Miao became a focal point of this hostility, and ultimately Sheng-pao's rivals all rose up to impeach him, using Miao's case as an essential item in their accusation.[101] The policy generally enhanced the power of the turbulent forces rather than diminished that of the Nien. It increased the cleavage on the loyalist side instead of dividing the enemy.

Weng T'ung-shu, governor of Anhwei from 1858-1860, was another official who tried to employ the local forces. Unlike Sheng-pao, who had a considerable army of his own, Weng was well known as being lenient and unmilitant.[102] Consequently, his way of using the local corps differed from that of Sheng-pao. He called the local corps to his support without adding any training or

---

97. Fang-lüeh, 78/17-19; 79/9-11; 40/19-20.
98. Ch'ing-shih-kao, Biographies, 145/5; Fang-lüeh, 144/25-26; 148/20.
99. Wang Ting-an, Ch'iu-ch'üeh-chai ti-tzu chi, 15/19; Yüan Chia-san, Memorials, 19/5; Fang-lüeh, 224/8.
100. Fang-lüeh, 167/16.
101. Ibid., 147/14-15; 150/32-36; 163/6-8; 168/28.
102. Ch'ing shih-kao, Biographies, 214/6.

indoctrination to their original organization. In 1859 the governor, retreating from Ting-yüan to Shou-chou, reduced himself to dependency upon the local corps chiefs, Hsü Li-chuang (徐立壯) and Sun Chia-t'ai (孫家泰). In view of the fact that he could not demand obedience from the chiefs, the governor attempted to exploit the rivalry between Hsü Li-chuang and Sun Chia-t'ai on the one hand and Miao P'ei-lin on the other.[103] Weng hoped that as long as Hsü and Sun remained hostile to Miao, they would submit to his leadership in defending Shou-chou against the common foe. The development of events, however, proved that Weng was too optimistic. Miao, jealous because the governor was in the hands of his rival, sought a chance to liquidate Hsü. As stated above, Miao captured Shou-chou in the tenth month of 1861. On his entry, besides killing the whole family of Sun Chia-t'ai, Miao butchered the local chiefs who had helped to defend the city, yet spared the pitiable governor. He preserved the governor because he thought the governor would be useful to him, too. Instead of using the local corps chiefs, Governor Weng let himself be used by them. Weng's fate in the contest for local support was far more tragic than that of Sheng-pao.

In contrast to the difficult position held by the central officials, the commanders who came up from the masses of the people found it easy to win local support. For example, Li Meng-ch'ün (李孟羣), once a commander of the Hsiang Army, applied the experience he had gained from that new organization to the local corps in Anhwei when he became financial commissioner of that province.[104] He selected two thousand men from the local corps of Liu-an and Huo-ch'iu and formed them into a militia. As for the corps themselves, he proposed that the government should grant them active support and guidance but should avoid unnecessary intervention in their internal affairs. He called this "moderate control."[105] His devotion to the work of rehabilitating the refugees of Liu-an aroused Sheng-pao's jealousy but sowed the seeds of sympathy among the people. With all sources of revenue cut off by Sheng-pao, Li held desperately to his post in the town of Ch'ang-ch'eng (長城) for half a year until the native people could no longer provision him and most of his starved soldiers had deserted. After the fall of Liu-an to the Taipings, he was captured

---

103. Hsü Li-chuang started organizing local corps in collaboration with Miao, but later Hsü's force grew to such a degree as to challenge Miao. Miao murdered Hsü's whole family and dug up the ancestral graves. (Ch'ing-pai-lei-ch'ao, 7/159-163; Hsü-hsiu Meng-ch'eng hsien-chih, 6/9) Later a Hsü clansman exposed Miao's ancestors' bones in retaliation. (Anhwei t'ung-chih, 106/11)

104. Later he succeeded Fu-chi (福濟) as acting governor of Anhwei.

105. Fang-lüeh, 34/13-14.

and killed (the second month of 1859).[106] With Li's death, the last spark of hope for organizing local forces was extinguished.

If Li Meng-ch'ün failed to complete his plan of using local forces because death deprived him of the chance, Yüan Chia-san failed because he did not pick up the chance. Yüan, a native of Hsiang-ch'eng, a district of Honan bordering northwest Anhwei and connected with the marginal Nien area, was a popular Huai man in his native area. After the Taipings had occupied Nanking and invaded northern Anhwei in 1853, Lü Hsien-chi,[107] a native of Anhwei, was sent there from Peking to organize local corps. At Lü's request, Yüan, with the title of censor, was ordered to assist in this task. Later in the same year Yüan was entrusted with the command of the militia which had previously been under Chou T'ien-chüeh, commissioner of local corps affairs. So in 1853 Yüan's specific assignment was to organize local corps, not to command the regular army.[108] Yüan was merely one of several officials who were sent out by the Emperor because it was believed that they could appeal to their countryfolk's loyalty.[109]

Indeed, Yüan had devoted his efforts to this mission in the early years.[110] He selected three thousand men from the Su-chou corps and organized them into five companies.[111] When he was transferred to Lin-huai in 1854, he ordered them to return to their farms. In 1856 he returned to the Honan-Anhwei border, where he found that his popularity ran so high that his old adherents, who were also his countrymen, returned to his camp with hope and enthusiasm.[112] In a few days he obtained three thousand men. Nevertheless, instead of utilizing this loyalty as a core for a new force, he relied on the remnants of the Shensi-Kansu regulars as the nucleus of his army.

Two considerations restrained Yüan from going further in the development of local forces. First, he distrusted them. Ch'ung-en, governor of Shantung, held that, though the local corps were a good instrument with which to cope with the Nien, in the long run they would be used by ambitious chiefs to disturb peace and order.[113] Yüan shared Ch'ung-en's viewpoint. He always guarded against using the local corps indiscriminately.[114] Even toward the so-called "good local corps," Yüan's attitude became more and

---

106. Kuang-chou chih-li-chou chih, 5/68.
107. Ch'ing shih-kao, Biographies, 186/1; Lü Hsien-chi, 1803-1853, Hummel, p. 949.
108. Yüan Chia-san, Memorials, 2/33.
109. Ibid., head volume, B, p. 2.
110. Ibid., 2/35; Fang-lüeh, 6/5-6.
111. Su-chou chih, 10/24; Yüan Chia-san, Memorials, 3/51.
112. Yüan Chia-san, head volume, B, p. 18.
113. Fang-lüeh, 55/9.
114. Yüan Chia-san, Memorials, 2/38.

more passive, that is, he tried to keep them neutral instead of reorganizing them for his own use.[115] Later on, the strife among the Shou-chou local corps chiefs convinced Yüan that the local corps chiefs were uncontrollable. Finally, the outright revolt of Miao P'ei-lin convinced him that it was impossible to deal with the local corps.

Secondly, Yüan underestimated the local corps' fighting power. His remarks in 1853 represent this attitude. As he saw it, "the local corps may be used for native campaigns but can never be used for distant expeditions. In appearance the use of the local corps makes the army seem more imposing; in reality the corps are useless before the onslaught of the turbulent bandits."[116] Therefore, throughout the whole period of his command, the most he expected from the local corps was that they augment the apparent strength of his army.[117] In 1858 the Nien destruction of the Feng-hsien local corps frightened the garrison forces of both south Shantung and north Kiangsu.[118] In the next year the Hsü-chou local corps, which were composed of thirty thousand men, collapsed.[119] The defeat of this vast force destroyed whatever confidence the officials still possessed in the fighting power of the local corps.

When Yüan and his colleagues became convinced that only simultaneously dispatched regulars from three provinces, together with cavalry from outside the Great Wall, could handle the Nien's fortresses and mounted bands, respectively, then the suspicion of, and contempt for, the local forces became unshakable. Yüan did not comprehend the fact that discipline could affirm fidelity and training could heighten fighting power. If Yüan had continued his earlier measures regarding the local corps of his native area, he might have succeeded not only in preventing further defection of his countrymen but in organizing the local forces into a new army in the Huai region to rival the Nien. This new force might have been superior in strength and morale to the heterogeneous troops drawn from various provinces to the Huai Basin.

Such a new regional force was exactly what the Huai theater lacked. Censor Hou Teng-yün (侯登雲) realized in 1856 the necessity for a new army in the Huai region.[120] He proposed to the Court that the armies drafted from four provinces be replaced with a special militia, and recommended Yüan Chia-san as its commander. Of course what the censor intended was to substitute

---

115. Ibid., 7/4, 16; 8/17; 3/16, 32.
116. Ibid., 2/49; 3/32.
117. Ibid., Letters, 1/5; Fang-lüeh, 71/25.
118. Shantung chün-hsing chi-lüeh, 2A/14-15.
119. Fang-lüeh, 72/1.
120. Fang-lüeh, 15/8.

98

for the Green Standard troops a newly organized militia on the model of the Hsiang Army.

Did Yüan Chia-san seriously consider Hou's proposal? He disappointed Hou, for he organized his army on a pattern similar to that followed by his colleagues, such as Sheng-pao and T'ien Chai-t'ien. In 1856 he stopped recruiting his forces from local corps. When casualties made his patched army thinner and thinner, he continually resorted to regular reinforcements from the various provinces, considering the native recruits to be acceptable only as the last choice.[121] But few of the provinces responded to his plea promptly. In 1861, despairing of the regular armies, Yüan attempted to draft local corps again. He reckoned it possible to draw twenty to thirty thousand men from the Hsü-chou earthwall communities.[122] Since they would provide their own provisions, they would cost Yüan very little. He expected that half a year's training would mold the Huai-pei area into a formidable army. Half a year passed. This formidable army still remained on paper.

Yüan failed to organize a new army in his native region, perhaps because he lacked the sagacity to appreciate the power potential of the local forces, perhaps because he lacked the vitality to undertake this hazardous task.

Since the officials had lost their opportunity to win over the populace, leadership naturally fell into the hands of either the Nien or the ambitious local corps chiefs. We have pointed out that the Nien had absorbed many of the local corps during the course of their expansion. As for the local chiefs, Li Nan-hua (李南華), a chief of the Meng-ch'eng corps, took over the defense of that city in opposition to Miao P'ei-lin, struggled with the latter for the support of other corps, and withstood Miao's furious assault for several months in 1863.[123] The Shou-chou chiefs like Hsü Li-chuang, Sun Chia-t'ai, Meng Shih-chung (蒙時中), and Chi Hsüeh-sheng (吉學盛), as shown elsewhere, were strong enough to take over the governor's temporary site as their base for power competition with Miao.

Miao himself first extended his influence to the west of Meng-ch'eng and then to the southwest.[124] The city corps, though determined to resist, knew their strength did not equal their determination, and contented themselves with the defense of the city alone.[125] In view of Miao's expansion, Yüan Chia-san ordered him to advance to the north bank of the Hui where the Nien were spreading. Yüan's intention was to let Miao and the Nien check--

121. Yüan Chia-san, Letters, 1/14-15, 27, 37; Memorials, 13/55.
122. Fang-lüeh, 112/11.
123. Hsü-hsiu Meng-ch'eng hsien-chih, 9/26-32.
124. Ibid., 6/7.
125. Hsü-hsiu Meng-ch'eng hsien-chih, 6/8-9.

and thus weaken--each other.[126] However, when Yüan was congratulating himself on the success of his policy of "one stone for
two birds," Miao took the opportunity to round off his sphere of
influence to the southeast of Su-chou.[127] Yüan had been outwitted.

Early in 1861, before Miao started the Su-chou siege as a
sign of revolt, he had accomplished the absorption of the corps on
both sides of the Hui.[128] From there he enveloped areas as far as
southwest of Lin-pi.[129] In the autumn of 1862, after Miao had acknowledged the government's rule again, Yüan claimed that the
Hsiang Army under Chiang Nin-hsüeh (蔣凝學) had recovered two
hundred earthwall communities east of Huai-yüan, while he himself had recovered more than two hundred in the Hui Basin.[130] The
so-called recovery was unreal, for the association between the
chiefs and Miao was too tight to break. Half a year later, in response to Miao's second revolt, all the corps along the Hui banks
again defied the government authority.[131]

Behind the Nien front, the officials failed to detach the
masses from their leaders even when victorious campaigns
brought them to the heart of the Nien realm. In the outlying areas,
the officials failed to set up a new army on the basis of local
forces but let some local corps chiefs utilize this source of power.
By 1862 two regional forces, one under Chang Lo-hsing and
another under Miao P'ei-lin, accomplished the division of the
Huai Basin, with the Imperial influence almost entirely driven out.
The task of winning over the people and of turning them to the
government's use had to be postponed until the Hsiang-Huai
leaders appeared in the north.

4. Measures Adopted by Tseng Kuo-fan

The appointment of Tseng Kuo-fan as Imperial Commissioner
to succeed Seng-ko-lin-ch'in opened a new phase in the Nien story.
It is well known that Tseng transferred from the Yangtze Basin to
the north the Huai Army which finally suppressed the Nien. We
can call this a new phase, not because the Nien were suppressed
three years after the entry of Tseng but because his entry made
their suppression possible. Tseng understood the nature of the
Nien organization which had puzzled his predecessors for twelve
years.

On receiving the news of Prince Seng's catastrophe, the

126. Yüan Chia-san, Memorials, 9/24.
127. Ibid., 14/11; Letters, 2/4; Fang-lüeh, 92/16.
128. Yüan Chia-san, Memorials, 18/21-23.
129. Ibid., Letters, 1/36-37.
130. Ibid., Memorials, 19/2; Fang-lüeh, 165/5.
131. Yüan Chia-san, Letters, 2/22.

Court issued a hurried edict, in the fifth month of 1865,[132] commanding Tseng to turn his spearhead northward. Since the Nien were still wandering about in south Shantung, the Court was concerned about the security of Chihli where the capital was located. Tseng Kuo-fan, the suppressor of the Taipings, became the man of the hour. The government hoped that he would change the unfavorable situation left by Prince Seng. Tseng, however, did not hurry to the north, for his army was not of Prince Seng's type. According to his own judgment, slowness was characteristic of his army, and he still preferred to be prudent.[133] Departing from Nanking, he proceeded to Lin-huai, then to Hsü-chou and finally to Tsi-ning, which he selected as the site for his headquarters. This slow trip through three provinces furnished him with invaluable information. By personal inspection and observation, Tseng gained a concrete idea of the Nien's homeland. First, he discovered that the Nien were not roaming bandits as his contemporaries presumed. In his observation, "roaming bandits are always like water without a source, flooding aimlessly. But this type of bandit has a deep attachment to his nest in the Meng-ch'eng and Po-chou area. While land and houses have been ruined in surrounding districts, his own land and house in Meng-Po are kept intact and provide the comforts of home."[134] Then he pointed out, "the Po-chou peril [the Nien Rebellion] originated in that the rural ignorants [the common people] were seduced by the Nien. Later the wavering earthwall community chiefs joined the Nien because of fear."[135]

The fact that the Nien had popular support had also surprised the previous commanders. But the previous commanders had not considered this the key to the Nien's ascendancy. In their minds, if there was anything standing in the way of the Nien's suppression, it was the earthwalls which transformed every Nien community into a fort. So whenever they overcame a Nien earthwall community, the first step they took to complete the conquest was to tear down the earthwall. Now Tseng brought to light both the people and the chiefs as the real objects for which he was resolved to fight. Whether he eventually gave the problem a basic solution is another question. That he pointed out the crux of the problem proves he had greater insight than his predecessors. He never proposed to destroy the earthwalls. On the contrary, he ordered the villages to erect more earthwalls and to dig more trenches.[136] Why could the government officials not use the

132. Fang-lüeh, 230/20-21.
133. Wang Ting-an, Ch'iu-ch'üeh-chai ti-tzu chi, 11/4-5.
134. Shantung chün-hsing chi-lüeh, 4C/9-10.
135. Tseng Kuo-fan, Tseng Wen-cheng-kung ch'üan-chi, Comments on reports, 3/40.
136. Wang Ting-an, Ch'iu-ch'üeh-chai ti-tzu chi, 11/10.

enemy's own weapon against them? Ch'iao Sung-nien (喬松年), governor of Anhwei, agreed with Tseng without reservation. He believed, "The extermination of outlaws depends on whether the government is able to separate the wheat from the chaff, not on the destruction of earthwalls. While former rebellious earthwall communities have already been destroyed, loyal ones should be spared so as to meet the emergency of bandit raids."[137]

Tseng not only talked but acted. Corresponding to his assumption that the inhabitants of the communities and their chiefs were the two important factors to deal with, he issued a proclamation in two sections; one dealt with the people, one with the chiefs.[138] In this proclamation he divided the people into two categories: the loyal and the seditious. Commissioners were to be sent to each earthwall community to investigate thoroughly and to prepare two lists, in which the names of the people in the two categories would be registered. Excepting those who led the rebellion and those who faithfully adhered to their leaders, most would be regarded as loyal subjects, including those who followed the bandits by accident or were forced to join. The seditious ones would be hunted down until they got their due punishment, that is, were beheaded. The loyal ones should present the chief with a guarantee that, within groups of five families, each family would be responsible for the behavior of the other four.[139] The chief had to present a similar guarantee to the local magistrate and was held responsible for his earthwall community as a whole. The proclamation concerning the chiefs abolished the title "lord of the earthwall community" (yü-chu 圩主), and replaced "lord" (chu 主) with "head" (chang 長), because "lord" was a symbol of usurpation. The head was to be elected by the inhabitants, with the election supervised by the local governments and recognized by an appointment from Tseng himself. To affirm the officially appointed chief's position and to tighten his connection with the government, Tseng would grant each of the chiefs a license bearing the Imperial Commissioner's seal. Each chief was charged with the responsibility of purifying his community; that is, he was to seize any dweller who still communicated with the Nien. The community which delivered the most bandits to the

137. Po-chou chih, 8/34.
138. Wang Ting-an, Ch'iu-ch'üeh-chai ti-tzu chi, 11/10-11. In the last part, we have pointed out that in an earthwall community the big clans and gentry usually provided leadership, while the rest of the inhabitants were peasants. The word "people" used here should be considered a general expression for peasants.
139. This idea of mutual guarantee was obviously derived from the centuries-old pao-chia (保甲) system. This system is discussed in an unpublished manuscript by Hsiao Kung-chuan, "Rural China, Imperial Control in the Nineteenth Century."

government would be rewarded; on the other hand, if any community was found harboring treacherous persons, its chief would be dismissed and punished.

Tseng was aware of the power held by a chief, whose will usually decided which side the entire community would take.[140] Thus what Tseng sought was the chiefs' submission. When someone suggested that the small earthwall communities be combined into larger units in order to facilitate the government's control, Tseng replied that unification was impractical and was of secondary importance. He preferred to cast out the old chiefs and to give the new ones guidance and instruction. He did not hesitate to use the death penalty to punish disobedience or rebellion.[141]

The investigation of villages began in the ninth month of 1865, three months after the Nien had been driven from Huai-pei by the Huai Army under Liu Ming-ch'uan and Chou Sheng-po.[142] Before sending commissioners to survey the earthwall communities, Tseng first adopted a drastic measure. He ordered Liu Ming-ch'uan,[143] one of the leading commanders of the Huai Army, to inquire of the gentry and elders in the districts of Su-chou, Meng-ch'eng, and Po-chou about the residences of the famous Nien leaders.[144] Then Liu was to go directly to the earthwall community which was identified and demand delivery of the rebel. Resistance was to be answered with suppression. But the theme of Tseng's policy was to detach the followers from their leaders. A harsher measure would run counter to the principle of winning the people and thus isolating the leaders. Liu's mission was to deal with the leaders. To the people Tseng sent a group of civil officials, who were to use persuasion instead of threats.[145] They treated the pardoned followers just as they treated loyal subjects.

The task of investigation was extended to the earthwall communities under the jurisdiction of the prefectures of K'ai-feng, Kuei-te, and Ch'en-chou in Honan.[146] Tseng warned the commissioners against hasty and slovenly inspection; until they were confident that they had accomplished their work in one district, they should not go on to the next. He taught them that only sincerity could rid the people of their suspicion of the government

140. See Part I, section 3.

141. Tseng Kuo-fan, Tseng Wen-cheng-kung ch'üan-chi, Comments on reports, 3/66-67. We regret that these instructions are not available.

142. d. 1888. Hummel, p. 526.

143. 1836-1896. Hummel, pp. 526-528.

144. Tseng Kuo-fan, Tseng Wen-cheng-kung ch'üan-chi, p. 28.

145. Su-chou chih, 10/39; Hsü-hsiu Meng-ch'eng hsien-chih, 6/24. Materials regarding persuasion are also extremely scanty.

146. Tseng Kuo-fan, Tseng Wen-cheng-kung ch'üan-chi, Comments on reports, 3/56.

and bring them to the side of the government armies. He did not believe that out of a thousand earthwall communities in those districts there was not a single one willing to accept the government's good will.

Nevertheless, Tseng's policy of investigation might never have been successful if he had not been able to bar the Nien from this area. In the eleventh month, two months after he began the investigation of villages, he selected four key posts in the four corners of the area; at these posts vast forces were to be massed. Thereupon Lin-huai in Anhwei, Hsü-chou in Kiangsu, Tsi-ning in Shantung and Chou-chia-k'ou in Honan became the so-called "four posts." All of them enjoyed river facilities for supply transportation.[147] The first function of the four posts was to relieve the first one which was attacked. In that way they stood as a barrier surrounding the Huai region, into which the home-loving Nien could hardly penetrate. Their second function lay in the fact that their presence, even without fighting, would guard against the revival of disturbance within this area.

Originally Tseng intended to revert to Prince Seng's policy of pursuit, but he changed the policy of pursuit to a policy of checking the enemy along their front, so as to contain the fluid bandit forces with stationary armies.[148] Obviously Tseng did not expect that this reversal of policy would effect the suppression of the Nien who remained unharmed outside the barriers. What he emphasized at this time was the protection of north Anhwei, north Kiangsu, south Shantung, and west Honan against Nien invasion, so that he could carry out his project of converting the Nien nests. In order to concentrate his efforts on this region, he even declined the government's offer of the command of Chihli, east Honan, and Hupeh.

The Nien, unable to move eastward, trampled at will west Honan and north Hupeh, because the weak provincial armies made those areas almost defenseless. Tseng found it unwise to let his main forces stand idle at the four posts. In the next spring (1866), he revised his strategy. He shortened his defensive line to three rivers so as to release more troops to carry on mobile warfare with the Nien. On the north, he guarded the Grand Canal; the sector from Ch'ang-kou (長溝) to Huang-shu-chuang (黃樹莊) was assigned to the Huai Army, the sector north of Ch'ang-kou to the Shantung Army, and the sector south of Huang-shu-chuang to the Kiangsu Army.[149] In the west, he built a line along the Sha and

---

147. Fang-lüeh, 239/11. Chou-chia-k'ou and Lin-huai used the rivers Huai and Ying as provision routes, while Tsi-ning and Hsü-chou used the Grand Canal.

148. Ibid., 242/17.

149. Fang-lüeh, 233/11; 258/21; Ting Pao-cheng, 1/32.

Chia-lu rivers and entrusted the central section to the Huai Army, assisted by the Honan Army on the right flank and by the Anhwei Army on the left.[150] Between the headwaters of the Chia-lu and the Yellow River course there was a gap where a trench was to be dug. However, before the trench was completed, the Nien slipped through into Shantung.[151] The defense chain, linked by the rivers, thus crumbled. The general situation again appeared to be as distressing as in Prince Seng's time. Impatience grew among the Shantung and Honan people, criticism arose in the capital, and Tseng himself began to question the policy of "checking the roving bandits with stationary armies."[152]

Nevertheless, Tseng's defensive policy was a success in that it rendered possible the destruction of the Nien's home organization. During 1866-1867, the Nien made a series of desperate thrusts toward the east. One of their main objectives seems to have been to acquire provisions,[153] but, in comparison with their determination to return home, the desire for supplies was secondary. In the tenth month of 1865, they dashed from Ts'ao-chou, south to Hsü-chou and then west to Hsiao-hsien and Tang-shan, with the sole intention of reaching Huai-pei.[154] In the second month of the next year, they exhausted every means to break through the Canal embankments, first at Yün-ch'eng and then at Su-ch'ien, lingering in the Ts'ao-Hsü-Huai-Szu area for two months, without realizing their dream of reaching Huai-pei soil.[155] Another group in Honan pursued the same objective and met the same rebuff.[156] All moves were directed towards a common goal--the recovery of the home domain; but all attempts were in vain. The four garrison posts and later the river defense lines functioned effectively. "Since the four posts had defined garrison locations, the roving bandits came in collision with the defense network wherever they tried to break through."[157] In the meantime, Tseng came to an agreement with the natives of the former Nien area: in case the Nien succeeded in piercing the defense line and emerged in the area, the earthwall community under attack was required to hold

150. Ibid., 257/15-16.
151. Fang-lüeh, 259/27-28.
152. Wang K'ai-yün, 14/10; Fang-lüeh, 259/24; Tseng Kuo-fan, Tseng Wen-cheng-kung shu-cha, 25/19.
153. Tseng Kuo-fan, Tseng Wen-cheng-kung shu-cha, 25/17; Fang-lüeh, 255/2; 264/16; 277/10. They desired to cross the Grand Canal so as to gain access either to east Shantung or to north Kiangsu, for both of these regions were considered rich and undisturbed. Rebuffed in that direction, they turned toward Hupeh with the same objectives.
154. Chou Shih-ch'eng, Huai-chün p'ing-nien chi, 1/23.
155. Ibid., 2/10.
156. Fang-lüeh, 252/11.
157. Chou Shih-ch'eng, Huai-chün p'ing-nien chi, 2/3.

out for at least half a month; if it submitted within this time limit, the said earthwall community would be held responsible for its own fall.[158] If rescuing forces failed to come within half a month, Tseng announced that he himself would assume the blame. He demanded that the natives call back their relatives who had followed the Nien outside the area.[159] Also, the community chief was required to report those who left their home communities to join the wandering Nien. The deadline for summoning relatives and for reporting runaways was half a month. After this period of time, no more followers would be allowed to come back, and the chiefs who hesitated to report would be accused of giving improper protection to the bandits. Once this regulation was put into effect, the tie between the Nien and their home associates was effectively severed.[160]

The protection given Huai-pei against the Nien was significant in another respect. In Tseng's opinion, the devastation of the districts which surrounded the Nien area -- Feng-yang, Ying-chou, Hsü-chou, Su-chou, Kuei-te, and Ch'en-chou -- resulted directly in the growth of the Nien power.[161] According to Tseng, whenever the land of a hundred li had been made barren, the peasants within those hundred li had found in joining the Nien their only means of living. The wider the desolation was spread, the more recruits flowed to the Nien forces. Now, unless the officials could restore the peasants to their normal economic life, any measure to bring about political control would be impracticable. Thus Tseng assigned to the chiefs of the earthwall communities not only the garrison duties but also the task of intensifying agricultural work.[162] He was eager to see all the land ravaged by the Nien brought under cultivation again. The resumption of cultivation required a breathing space. Unless the officials could hold off the disturbing Nien, the necessary leisure and order could not be won.

After the ninth month of 1865, with their nests shattered and their forces being pursued, the Nien began a succession of attempts to return home. All were unsuccessful. They had no option but to continue wandering. Along their circuitous line of march, they were confronted with earthwalls, the same weapon

---

158. Wang Ting-an, Ch'iu-ch'üeh-chai ti-tzu chi, 11/10-11.

159. The Nien, though wandering outside, still maintained secret communication with their relatives at home.

160. Wang Ting-an, Ch'iu-ch'üeh-chai ti-tzu chi, 12/18.

161. Shantung chün-hsing chi-lüeh, 4C/9. The land which the Nien laid waste was in the districts surrounding the Nien area, not within the area itself.

162. Wang Ting-an, Ch'iu-ch'üeh-chai ti-tzu chi, 11/11. At the beginning of this chapter, I have pointed out that though the Nien laid waste the soil around their homeland, their own farmwork remained intact. Tseng, of course, did not need to apply his measure to the heart of the Nien nests.

which they had used against government attackers. Earthwalls also sprang up in other provinces.

In Central China, the elimination of the Taiping remnants by the loyalists at the Hupeh-Anhwei border in the tenth month of 1864 virtually put an end to organized rebellion except that of the Nien.[163] On the other hand, the governors in those provinces became stronger than they were before the fifties, so that rebellious aspirants who still persisted in the villages found it difficult to start new insurrections. Meanwhile the dislocated and war-weary peasants desired the restoration of peace and order. To be sure, the Nien were still there, but the situation had changed. Now they were wandering, rather than holding a piece of stable territory. On their routes of gallop, they had neither the basis nor the leisure with which to organize the local forces and thus to establish themselves in control of a new dominion. Nor could they continue the policy of providing the masses with protection and provisions as they had done in the fifties. Now the villages which suffered from the plundering troops and crushing cavalry of the Nien had to turn to the government for protection or to plan self-defense.

In 1865-1867, the governor of Hupeh, Tseng Kuo-ch'üan,[164] encouraged the villagers of Hupeh to imitate what the Nien had done in Anhwei in the fifties, that is, to store the harvests of the fields in earthwalls, clear up the outlying land, and close the walls to the homeless enemy.[165] Honan applied the same tactics.[166] In Shantung, under the direction of Governor Ting Pao-chen,[167] the earthwalls were even more plentiful. The peasants either opened their wall gates and surprised the passing Nien with unexpected attacks or followed up the government victories with sudden massacres of those who survived.[168] In the 1850's it was the government troops who, as aliens in a hostile country, had fallen helpless in front of the Nien's earthwalls. Now it was the Nien's turn to suffer the same fate in provinces hostile to them. This reversal marked the end of the Nien.

---

163. The suppression of the Taipings did not result in a regeneration of the Manchu rule. Out of the upheaval, a new force grew up, namely the regional force represented by the governors. They succeeded in suppressing the rebels, but at the same time they challenged the central power.

164. 1824-1890. Hummel, pp. 749-751.

165. Hupeh t'ung-chih, 73/1868; 74/1875-77.

166. Yü-chün chi-lüeh, 8, Wan-fei 7/13.

167. 1820-1886. Hummel, pp. 723-725.

168. Ting Pao-cheng, 2/42; 5/16; Li Hung-chang, Letters to Friends and Colleagues, 7/21; Fang-lüeh, 263/1-2; 290/10; 291/24.

5. The Suppression of the Huai Rebels
by the Huai Army

Tseng Kuo-fan made up for his predecessors' failure in separating the masses from the Nien; however, the reader should not make the mistake of thinking that Tseng ever tried to substitute a political solution for military expediency. Although Tseng strove to detach the Nien followers from their leaders, he had no comprehensive plan for ridding the people of political oppression and economic and social injustice, so as to root out the source of rebellion once and for all. What I want to emphasize here is that Tseng not only detached the peasants from their leaders but actively organized them into a new force in opposition to the Nien. In this respect Tseng succeeded where his predecessors had failed.

Tseng said to Li Hung-chang in 1859 that the people in Huai-nan and Huai-pei were turbulent and vigorous, as enthusiastically inclined to rebellion as a long-absent native is to return home; but that their simple ways and brave spirit were also suitable to the formation of a new army.[169] This indicates that Tseng, unlike Yüan Chia-san, neither suspected, feared, nor underrated the Huai people. With the same attitude, he had succeeded in building up the Hsiang Army in his native place nine years before. After making the above observation, he ordered Li Hung-chang, a native of Ho-fei, to call five hundred volunteers in Huai-nan as an experiment. In the next year, 1860, when he ascended to the governor-generalship of Liang-Kiang, Tseng intensified his efforts to carry out the plan. In the second month of 1861, the Huai Army was established in Anking.

The establishment of this new force was merely one of Tseng's devices to deal with the general military situation north of the Yangtze. His purpose was far-reaching; he aimed at replacing the worn-out Hsiang Army with the fresh Huai Yung.[170] This farsighted plan was also aimed at the Nien. In the same year that the Huai Army came into being, and three years before he undertook the command in the Huai area, Tseng assured Li that "after the Huai Yung grows popular and strong enough, we can rely on it for suppressing the Nien and stabilizing the central land";[171] he considered the Huai volunteers more adaptable to geographical conditions than the Hsiang Army.[172] Li Hung-chang

169. Lo Erh-kang, Hsiang-chün hsin-chih, 13/1.
170. Tseng Kuo-fan, Tseng Wen-cheng-kung shu-cha, 24/13.
171. Ibid., 18/27.
172. Ibid., 24/9. In 1859 Tseng had told Yüan Chia-san, "The Hsiang Yung are not used to eating wheaten food and to enduring hardships, and besides, they are homesick, always longing for a

shared the same feeling. He knew that although Li Hsü-i and
T'ang Hsün-fang had used the Hsiang Army in the Huai-pei battlefield, and Liu Ch'ang-yu had employed the Hsiang volunteers to
fight the Chihli mounted bandits, both attempts had proved inef-
fective.[173] The provincial armies of Honan and Anhwei looked
even more discouraging. From Li's viewpoint, these forces were
impotent, divided, and undisciplined.[174] Moreover, he did not
have a high opinion of Prince Seng.[175]

 With the provincial forces and those of Prince Seng written
off, Tseng saw in the Huai Army the only hope, and Li himself
was full of confidence. Especially when the struggle with the
Taipings dragged on, it became evident that the Hsiang Army was
used up. The "evening spirit" dominated the whole army.[176] A succession of mutinies after the fall of Nanking frightened Tseng.[177]

leave. If they are transferred to Huai-pei, physically they will
not be able to stand the northern climate and mentally they are not
willing to go so far from home. The outside world is impressed by
the Hsiang Yung's merits only, but I am familiar with their defects
as well." (Ibid., 9/19)

 173. Fang-lüeh, 245/22-23. At the beginning of the T'ung-chih
reign, the northern provinces copied the Hsiang Army system. Yen
Shu-sen (嚴樹森) replaced the Honan provincial army with Hsiang
volunteers. Liu Ch'ang-yu trained the Chihli Army on the model of
the Hsiang Army. (Fang-lüeh, 189/25) T'ang Hsün-fang, acting
governor of Anhwei, applied the Hsiang Army regulations to the
Anhwei Army. (Fang-lüeh, 170/4) Liu Jung, governor of Shensi, formerly a follower of Tseng Kuo-fan, recruited his army of over ten
thousand men from Hunan. (Ch'ing Shih-kao, lieh-chuan 212/4) Ting
Pao-chen, governor of Shantung, brought eight thousand Hunan
volunteers with him to Shantung. (Ting Wen-ch'eng-kung chou-kao,
1/5) In training the Shantung Army, he mingled two hundred Hunan
volunteers with three hundred Shantung volunteers in each battalion.
(Shantung chün-hsing chi-lüeh, 15C/6) None of these new armies on
the pattern of the Hsiang Yung gained the same triumphs as their
countrymen did in the south. In Shensi, Chang Tsung-yü completely
destroyed Liu Jung's Hsiang Yung. (Fang-lüeh, 268/20-21) Chang
Chih-wan, governor of Honan, even requested the Emperor to cancel
the Imperial order directing the Hupeh-Hunan armies to enter Honan.
According to Chang, the Hupeh-Hunan armies were weak in discipline
and unskilled in fighting the Nien. (Fang-lüeh, 228/6)

 174. Li Hung-chang, Letters to Friends and Colleagues, 6/23.

 175. Ibid., 6/5.

 176. The defects of the degenerated Hsiang Army can be enumerated: (1) both soldiers and commanders were weary and sick of
military life, (2) they were corrupted by the traditions of officialdom, (3) their military units were far under strength, (4) they
made trouble for the people, (5) the officers regarded their camps
as temporary lodging, which they were free to enter and leave at
will, (6) if they lost a battle, they declined to rescue one
another. (Lo Erh-kang, 12/1)

 177. The troops under Pao Ch'ao mutinied in Chin-k'ou, Hupeh,

Meanwhile, his supremely meritorious service aroused jealousy and suspicion. Self-restriction, the result of long years of cultivating neo-Confucianism, made him resolve to dissolve his own force so as to save its revenue for the Huai Army, on which he would rely for his power, subsequent career, and even his personal safety.[178] Thus, weariness, lack of discipline, Imperial suspicion, and financial considerations were the reasons for the demobilization of the bulk of the Hsiang Army.[179]

Tseng then led the Huai Army to the north and made contact with the northern provincial forces. Facts soon confirmed his former calculation about them. He congratulated himself on his wisdom in establishing the Huai Army. He was proud that "people usually like to talk of a united offensive against the Nien, unaware that throughout San-Kiang (Kiangsu, Chekiang, and Kiangsi) Liang-Hu (Hupeh and Hunan), Shantung and Honan, the Huai Yung is the sole force which can be entrusted to fight field warfare as well as to defend."[180] One may ask why the Huai Yung, who were largely drafted from the districts south of the Huai, should be considered as a new formation particularly suitable for suppressing the Nien, who were from the area north of the Huai. Li Hung-chang himself remarked: "My soldiers belong to Lu-chou, Liu-an, Anking, and Yangchow, different from the men from the north of the Huai [in character and in customs]."[181] Moreover, before 1865 it was the Taipings instead of the Nien which the Huai Army fought.

Before answering this question, let us make a brief inquiry into the origin of the Huai Army commanders. The Huai-chün p'ing-nien-chi makes it clear that veteran commanders of the Huai Army had previously led local corps in their native districts, and that Li's popularity was dreaded by the Nien.[182] Whether Li was really feared by the Nien before 1867 remains to be verified. But the fact that the Huai Army commanders were originally leaders of local corps is indisputable; even Li Hung-chang himself had once been a local corps chief fighting against the Nien. In response to Wang Mou-yin's (王茂蔭)[183] proposal to send central govern-

in consequence of their commanders' inability to pay them the sum earned in the past years. The movement spread to south Anhwei, where mutineers injured their superiors. (Tseng Kuo-fan, Tseng Wen-cheng-kung ch'üan-chi, Comments on reports, 3/22; Li Hung-chang, Letters to Friends and Colleagues, 6/24) The troops under Chang Lien-chün, Chiang Nin-hsüeh, and Ch'eng Ta-chi followed suit. (Tseng Kuo-fan, Tseng Wen-cheng-kung shu-cha, 24/35; Fang-lüeh, 249/2.)

178. Tseng Kuo-fan, Tseng Wen-cheng-kung shu-cha, 25/5, 18; Lo Erh-kang, chap. 1.

179. Lo Erh-kang, 12/1.

180. Tseng Kuo-fan, Tseng Wen-cheng-kung shu-cha, 25/18.

181. Fang-lüeh, 254/22-23.

182. Chou Shih-ch'eng, Huai-chün p'ing-nien chi, 1/3.

183. Junior Vice-President of the Board of Finance.

ment officials back to their native places to raise local forces, the Court sent Li Wen-an (李文安) to Lu-chou. When Li Wen-an passed Lin-huai in the eleventh month of 1853, Yüan Chia-san retained him to assist in enrolling volunteers.[184] At the beginning of that year, Li Hung-chang, Wen-an's son, had already followed local corps commissioner Lü Hsien-chi to Lu-chou, and had served under the acting governor, Chou T'ien-chüeh, as a staff member. The acute situation in Ying-chou, which resulted from the defeat of government forces by the rising Nien, drew Chou's attention to the north. There Li and Sun Chia-t'ai, led by Chou, fought with his local corps against the Nien.[185] The government's order sending officials back to the Huai Basin was intended to contain the rebellious agitation, including the Nien insurrection, in that area. Men such as Chou T'ien-chüeh, Yüan Chia-san, and Lü Hsien-chi, with whom Li was associated at this time, are familiar from the Nien uprising in the early fifties. Sun Chia-t'ai has been mentioned in previous passages regarding Miao P'ei-lin. In fact, Li had followed them to check the Nien tide which over-flowed in Ying-chou, a prefecture located in the north of the Huai instead of the south. Therefore, Li's return to the Nien affair in 1866 was nothing more than a resumption of his earlier career.

Liu Ming-ch'uan (劉銘傳), Li's first lieutenant, followed his father in leading a local corps when he was only eighteen years of age.[186] Chang Shu-sheng (張樹聲) and his brother, Shu-shan (樹珊), defeated Chang Lo-hsing in the Kuan-t'ing (官亭) battle in 1857.[187] P'an Ting-hsin (潘鼎新), Wu Ch'ang-ch'ing (吳長慶), Chou Sheng-po (周盛波) and his brother, Sheng-ch'uan (盛傳), started their careers in the same way.[188] All of these men, who later became commanders of the Huai Army, began their careers as local corps chiefs in the Lu-chou area, in a manner similar to that of Sun Chia-t'ai, Hsü Li-chuang, Li Nan-hua, and others to the north of the Huai. The difference was that in the north there was no Tseng Kuo-fan to appreciate the potential power of the local forces and to take the initiative in elevating their organization to a higher plane. Sun Chia-t'ai's case demonstrates this difference. Sun had fought shoulder to shoulder with Li Hung-chang against the Nien and later offered protection to Governor Weng T'ung-shu. But the governor, instead of elevating Sun's military force to a

184. Hsü-hsiu Lu-chou fu-chih, 96/1-2.
185. Idem.
186. Ch'ing shih-kao, Biographies, 203/3. Liu Ming-ch'uan, 1836-1896. (Hummel, pp. 526-528)
187. Ibid., 203/4-5; 234/4.
188. Ch'ing shih-kao, Biographies, 203/6-9; Li Hung-chang, Letters to Friends and Colleagues, 6/19. P'an Ting-hsin, d. 1888; Wu Ch'ang-ch'ing, 1834-1884; Chou Sheng-po, d. 1888. (Hummel, pp. 745; 483; 526)

higher organization, used Sun's life as a price for appeasing Miao P'ei-lin. Maybe Sun was as "turbulent" as Miao, but the officials' neglect of the local forces ruled out every chance for their mobilization on a large scale.

The Huai Army was not entirely recruited from the people south of the Huai. When Tseng Kuo-fan set his foot in Hsü-chou, he was so moved by the animated character of the Huai-pei people that he conveyed his impression to Li Hung-chang immediately:

> Hsü-chou, as a battlefield since the ancient times, produces plenty of gallant commanders and valiant fighters. Its tempo resembles that of your native place. Provided we can instill them with loyalty and faithfulness in place of turbulence, the Huai Yung's prospect of development will be like a broad wave-ridden sea and a densely branched tree.[189]

Tseng evaluated the Huai-pei people exactly as he did the Huai-nan volunteers. He even saw in the inclusion of the Huai-pei elements the future grandeur of the Huai Army. Li Hung-chang, bearing this evaluation in his mind, made up the Huai Army's losses by drafting male adults from the intersection of Anhwei, Hsü-chou, Honan, and Shantung, and by reorganizing the surrendered Nien.[190] When the war ceased in 1868, the composition of the Huai Army had changed to such an extent that seventy per cent of the soldiers were from Ying-chou and Po-chou,[191] the former central Nien area. Because the Huai-pei newcomers outnumbered the original elements from Huai-nan, the entry of the Huai Army in the north succeeded not only in drawing the Nien's supporters from their leaders but in incorporating them into the Huai Army to fight their countrymen. The success in using the surrendered Nien to fill gaps left by casualties is even more astonishing. It meant using the pardoned Nien to suppress their comrades who had preferred to fight to the end.

The enlistment of Huai-pei male adults was not confined to the Huai Army. After 1863 there was a movement to reorganize the provincial armies in the provinces of Chihli, Shantung, Honan, and Anhwei, with the intention of enabling them to stand on their own feet in defense of their respective territories. Attracted by Western guns, the Shantung governor, Yen Ching-ming (閻敬銘),[192] established a battalion, to which he gave special training in the

---

189. Tseng Kuo-fan, Tseng Wen-cheng-kung shu-cha, 24/32.
190. Fang-lüeh, 319/29.
191. Fang-lüeh, 317/24-25. In Meng-ch'eng alone, several thousand men came back from the armies after the war was over. (Hsü-hsiu Meng-ch'eng hsien-chih, 6/24)
192. 1817-1892. Hummel, p. 724.

use of the new weapons.[193] At that time, the successful adoption
of Western weapons by the Huai Army produced the impression
that the Huai Yung were the most suitable users of these weapons.
Then the Shantung governor specially enlisted two thousand
volunteers from the Huai area.[194] In Honan, Governor Chang
Chih-wan (張之萬)[195] had reformed the Honan Army in 1864, entitling it the "Yü Army" after the manner of the Hsiang and Huai
armies.[196] Two years later his successor added more than ten
thousand men to the original fourteen thousand, and withheld as
funds for the new army the "capital revenue"[197] and also the subsidies assigned to help other provinces.[198] However, this new
Honan Army was also recruited from Huai-pei volunteers. In the
closing year of the Nien Rebellion, sixty per cent of the Yü Army
were from Huai-pei,[199] as was the "Wan Army," the refreshed
Anhwei Army on the model of the Hsiang-Huai armies. This new
force was founded on reorganized local corps and continued to be
commanded by former local corps chiefs like Li Te-sheng (李得
勝) and Niu Shih-han (牛師韓).[200] The components, of course,
were entirely the natives of the Ying-Po area.[201] Though the
Hsiang-Huai leaders did not consider the provincial armies as
main forces in the task of handling the Nien business, the reformed armies of Shantung, Honan, and Anhwei played an active
part in collaborating with the Huai Army. Their contribution lay
in preventing the Nien's roaming at will from province to province,
in sending troops to Shantung to share in garrison duties on the
blockade lines, and in aiding in the Nien's final elimination. Since
these provincial forces and the Huai Army all drew replacements
from the Huai-pei recruits, it is no exaggeration to say that the
Huai-pei people themselves suppressed the Nien who had once been
masters of that region.

The service rendered by the Huai-pei peasants to the government armies exposes the limitation of their loyalty to the Nien.
Before 1865 clan and communal bonds bred passionate allegiance
between the peasants and their leaders. In addition to these bonds,
the leaders took the place of the officials as rulers of the rural
areas and sought to relieve the peasants from famine and to

193. Shantung chün-hsing chi-lüeh, 4C/16-18.
194. Ibid., 5A/10.
195. 1811-1897. Hummel, p. 32.
196. Fang-lüeh, 217/13.
197. The land tax and grain tribute which should be forwarded
to the capital.
198. Yü-chün chi-lüeh, 12, Wan-fei 20/4-6.
199. Fang-lüeh, 317/25; 320/14.
200. Hsü-hsiu Meng-ch'eng hsien-chih, 9/32; Wo-yang feng-t'u
chi, 12/67-71.
201. Fang-lüeh, 317/24.

protect them from injury. In other words, the Nien leaders took over the positions as well as the functions of the officials. Yet these social and political ties depended for perpetuation on one condition, namely, the leaders' continued hold on their territory. After 1865 this condition ceased to exist. The officials, under the direction of Tseng Kuo-fan, reestablished their authority in Huai-pei and repulsed the Nien's feverish attempts to return home. In the first place, with the leaders gone, the binding force resulting from clan or communal relationship relaxed. Secondly, insofar as the Nien leaders had been the prominent personalities in their communities, capable of welding the peasants into an organization, their departure meant the recession of that organizing power. Thirdly, Tseng Kuo-fan encouraged the reclamation of the ravaged land bordering the Nien realm, in part a substitute for the previous Nien policy of feeding the hungry people. The adequate pay offered by the Huai Army to the recruits from Huai-pei opened another way to earn a living.[202] Finally, just as the Nien leaders had used their position as rulers to command the peasants' loyalty, so now the new rulers used their power over the peasants. The peasants, lacking sharp political consciousness, tolerated existing authority, seldom resorting to revolt unless natural calamities or official oppression pushed them to extremity. Even during the revolt, they fought less for an abstract principle than for concrete objectives, for example, to survive famine. With the Nien leaders and veterans wandering outside, the peasants left in the Huai-pei nests were unable and unwilling to refuse to serve the new rulers, especially when such service provided a means of living.

Although the invigoration of the Huai Army by the Huai-pei masses provided the key to the Nien's suppression, other conditions were needed to achieve success. First, the command by Li Hung-chang was indispensable. The establishment of the Hsiang-Huai armies set the standard for personal contact between the army and the commander.[203]

Tseng Kuo-fan's defensive policy, as noted above, had aroused resentment. In the eleventh month of 1866 the veteran commander in chief of the Hsiang-Huai forces retired from the front. In his memorial Tseng regretted that he was not shrewd enough to draft more effective plans of strategy, and that his slowness and scruples were unsuitable for dealing with the mobile and deceptive Nien.[204] But this was not the only reason for his retirement. In spite of the fact that Tseng was responsible for the

---

202. The Huai Army could afford to offer adequate pay because its financial condition was much better than that of the armies before 1865. See later passages.
203. Lo Erh-kang, 13/6.
204. Fang-lüeh, 261/27.

formation of the Huai Army, and that Li Hung-chang respected
Tseng as his master for thirty years, the real master of the army
was Li. During the interval of Tseng's command, Li stayed in the
rear as acting governor-general of Liang-Kiang, commissioned to
sustain the front. Nevertheless, as the possessor of the army, Li
not only felt that he had to have his say on crucial occasions, but
also he could not help intervening in routine concerns. This disturbed Tseng. He wrote to Li in a direct manner: "At the present
time, since the command of the Huai Army is shifted to me, you
should keep yourself completely aloof, so that the generals can
have a unified guidance and, meanwhile, I may direct them
smoothly."[205] Nevertheless, three months prior to this complaint
(the third month of 1866), a year's experience had convinced Tseng
that no force other than the Huai Army would be able to suppress
the Nien, and no persons other than the Li family could command
the Huai Army.[206] With this conviction, he promised Li that if no
sign of progress appeared by summer, he would recommend Li as
his successor. He frankly admitted, "Whereas I am not able to
ride and conduct battles in the field, you [Li] can gallop at the
head of the army. After your personal attendance in the battle but
once or twice, the combatants' morale will mount a hundred times
higher."[207]

Though the commanders of the Hsiang Army established personal control over their men, it was Li who tightened the link
between himself and his lieutenants, and thus was able to dominate
all of their activities. According to Tseng's judgment, "the Huai
commanders were always beneath the heels" of Li.[208] Now Tseng
found it necessary to give way to his pupil. After accepting
Tseng's resignation, the Court ordered him to exchange positions
with Li.[209] Though the latter still followed in the former's foot-

205. Tseng Kuo-fan, Tseng Wen-cheng-kung shu-cha, 25/33.
206. Ibid., 25/23, 25. Tseng, though founder of the Huai Army,
felt incapable of commanding it; others were even less able to do
so. In the third month of 1865, one month before the death of Seng-
ko-lin-ch'in, the Huai troops under Chang Shu-sheng, Liu Ming-
ch'uan, and Chou Sheng-po had already reached Hsü-chou, very close
to Ts'ao-chou where Seng-ko-lin-ch'in was struggling bitterly.
(Chou Shih-ch'eng, Huai-chün p'ing-nien chi, 1/1) Instead of crossing the border to his relief, the Huai commanders contented themselves with safeguarding the Kiangsu frontier, for whose security
Li, as governor of that province, was responsible. Li frankly
declared that he would never let Prince Seng command his army, and
therefore did not let his army go beyond the border. For this he
dared disobey the pressing Imperial edicts several times. (Li Hung-
chang, Letters to Friends and Colleagues, 6/18)
207. Tseng Kuo-fan, Tseng Wen-cheng-kung shu-cha, 25/23, 25.
208. Ibid., 25/33.
209. Originally the Court summoned Tseng to audience in the
capital. His advisers suspected that the Court would detain him,

steps in regard to the principle of limiting the Nien's range of
activities with river defense lines, his presence inspired in his
lieutenants a new spirit. For him they were willing to fight and,
if necessary, to die.

The fact that the Huai Army enjoyed adequate revenues was
the second favorable condition contributing to its final triumph.
Li Hung-chang himself laid stress on this point.[210] He said that
during 1853-1858, when he was assisting in managing military
affairs in north Anhwei, he saw how revenue shortages caused the
collapse of the armies under Ho-chün (和 春),[211] Cheng K'uei-shih
(鄭魁士), Yüan Chia-san, and Weng T'ung-shu. On the other hand,
Li continued, the successes gained by Hu Lin-i, Tseng Kuo-fan,
Tso Tsung-t'ang, and himself in the Taiping campaigns resulted
from various and sufficient sources of financial support. But the
financial factor, as shown earlier, was not decisive in the outcome of the contest between the government forces and the Nien.
In the case of the Huai Army, it was not because Tseng had been
assured ample funds that he determined to create a new force.
Adequate revenues, however, became indispensable once the army
came into being. Especially after 1867 money became a chief
means to induce the Nien to surrender; an additional inducement
was the fact that they were fed well after they had been incorporated into the army on a mass scale. The Huai Army's mastery of
the wealth of the Yangtze Delta distinguished it from the impov-
erished provincial armies. When it started the northern campaigns,
the Huai Yung numbered more than fifty thousand.[212] The monthly
expenses for remuneration and procurement of munitions and
supplies amounted to 500,000 liang of silver, of which two-thirds
were drawn from the Kiangsu taxes and likin and the Huai-nan
salt likin.[213] Kiangsu was the only province which could afford
such a large sum for military purposes; and Li Hung-chang
occupied the governorship of that province. To use Li's own
words, whereas his predecessors in the Huai area had to establish headquarters in "strange lands," he raised revenue in a

---

and he himself felt uneasy. Then Li hinted in his memorial that he
needed Tseng to manage revenues in the rear. This resulted in the
Imperial order which sent Tseng back to the governor-generalship of
Liang-Kiang. (Lo Erh-kang, 6/3)

    210. Chou Shih-ch'eng, Huai-chün p'ing-nien chi, 1/19.

    211. d. 1860. Hummel, p. 293.

    212. Chou Shih-ch'eng, Huai-chün p'ing-nien chi, 1/3.

    213. Ibid., 1/8; 11/16-18. Of the 500,000 total, 300,000 were
spent for the Huai Army's salaries and rations and 70,000 for the
Hsiang Army which had not been dissolved. (Fang-lüeh, 263/10-11)
Likin was a new tax utilized on a large scale by the Hsiang Army
and copied by some other provinces. It was imposed on merchandise
in inland transit.

province where he possessed administrative power.[214] Li's
remark is convincing, especially when one recalls how poverty-
stricken were those armies living on subsidies from other provinces. In the winter of 1860 Tseng returned from the front to
Nanking, where he fulfilled to the utmost degree the mission of
financing the front.[215] The marriage of the Kiangnan resources
and the Huai-pei manpower was an unrivaled masterpiece produced
by the partnership between Tseng and Li.

In addition to the abundance of revenues and supplies, Li
employed modern facilities to speed up transportation. Before
1863 disorder in Huai-pei disrupted the supply lines of the government forces. On the other hand, the Nien did not have this
problem. At home, they kept all the productive land of their
village communities intact, and all the farming work went on undis--
turbed. Abroad, they looted for provisions along their line of
march. During 1865-1866 the order which Tseng restored in
Huai-pei made the Ying and Huai rivers, together with the Grand
Canal, navigable again. Provisions flowed to the four garrison
posts over these water routes. Meanwhile, the fate of the
homeless Nien became worse. They found it no easy task to
procure grain in front of the hostile and well guarded earthwalls.
Li Hung-chang, after having arrived at the front, made another
great advance. In the summer of 1867, he set up a supply bureau
in Chiao-chou, on the coast of Shantung, to receive munitions and
rice shipped by sea from Shanghai.[216] At this time the blockade
enforced by the Huai Army had narrowed the area of military
operations to the Shantung Peninsula. While the Nien found it
difficult to acquire grain stored by the native people not far away
from them, the Huai Army enjoyed rice imported from places as
remote as Shanghai and Fukien.

In the next year, Li requested Ch'ung-hou (崇厚),[217] trade
commissioner of the three northern ports, to provide the Huai
Army with Imperial tribute grain to make up the deficiency in his
own supply. Simultaneously he requested Shen Pao-chen (沈葆楨),[218]
commissioner of ship affairs in Fukien, to send him additional
rice from the south.[219] Ch'ung-hou responded to the demand
promptly. He diverted 13,000 tan of foreign rice, intended for the
central government, to Shantung.[220] In the south, Ch'ung-hou
proposed to buy 100,000 tan of rice with shipbuilding funds, and to

214. Li Hung-chang, Letters to Friends and Colleagues, 6/48.
215. Tseng Kuo-fan, Tseng Wen-cheng-kung shu-cha, 26/19.
216. Li Hung-chang, Letters to Friends and Colleagues, 7/14.
217. 1826-1893. Hummel, p. 209.
218. 1820-1879. Hummel, p. 642.
219. Chou Shih-ch'eng, Huai-chün p'ing-nien chi, 10/20.
220. Tientsin hsien-chih, 16/22-24.

use steamers to ship it to Tientsin.[221] In the last year of the Nien campaign, Tientsin served the Huai Army as a supply depot through which provisions conveyed by the sea, together with revenue raised in Shanghai, streamed to the Shantung front.[222]

Among the supplies transported by steamships along the sea-coast, the most important item was Western weapons.[223] After 1864 every battalion of the Huai Army had invited Western

221. Ibid., 16/27-28.

222. Ibid., 16/29.

223. The use of firearms had not been confined to the government forces. The Nien adopted the same weapons. When they besieged Shen-ch'iu in 1853, the Nien already had guns with which they bombarded the city. (Fang-lüeh, 4/1) In the next year, in a single battle with the Nien under Li San-nao (李三閙), the government forces gained from their enemy the astonishing booty of six hundred guns of various types and two thousand catties of gunpowder. (Fang-lüeh, 5/6) In the early fifties the Nien frequently raided government boats loaded with guns or the arsenals. (Fang-lüeh, 8/12; 9/2) Li San-nao, though a Nien leader, had once submitted to the officials, with his bands organized as militia. It was likely that his bands obtained their guns from the officials during the period of submission. However, throughout the rebellion the Nien had not expanded the use of firearms, and, as shown elsewhere, they preferred long spears, perhaps because they could not afford to make up losses in spite of their occasional gains by raiding government equipage, or because their elusive tactics did not require firearms in large quantity.

The government troops were capable of procuring more guns and more gunpowder, but they relied on them only in attacking the Nien's strongholds. When they met the Nien in the field, the power of firearms was paralyzed; the Nien cavalrymen often charged their immediate front before they had time to load powder and balls. (Wang Ting-an, Ch'iu-ch'üeh-chai ti-tzu chi, 11/1) Usually the Nien rode far beyond the range of guns. Therefore, before 1865 firearms played a minor part in the Nien campaigns.

In the Huai Basin all the firearms we talk about were muzzle-loaders. The revolution of weapons did not take place until the entry of the Huai Army. The so-called Western guns in this period, though still muzzle-loaded, were improved with rifle lines; bullets replaced powder and balls. Of course, in the late fifties, this type of weapon had been well known in the Huai area. Sheng-pao had bought 10,000 liang worth of Western cannons to equip his gunboats in 1859, and T'ien Tsai-t'ien, garrison commander of Hsü-chou with the title of provincial commander in chief, had formed a special corps of Western rifles in 1862. (Fang-lüeh, 65/20-21; 137/28) An official called Chin An-ch'ing (金安清), commissioned to raise revenues in Chekiang in behalf of Anhwei, not only gave advice to Sheng-pao and Weng T'ung-shu in favor of the use of Western weapons but took action to furnish them with three hundred cannons and six hundred rifles from Shanghai. (Huang-ch'ao ching-shih wen hsü-p'ien, 95/70) The trouble was that the extreme scarcity of revenue, the

instructors to teach them how to use the new weapons.[224] Each
battalion was equipped with four hundred rifles, and thus the entire force composed of fifty thousand men possessed thirty to
forty thousand rifles.[225] Besides, Li supplemented his army with
four artillery battalions and with a thousand riflemen left by
General Gordon.[226]Steamships sailing along the coast solved the
problem of transporting the cannons, which could not easily be

loss of most of Kiangsu and Chekiang to the Taipings after 1860,
and the recall of Sheng-pao cut short this new measure.
    224. Chou Shih-ch'eng, Huai-chün p'ing-nien chi, 1/9. Liu
Ch'ang-yu had enforced a reorganization of the Chihli Army in 1863.
Later, the reorganization was extended to the Peking Field Force;
that is, a certain number of its rank-and-file members were selected for special training. (Ch'ing-ch'ao hsü-wen-hsien t'ung-k'ao,
217/9635-36) These Chihli and capital lien-chün (練軍), the reorganized army, were equipped with Western weapons. (Tientsin
hsien-chih, 16/19-21; Fang-lüeh, 175/8) When the West Nien invaded
Chihli and then entered north Shantung in 1868, the Chihli lien-
chün collaborated with other armies in the battles of its own province, and even advanced to Tung-ch'ang in east Shantung and to the
Chien River (減河) at the Shantung-Chihli boundary for the purpose
of completing the blockade. (Shantung chün-hsing chi-lüeh, 4C/5) On
his arrival at Hankow in January 1867, on the way to Shensi where
the Moslem uprising was at its height, Tso Tsung-t'ang, in an
effort to re-equip his army, provided 50 to 60 per cent of the
soldiers with rifles. (Tso Tsung-t'ang, Tso Wen-hsiang-kung shu-tu,
9/15) Before he reached Shensi, he received an Imperial order
commanding him to engage the West Nien who had spread carnage in
that province. In the next year Tso, unable to block the Nien in
Shensi, followed them to Chihli and then to Shantung. After Tseng
Kuo-ch'üan (1824-1890. Hummel, pp. 749-751) became governor of
Hupeh in 1865, he fought the Nien from time to time at the Hupeh-
Honan border with a regrouped force based on the Hsiang Army
veterans. He also urged adoption of the new munitions. (Tseng Kuo-
ch'üan, Tseng Chung-hsiang-kung shu-cha in Tseng Chung-hsiang-kung
ch'üan-chi, 8/44) To Shantung, where the vital battlefields lay
during the final years, Governor Yen Ching-ming brought a thousand
rifles in 1866. (Shantung chün-hsing chi-lüeh, 5A/10) The enthusiasm for the use of Western firearms on the model of the Huai Army
prevailed in the years 1865-1868, just as the application of the
Hsiang Army system to the provincial armies prevailed around 1860.
    Regardless of its subsequent development, the change of weapons
at this moment was aimed at suppressing the Nien. In fact, all the
armies mentioned above had attended the Shantung campaigns in 1867-
1868, though the battles were no longer fought in their respective
provinces.
    225. Chou Shih-ch'eng, Huai-chün p'ing-nien chi, 1/9; 12/3;
Fang-lüeh, 234/3. According to the Hsiang-Huai system, each battalion was composed of five hundred men excluding officers and
laborers.
    226. Ibid., 1/9-12.

shipped by old-fashioned river boats.[227] Li thought that the risks
resulting from long-distance transportation could be avoided by
setting up an arsenal in Tientsin. He called technicians and
artisans from the Shanghai Machinery Bureau to Tientsin, where
cannon shells were to be manufactured.[228] Thus military necessity founded the subsequent Tientsin Machinery Bureau.

In face of the onrushing tide of modern arms, the Nien's long
spears fell helpless. The long-range rifle fire caught numerous
soldiers as well as the Nien chiefs who tried to gallop away from
the enemy. Since the chiefs usually held flags in their hands as a
signal for directing the course of attack, it was easy for the
government rifle-bearers to recognize the Nien leaders as worth-
while targets. Jen Chu, one of their able leaders, died in this
manner.[229]

Faced with this desperate situation, the Nien resorted to their
old craft. They raided the Huai Army's munitions. In the summer
of 1867 the garrison forces on the Grand Canal found that the
mounted Nien not only carried rifles but were also skillful in
firing them.[230] Five months later the Nien maneuvered eleven
cannons in the battle near Tsou-hsien.[231] The West Nien who
entered Shantung in the next year followed suit; they stole many
rifles from the government troops.[232] Since robbing was not a
dependable means of supply, the Nien sought a more direct source.
"There are two foreign bandits in the Nien, through whom Jen Chu
and Lai Wen-kuang had an interview at Lao-shan (勞 山) with more
than a hundred foreigners, whom Jen and Lai entrusted with the
mission of purchasing Western guns."[233] This story came from a

227. Fang-lüeh, 235/3.
228. Chou Shih-ch'eng, Huai-chün p'ing-nien chi, 12/4. The
Shanghai bureau was started by Li in 1863.
229. There are diverse records of the death of Jen Chu. According to Li Hung-chang's memorial, a lieutenant of Jen's, P'an Kuei-
sheng (潘貴升), had surrendered to the Huai Army and made a deal
with his new superior that he would kill Jen at the first opportunity. In the tenth month of 1866, when a battle was raging on the
Shantung-Kiangsu border, a thick fog hid P'an who assumed the
Nien's flag falsely. He succeeded in infiltrating into the Nien's
ranks and finally shot Jen Chu down from his saddle. (Fang-lüeh,
288/22) Another source states that it was Liu Ming-ch'uan and
another general, Ch'ing-shan, who, rushing ahead of their troops,
shot Jen, but that the clever P'an came out to claim the merit. In-
tending to encourage the former Nien chief, Liu and Ch'ing-shan
made a concession to P'an's claim. (Shantung t'ung-chih, 117/3332)
The latter report is less credible. Anyhow, the two stories both
tell us that Jen, whom Li Hung-chang praised as the number-one
cavalry commander of his age, was shot by a rifle.
230. Ting Pao-cheng, 2/21.
231. Fang-lüeh, 286/2-3.
232. Ibid., 309/10.
233. Ting Pao-cheng, 2/48.

captured Nien's confession in the seventh month of 1867, five months before the suppression of the East Nien. The credibility of the confession is not too high, nor is there any evidence showing that the Nien's plan for buying Western guns ever materialized. This story only indicates how eagerly the Nien desired the new arms in their final struggle, and to what an extent those weapons had enhanced the Huai Army's success.

Of almost equal importance with these Western weapons was the Huai Army's cavalry. The Huai Army did not have cavalry until it was ordered to defend Anhwei against the Nien.[234] From the third month of 1865 on, the Huai Army commanders purchased horses from Chahar and Suiyuan. By the autumn of 1867, after a period of two and a half years, the horses which had been bought by the Huai Army and the remaining Hsiang Army amounted to eight thousand, the camels to about a thousand.[235] This was three times as large as Prince Seng's cavalry, which was the strongest cavalry opposing the Nien before 1865. Of this number ninety per cent--over seven thousand--went to the Huai Army; of these seven thousand, more than one-third belonged to the corps under Liu Ming-ch'uan.[236] Liu's corps already enjoyed renown as the most powerful and most disciplined among the Huai Yung. This gigantic mounted troop now made his corps as mobile as those of the Nien. Indeed, Liu did not depart from the policy of pursuit followed by Prince Seng.[237]

It seems evident that the Huai Army laid more stress on horses than did any previous force. Such a strong cavalry encouraged them to follow Seng-ko-lin-ch'in's strategy. Yet why, if over-emphasis on cavalry was clearly a fallacy, and if Seng-ko-lin-ch'in's policy had cost him irrecoverable losses, did the Huai Army repeat the same error? In the first place, the Huai Army's emphasis on cavalry did not distract the attention of Tseng and Li from the execution of their basic policy of destroying the Nien nest at its foundations. In other words, the cavalry only provided them with an instrument Secondly, even as an instrument, it represented only a part of the whole machine. Tseng and Li had never blindly and exclusively put their whole faith in cavalry.

---

234. Chou Shih-ch'eng, Huai-chün p'ing-nien chi, 11/9.

235. Ibid., 11/9-10; Fang-lüeh, 228/25.

236. Chou Shih-ch'eng, Huai-chün p'ing-nien chi, 11/10; Fang-lüeh, 283/19. According to the Huai Army's regulations a mounted battalion comprised 276 horses. (Chou Shih-ch'eng, 11/2-3) Liu had thirteen battalions out of the total twenty-eight. (Li Hung-chang, Letters to Friends and Colleagues, 7/2; Chou Shih-ch'eng, 11/10) Among the seven thousand horses, eight hundred were received from the dissolved T'ing-chün (a corps of the Hsiang Army under Pao Ch'ao).

237. Li Hung-chang, Letters to Friends and Colleagues, 6/29.

Moreover, the Huai Army's financial capacity was sufficient to afford eight thousand horses. It could thus embark on the policy of using cavalry on a large scale.[238] In this respect, no former armies under Sheng-pao or Yüan Chia-san could compare.

As soon as Tseng Kuo-fan took over the command in the north, he proposed to establish a Yellow River water force. In support of this proposal, Liu Ch'ang-yu, the governor-general of Chihli, replaced the merchant ships in his old fleet with gunboats.[239] For the Shantung sector of the river, Tseng advocated the same policy, even though the Grand Canal fleet in north Kiangsu had been moved to Shantung.[240] In the next year, Governor Yen Ching-ming assembled a fleet of sampans loaded with guns.[241] In 1868 Li Hung-chang, in addition to the water forces belonging to the Huai Army, concentrated the Huai-yang (淮揚) fleet under Huang I-sheng (黃翼升)[242] to patrol the Grand Canal in Shantung.[243] Without these naval forces, it might have been hard for the Huai Army to enforce the blockade that was to encircle the Nien with natural barriers, most of which were rivers. In the late fifties, Sheng-pao and Yüan Chia-san had once employed water troops to assist in campaigns along the Huai, but those feeble fleets were broken by the Nien's water forces.[244]

Finally, the Huai Army owed its triumph over the Nien to Li Hung-chang's strategy. Whereas Sheng-pao emphasized the policy of pardon, Seng-ko-lin-ch'in that of pursuit, and Tseng Kuo-fan that of defense, Li blended these three measures and carried them through simultaneously.[245] We have seen that he not only pardoned the surrendered Nien but incorporated them into his army. But his pardoning was by no means appeasement. The pardoned Nien, after reorganization and reindoctrination, furnished the Huai

---

238. At the same time, Tso Tsung-t'ang also spent more than a hundred thousand _liang_ to buy horses from Inner Mongolia. (Tso Tsung-t'ang, Tso _Wen-hsiang-kung shu-tu_, 9/26; Fang-lüeh, 286/12) Governor Yen Ching-ming bought five hundred horses for Shantung in 1865. (Shantung _chün-hsing chi-lüeh_, 4C/17) His successor, Ting Pao-chen, enlisted mounted volunteers from Manchuria in the next year. (Fang-lüeh, 267/16-17)

239. Wang Ting-an, _Hsiang-chün chi_, 20/12.

240. Fang-lüeh, 229/18.

241. Shantung _chün-hsing chi-lüeh_, 5A/10; Shantung t'ung-chih, 117/3330.

242. 1818-1894. Hummel, p. 526.

243. Wang Ting-an, _Hsiang-chün chi_, 20/12.

244. When Sheng-pao advanced towards Cheng-yang-kuan, he was confronted with two to three hundred Nien ships "with their masts and sails covering the Huai River like woods." (Fang-lüeh, 29/10) In a single battle at Liu-an, the government forces were reported to have captured a hundred and twenty boats from the Nien. (Fang-lüeh, 44/1)

245. Huang-ch'ao ching-shih wen hsü-p'ien, 95/70.

122

Army with new blood; they did not make Li's camps their temporary lodgings until the time became ripe for another revolt. The
fact that Li increased the Huai Army's cavalry to seven thousand
horses shows that Li not only continued the policy of pursuit but
intensified its enforcement. "The troops endured cold and hunger
on their thrusts of more than a hundred li a day. Laying aside
baggage wagons and then even cooking-pots and tents, they only
carried dry provision for their day and night pursuit."[246] Li himself held that such a rapid progression set an unprecedented
record in his army.[247] This record, however, was made only in
an encircled zone following the summer of 1867 rather than in an
unlimited area of several provinces. Here the policy of blockade
was functioning.

During the first half-year after he had replaced Tseng, Li
altered little of Tseng's river defense system, especially the
barriers built along the east bank of the Grand Canal. The only
change he made was to turn the garrison of the defense line in
Shantung over to the Shantung Army, so as to release the Huai
forces, which were responsible for the section south of Ch'ang-
kou, to strengthen the troops which were pursuing the Nien.[248]
The extension of the Shantung Army's line to the south thinned the
garrison forces on the north section. It was through this weakened
section that the Nien, driven by the desire to plunder the three
wealthy prefectures east of the Grand Canal, broke the two-year-
old defense system in the fifth month of 1867.[249] The Nien success
in reaching east Shantung made the defense works on the east bank
of the Grand Canal meaningless.[250]

---

246. Chou Shih-ch'eng, Huai-chün p'ing-nien chi, 8/6.
247. Ibid., 9/2.
248. Ting Pao-cheng, 1/32; Fang-lüeh, 279/2-3.
249. Shantung chün-hsing chi-lüeh, 6A/3; Chou Shih-ch'eng,
Huai-chün p'ing-nien chi; the so-called three east prefectures comprised the districts under the jurisdiction of Teng-chou, Ch'ing-
chou and Lai-chou.
250. This defense system had not done much harm to the Nien.
After the ninth month of 1866, when the Nien were rebuffed in
southwest Shantung, they returned to Honan where they separated
into two branches with Chang Tsung-yü entering Shensi. (Fang-lüeh,
261/24) The Nien had separated several times after 1865, but this
time they were never reunited. The corps under Chang Tsung-yü,
which turned to Shensi, was called the West Nien, while the corps
under Jen Chu and Lai Wen-kuang, which remained wandering in Honan
and then in east Shantung, was called the East Nien. Thus the Nien
terror spread far beyond the control of the Imperial commissioner.
In the autumn of 1866 Tseng Kuo-fan entrusted to Pao Ch'ao the
defense of the areas west of the Chia-lu River. In the Nien campaigns, however, luck was not on Pao's side as it had been in the
struggle with the Taipings. He moved back and forth in west Honan

However, Liu Ming-ch'uan saw in this setback a spark of new hope. He proposed that Li shift the barriers from the east bank to the west so as to contain the Nien in east Shantung.[251]

East Shantung confronted the boundless sea. According to Liu's calculation, if the government forces could shift the defense works to the west bank and turn their guns toward the east, east Shantung would become a trap for the Nien. Of course, Governor Ting Pao-cheng preferred driving the Nien out of his province to letting three prefectures be trampled by the Nien.[252] However, except for Ting, the neighboring governors all lent full support to the blockade policy on the ground that the sacrifice of three prefectures would save three provinces.[253]

The blockade zone was bounded by the Yellow River on the north and by the Grand Canal on the west and southwest. Along the Grand Canal, the Huai troops under Li Chao-ch'ing (李昭慶), Hung-chang's brother, undertook to guard the sector from Han-chuang (韓莊) to Mao-erh-wo (貓兒窩), the Anhwei Army from Mao-erh-wo to Su-ch'ien, and the director-general of the grain tribute from Su-ch'ien to the Ch'ing-kiang-pu and Huai-an area.[254] The Hupeh and Honan armies, though the Canal did not pass through their provinces, were drawn in to fill the gaps left by the Huai Army, and thus complete the garrison of the Canal line. On the Yellow River, the section west of Ch'i-ho (齊河), except Chang-ch'iu (張秋) where the Canal crossed, was assigned to the for several months without gaining a single engagement with the Nien. (Tseng Kuo-fan, Tseng Wen-cheng-kung ch'üan-chi, Comments on reports, 4/11; Fang-lüeh, 260/34) The Emperor ordered him to proceed to Shensi, but suddenly Tseng Kuo-fan summoned him back to Hupeh. This indetermination kept his army vacillating between the two objectives. Finally, in the first month of 1867, he and Liu Ming-ch'uan succeeded in contacting the Nien near An-lu (安陸), Hupeh; but a separate action taken by Liu spoiled the whole plan and caused Liu heavy losses. Though Pao's arrival at last saved the battle, mutual accusation arose between Pao and Liu. Li Hung-chang, of course, always sympathized with his own lieutenant. Pao, irritated by this injustice, requested leave to retire under the excuse of ill health. (Ch'ing shih-kao, Biographies, 196/9) With the dissolution of Pao's corps and the setback of Liu Ming-ch'uan, the Nien flame continued to blaze in the provinces east of the Grand Canal. The most the Canal defense line could do before the fifth month of 1867 was to protect Anhwei, north Kiangsu, and east Shantung. Once the ultimate goal of the Nien's suppression came up for discussion, the strategical significance of the Canal defense seemed not too great.

251. Fang-lüeh, 279/23-24; 290/10; Wang Ting-an, Hsiang-chün chi, 16/21.

252. Li Hung-chang, Letters to Friends and Colleagues, 7/10; Fang-lüeh, 279/23-24.

253. Shantung chün-hsing chi-lüeh, 6B/2-3; Fang-lüeh, 280/10-11.

254. Fang-lüeh, 281/25.

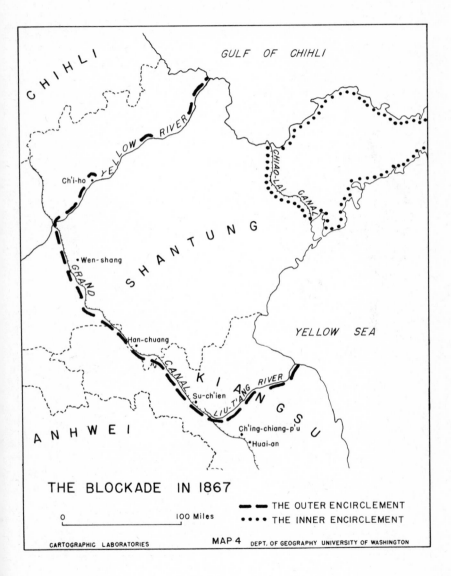

CHIHLI

GULF OF CHIHLI

YELLOW RIVER

Ch'i-ho•

CHIAO-LAI CANAL

SHANTUNG

•Wen-shang

GRAND

YELLOW SEA

Han-chuang•

CANAL

K I A N G S U

LIU-TIANG RIVER

Su-ch'ien•

Ch'ing-chiang-p'u•

•Huai-an

A N H W E I

THE BLOCKADE IN 1867

0   100 Miles

━ ━ THE OUTER ENCIRCLEMENT

• • • • THE INNER ENCIRCLEMENT

CARTOGRAPHIC LABORATORIES   MAP 4 DEPT. OF GEOGRAPHY UNIVERSITY OF WASHINGTON

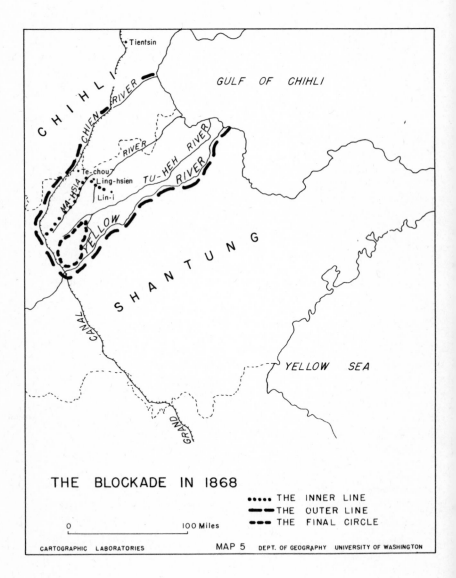

THE BLOCKADE IN 1868

•••••• THE INNER LINE
━━━ THE OUTER LINE
━ ━ ━ THE FINAL CIRCLE

0   100 Miles

CARTOGRAPHIC LABORATORIES   MAP 5   DEPT. OF GEOGRAPHY   UNIVERSITY OF WASHINGTON

Shantung and Chihli armies, while that east of Ch'i-ho was left to the combined forces of the Shantung Army and the Shantung local corps.[255] The troops massed along the two lines numbered 100,000.[256]

Within this encirclement, however, the Nien still had considerable room for maneuver. Besides, along the thousand-mile-long Canal line, it was impossible to harden the defense of every point. Li Hung-chang next turned his attention to the Chiao-lai (膠萊) Canal on the Shantung Peninsula. This canal, more than three hundred li long, was dug in the Yüan dynasty for grain tribute transportation, in order to avoid the dangers of the sea route near Ch'eng-shan (成 山), "with both its head and tail accessible to the sea."[257] At this juncture, the Nien had penetrated to the tip of the peninsula. Li calculated that as long as the Nien stayed on the east side of the Chiao-lai Canal, he could utilize that canal as an inner circle for his blockade framework. Thirty li up its north mouth, the canal became narrower and shallower. It was along this section that Li stationed the Shantung Army, and that the Nien, exploiting the Shantung Army's weakness, cracked the inner circle. The reader will recall that two months earlier the Nien had in the same manner swept the Shantung forces aside at Tai-miao (戴 廟), a defense post on the east bank of the Grand Canal. From the very beginning, Governor Ting Pao-cheng had disliked the blockade policy which turned his province into a battlefield. Now the breakdown of the inner circle deepened the ill feeling between Li and the governor. Ting charged that under the pretext of waiting for reinforcements from the Hupeh Army, Li had failed to release troops from the southern sections to strengthen the north mouth of the Chiao-lai River.[258] Li defended himself, saying that it was because Ting had neglected to solidify the defense works and had delayed the issuance of the soldiers' provisions that the Chiao-lai line was crossed by the Nien.[259] The justice of any criticism of Li Hung-chang depends on his awareness of the narrowness and shallowness of the north end of the river. As commander in chief, he was responsible for knowing such matters. If he had noticed it, he should have sent adequate detachments from the Huai forces to make up that natural defect. Instead, he allowed P'an Ting-hsin to shift four battalions of the Shantung Army to take charge of that section. From the correspondence between Tseng and Li, we know both of

255. Ting Pao-cheng, 10/12; 11/10; Fang-lüeh, 280/10.
256. Fang-lüeh, 280/26.
257. Chou Shih-ch'eng, Huai-chün p'ing-nien chi, 5/7-8.
258. Ting Pao-cheng, 3/3.
259. Fang-lüeh, 284/2.

them had no confidence in the provincial armies.[260] We are
curious to know why Li let an army which he despised garrison a
weak point.

With the inner circle broken, Governor Ting was the first who
proposed that the blockade be called off.[261] Even Tseng Kuo-fan's
confidence in this measure was shaken.[262] Li Hung-chang alone
was determined. He saw the outer circle linked by the Canal and
the Yellow River still intact. If the Nien could not be eliminated
within a blockade zone, the situation would be hopeless when the
Nien once escaped from the outside circle. This was Li's observation, and his confidence in his own decision resulted in the suppression of the East Nien five months later. Formerly, most
losses of the government cavalry were the result of exhaustion
from pursuit rather than of annihilation in battles. The shortened
distances now gave the vast cavalry of the Huai Army an opportunity to gather its strength for a decisive blow against the Nien.
Before the demise of the East Nien, four decisive battles were
fought within the blockade zone.[263] The second one, in which Jen
Chu was shot, was fatal. The last one, the battle of the Mi River
(漒河), cost the Nien thirty thousand casualties and prisoners,
and all their weapons, horses, and baggage wagons.[264] Lai Wen-
kuang, a Taiping remnant and the co-leader of the East Nien,
survived this finishing blow, and at the last moment (the twelfth
month of 1867) penetrated the blockade line by crossing the Liu-
t'ang (六塘) River. But the crossing left him only several
hundred mounted troops and postponed his death only a short time,
for Lai himself was captured alive near Hsü-i in northeast
Anhwei.[265]

This essay need not go into a detailed narration of the campaigns fought between the West Nien and the government forces in
Shensi. In the eleventh month of 1868, Chang Tsung-yü turned
eastward and crossed the Yellow River to Shansi, then to Chihli,
and finally to Shantung. The extermination of the East Nien taught

---

260. Li Hung-chang, Letters to Friends and Colleagues, 6/33;
7/16-17; 8/28; Tseng Kuo-fan, Tseng Wen-cheng-kung shu-cha, 25/25;
26/6; Fang-lüeh, 249/8.
    261. Ting Pao-cheng, 3/10.
    262. Tseng Kuo-fan, Tseng Wen-cheng-kung shu-cha, 26/16.
    263. The first one, the battle of An-ch'iu, took place on the
17th day of the 10th month, 1867; the death of Jen Chu on the 24th
day; the third one, the battle of Hai-chou on the 28th day; and the
fourth one, the battle of the Mi River, on the 10th day of the 11th
month. (Chou Shih-ch'eng, Huai-chün p'ing-nien chi, 6/12-17; 7/1-
14)
    264. Ibid., 7/15.
    265. Ibid., 7/13.

their western comrades that Shantung was a trap. It was the
checking and pursuing government forces which pushed them in
that direction. The Wo-yang feng-t'u chi records that Chang's
sortie from Shensi was in response to a plea for relief from Jen
Chu, whose forces were beaten within the Shantung blockade
zone.[266] I doubt that this was the chief reason. Originally Chang
Tsung-yü saw in Shensi a new sphere for expansion, where he
would cooperate with the Moslem rebels.[267] But after he had set
foot on that soil, he was disappointed by the shortage of provisions.[268] This move into Shensi ran counter to the Nien's main
purpose in wandering--to plunder for grain. Tso Tsung-t'ang's
entry into Shensi in the fourth month of 1867 made the situation
even more difficult for the West Nien. In addition to his Hunan
Yung, Tso had at his command the corps of Liu Sung-shan (劉松
山) and Kuo Pao-ch'ang (郭寶昌) sent from Anhwei by Tseng Kuo-
fan.[269] As long as Tso's forces stayed in Shensi, Chang Tsung-
yü had little room for expansion in that province. Moreover, Tso
was determined to suppress the Nien before he took any further
step to handle the Moslem problem,[270] and he intended to copy
the blockade strategy which was under way in Shantung.[271] If
Chang reckoned that he was unable to deal a crushing blow to Tso,
as he had done to Governor Liu Jung's (劉 蓉)[272] army, and that
a full-scale battle was at variance with the Nien tactics, he had no
reason to linger in Shensi waiting for the realization of Tso's
contemplated blockade. In the winter of 1867, Chang's only concern was to get out of Shensi. To do this, he forced his way to
north Shensi, from which he could easily cross the Yellow River
to Shansi. Chang's northward diversion affirmed Tso's conviction
that the Nien were anxious to pierce the Shensi-Shansi border.[273]
In Tso's calculation, the Shansi forces were no match for the
Nien. Tso was correct. In the eleventh month, Chang, taking

266. Wo-yang feng-t'u chi, 15/21.
267. T'ai-p'ing t'ien-kuo shih-wen ch'ao, 2/99.
268. Shensi, even in peacetime, was destitute of grain because
of the lack of water and fertile soil. Both Tso Tsung-t'ang and Pao
Ch'ao, when they were ordered to that province, regarded the shortage of provisions as their first problem. (Tso Tsung-t'ang, Tso
Wen-hsiang-kung shu-tu, 9/9, 38; T'ing-chün chi-lüeh, 11/7-8) The
same problem confronted the Nien.
269. Tso, on his way to Shensi, rebuilt his army with the recruits newly drafted from Hunan. (Fang-lüeh, 270/1-2) Liu's corps
was usually called "the old Hsiang battalion"; Kuo's corps was
detached from the Anhwei provincial army. Liu Sung-shan, 1833-1870,
Hummel, p. 765.
270. Fang-lüeh, 281/20.
271. Tso Tsung-t'ang, Tso Wen-hsiang-kung shu-tu, 9/56.
272. 1816-1873, Hummel, p. 538.
273. Tso Tsung-t'ang, Tso Wen-hsiang-kung shu-tu, 9/59.

127

advantage of the frozen river, entered Shansi almost unresisted.
By the time the Shansi governor "combed the provincial capital
garrisons, obtained three hundred men, and hurried to the south,"
the Nien had been driven by Liu Sung-shan to Honan.[274] In the
first month of 1868, the Nien slipped into south Chihli, directly
threatening the capital. At one time they reached the suburbs of
Tientsin. This alarm compelled the central government to throw
into battle the Peking Field Force, in addition to the Chihli Army
under Governor-General Kuan-wen (官 文),[275] the Tientsin
Western-equipped corps under the Three Ports Trade Commissioner, Ch'ung-hou, the army following the Nien from Shensi
under Tso Tsung-t'ang, the Shantung Army which came across the
provincial border, and finally the Huai Army. But this mass of
forces seemed helpless in face of the confusedly advancing Nien,
who ravaged at will the province where the sacred capital was
located. One consideration made the government armies hesitate
to exert great pressure on the Nien. Unless the southern edge of
the capital was well guarded, any move of the armies from the
south would result in pushing the Nien northward to the capital.[276]
In the Chihli plain, the river which could be used to check the
Nien was the Chang (漳). But it was extremely hard to build
defense works on its muddy banks.[277] Before Li Hung-chang completed his defense arrangement on the Wei (衛) River, the Nien
had burst across it. In the third month, the Nien made a drive at
Tung-ch'ang across the Grand Canal. Their drive was aimed at
pillaging Tientsin and its surrounding districts, but, repulsed
from the north, they were never able to return to the area west of
the Canal, and they met the same fate which had befallen the East
Nien the previous year.

The Nien's entry into the area east of the Grand Canal re-
kindled in Li Hung-chang's mind the blockade project.[278] Tso
Tsung-t'ang, though at odds with Li on almost every point, agreed
heartily with this plan.[279] The blockade around the West Nien in
1868, unlike that of the preceding year, was on the north side of
the Yellow River, with the Grand Canal lying on the west. Since
the north side still remained open, the Huai Army removed the
Canal's dam at Chieh-ti (捷 地), letting its water fill up the Chien
River which flowed eastward to the sea.[280] Later the Ma-hsia
(馬頰) River was used as an inner barrier and connected with
Lin-i (臨 邑) by a wall.[281] Finally, Liu Ming-ch'uan bottled up the

274. Shansi t'ung-chih, 78/37-38.
275. 1798-1871. Hummel, p. 427.
276. Fang-lüeh, 301/7.
277. Li Hung-chang, Letters to Friends and Colleagues, 8/7, 10.
278. Fang-lüeh, 309/6.
279. Tso Tsung-t'ang, Tso Wen-hsiang-kung shu-tu, 10/3-4.
280. Fang-lüeh, 310/2-3.   281. Ting Pao-cheng, 5/49.

Nien within a small circle bounded by the T'u-hsieh River (徒駭),
the Yellow River, and the Canal.[282] It was in this circle that
Chang Tsung-yü in desperation drowned himself in the river on the
twenty-eighth of the sixth month.[283] This was the end of the West
Nien.

While the enforcement of the blockade in the preceding year
had been under the unified command of Li, two princes and six
commanders in chief appeared at the same time within a small
area of several hundred li in 1868.[284] In principle, the garrison on
the west bank of the Canal was assigned to the forces under Tso
Tsung-t'ang, Kuan-wen, and Ch'ung-hou; but the section north of
Te-chou was shared by the Chihli-Shantung local corps, on the
grounds that the strength of the armies did not equal the length of
the line.[285] On the east bank, the sections from Lin-ch'ing to
Chang-ch'iu were assigned to the Anhwei Army, the Shantung
Army, and the Huai Army.[286] Thanks to the rising currents of the
Chang River and the Wei River, the heightened level of the Canal
afforded free passage for the patrolling Huai-yang fleet drawn
from the south by Li Hung-chang.[287] Within the zone, it was still
the Huai Army which shouldered the principal task of battering the
Nien. Under these circumstances, the presence of such important
figures as Tso, Kuan-wen, and Ch'ung-hou merely led to considerable confusion in the conduct of the war.[288]

In contrast to the division in the high command, most of the
Chihli and Shantung people were cooperative. The so-called
"people," according to sources available, included shen-min (紳
民), meaning both gentry and commoners. One should not confuse
these people with those who cooperated with the Nien before 1864.
The Nien's cooperators lived in south Shantung, especially at the
intersection of Shantung, Honan, and Chihli, where Nien nests
had once been scattered and where the Yellow River flood of 1855
had made the area a haven for bandits. The government's cooperators in 1867-1868 were the natives on the west bank of the Grand
Canal's Chihli sector and those on the south bank of the Yellow
River in Shantung. The latter areas were farther from the Nien's
influence. Devastation resulting from the Nien's circuitous

---

282. Fang-lüeh, 317/6.
283. Li Hung-chang, Letters to Friends and Colleagues, 8/48.
284. The six commanders in chief included Imperial Commissioner
Li Hung-chang, Imperial Commissioner Tso Tsung-t'ang, Governor-
General Kuan-wen, Trade Commissioner Ch'ung-hou, Manchu Garrison
General Te-hsing-a, and a Peking Field Force official.
285. Tso Tsung-t'ang, Tso Wen-hsiang-kung shu-tu, 10/9.
286. Fang-lüeh, 312/3.
287. Wang Ting-an, Hsiang-chün chi, 16/23; Wang Kai-yün, Hsiang-
chün chih, 14/16.
288. Li Hung-chang, Letters to Friends and Colleagues, 8/41;
Tso Tsung-t'ang, Tso Wen-hsiang-kung shu-tu, 10/11.

thrusts embittered the populace in these areas and made them eager to come to the assistance of the formidable Huai Army so as to end the misery sooner.

In the twelfth month of 1867, the Shantung people erected a wall a thousand and several hundred li long on the two banks of the Yellow River. The people themselves financed and managed the work and finished it within twenty days.[289] In the next summer the Chihli people accomplished the same thing along the west bank of the Grand Canal, under the encouragement and supervision of Chang Shu-sheng, then Chihli judicial commissioner, formerly a Huai Army general.[290] Behind the wall the local corps mobilized several hundred thousand men for its defense, raising their own provisions and equipment.[291] They shared the defense burden with the garrison armies, rather than playing an auxiliary role. Faced with this firm resistance, the Nien wandered up and down the Canal without gaining an opportunity to cross.[292] Within the blockade zone, especially after the completion of the circle made by the Ma-hsia River's dikes and walls, the villagers constructed a great number of earthwalls to shut out the weary and starved Nien. With the cooperation of the native people, the blockade deprived the Nien not only of escape but of the hope of survival.

---

289. Ting Pao-cheng, 4/40; Li Hung-chang, 8/27.

290. Chou Shih-ch'eng, Huai-chün p'ing-nien chi, 10/5; Li Hung-chang, Letters to Friends and Colleagues, 8/31.

291. Fang-lüeh, 312/13.

292. Fang-lüeh, 316/7. The cooperation of the natives did not rule out the fact that in some districts the people were hostile to the government armies. Some cities in east Shantung closed their gates to the Huai troops marching toward the Chiao-lai Canal. (Fang-lüeh, 284/11) Cases of armed conflict between the disturbing soldiers and the native people and of the murder of passing officers and soldiers recurred in Chihli, Shantung, and Honan. (Fang-lüeh, 304/22; 310/10; 314/39) However, these cases were local incidents. In comparison with the Chihli-Shantung people's hostile attitude toward the Nien, damage caused by these incidents was almost negligible.

CONCLUSION

The offenses like gambling, kidnapping, and robbery which the Nien committed in the prerebellion period tend to create the impression that the Nien were in no way different from the ordinary local bandits. The discovery of the connection between the Nien and the White Lotus sect, however, modifies this conception. The recurrent peasant insurrections which had been led by the White Lotus since the Southern Sung dynasty indicate that, in spite of temporary suppression by the rulers, the sect's underground existence persisted. The White Lotus would shoot out at any time that conditions seemed opportune for another outbreak. In the Ch'ing dynasty, in addition to the obstinate opposition to the oppressing rulers, an anti-Manchu feeling crept into the ideology of the sect. Bearing this in mind, one is not surprised by the sudden and simultaneous outbreak of revolts in the early 1850's in the dispersed localities north of the Huai, the area where the Nien elements prevailed.

The degeneration of the conquering dynasty rendered possible the upsurge of the long-suppressed local forces; recurring famine paved the road to rural unrest. Nevertheless, without organizational guidance, the rebellious movement might have remained local in nature and feeble in strength. Therefore, the fact that the Nien Society was itself an organized body was a factor of major importance. Unless one recognizes the fact that the Nien was a secret society distinguishable from ordinary violent mobs, one will find it difficult to understand how the Nien, as loosely banded insurgents, were able to knit together their own units, to assimilate outlying forces, and finally to turn Huai-pei into a solid fortress against the loyalists.

Thus, for the development of the Huai-pei local gangs into a regional force, the Nien furnished ideology as well as leadership.

To realize that the Nien base was located in the north rather than in the south is equally important. The topographical conditions of the North China Plain necessitated fortification by earthwalls and provided boundless wilds for mounted forces.

It has been reiterated that though the earthwalls were not confined to Huai-pei, they functioned in a peculiar way in the Nien region. Early in 1856 the Nien had worked out a banner system to correct the decentralized tendency of their scattered bands. But the unity expressed by the banners might have been short-lived had it not been supported by an underlying structure. The rapid appearance of earthwalls after 1853 gradually stabilized the fluid

Nien bands; the link-up of these earthwalls by Chang Lo-hsing during 1857-1859 brought into being an organic network and thus completed the unique Nien organization. Within this union, each earthwall community maintained a great deal of autonomy in dealing with its own internal affairs. A union of this type advanced the Nien organization to a higher stage, and yet at the same time it did not cause radical departure from the Nien tradition.

It was famine which prepared fertile soil for the revival of the White Lotus branches in Huai-pei and southern Shantung. In the years 1853-1859 the same distress lingered. The earthwalls assured the Nien's safety but could not guard against starvation. In front of the Nien domain was a vast plain reaching to the fairly wealthy and intact areas of Honan, Shantung, and northern Kiangsu. To extort resources like grain, livestock, and human captives from those areas became the most convenient way for the Nien to build up their economic strength. Earthwall units could not undertake this task. This was the function of the cavalry, to the formation of which the Nien devoted their efforts from the outset.

Earthwalls and cavalry--the one stationary, the other mobile--represented the dual nature of the Nien organization. The Nien's concentration on the maintenance of their homeland against the surrounding government forces for ten years did not prevent them from spreading their range of plunder to eight provinces.

The structure based on autonomous communal units, however, bred its own limitations. The status preserved by the yü-chu, or the lords of earthwall communities--most of whom were also ch'i-chu, or lords of banners--rendered it difficult for the Nien to develop a highly centralized regime. Secondly, the structure, though flexible enough to assimilate non-Nien local forces, could exist only where the Nien elements were of sufficient density. Because of this limitation, the Nien could hardly secure permanent occupation in such districts as Lin-pi and Su-chou to the east, Kuei-te and Ch'en-chou to the west, Feng-hsien, Tang-shan, Chin-hsiang, and Yü-t'ai to the north, and the areas south of the Huai, no matter how frequently they penetrated those places. In those places where the Nien elements were sparser, an administrative system attached to the Nien's heart area was necessary. But the Nien lacked this. Chang Lo-hsing, throughout the years of his rebellion, never broadened his sphere of domination far beyond the Hui on the east and the Sha on the west. Thirdly, since the Nien lacked a central organ, the undertaking of external expansion fell on the autonomous lords of banners. The lords, however, always concerned themselves with their respective home communities. Before 1863 their cavalry had trampled as far as the edge of east Shensi, but most of them did not stay out in the field for a longer time than was necessary to plunder. The caravan of spoils moved in one direction--homeward.

The limitation of the Nien organization may explain in part why the Nien seldom occupied cities. In the ninth month of 1855, Chang Lo-hsing captured Meng-ch'eng. But instead of retaining it, he tore down its wall and then turned to raid the northern country-side of Po-chou.[1] It was the combined forces of the Nien and the Taipings which achieved the capture of Liu-an, Anhwei.[2] Though the Nien held out in Liu-an until 1858, they did this only to keep it as an outpost for the Taipings in T'ung-ch'eng and Shu-ch'eng. For the defense of the city, the Taipings, besides using verbal per-suasion, poured in a great amount of provisions to strengthen the wavering Nien garrison.[3] The Nien's seizure of Huo-ch'iu, the occupation of Feng-yang, Huai-yüan, and Lin-huai in 1858, and the siege of Ying-chou in 1861-1862, were all either inspired and sponsored by the Taipings or undertaken by coalition forces.[4] To maintain a city was no easy task. Since the Nien lacked a machinery capable of administering cities, they could not turn them to serve Nien purposes and even had the feeling that the cities constituted a burden. With the encouragement and active support of the Taipings, the Nien did occupy some cities along the Huai in the years 1857-1859. But this compelled them to convey provisions from their homeland in Huai-pei to the city garrison forces. We have seen that the Nien's white banner under Sun Kuei-hsin, Chiang T'ai-lin, and Wang Huai-i withdrew from the Huai cities in 1858 and directly returned home. The reason given by Yüan Chia-san for this withdrawal was that Sun had disputes with Kung Te. But one can find the basic reason in the fact that after Sun had reached home he resumed his preparations for plundering Shantung and Honan. As Sun and his associates reaped no benefits from the retention of the Huai cities, they returned to their traditional activities. The occupation of the Huai cities by the Nien, with the support of the Taipings who controlled central Anhwei, did not result in turning Huai-pei and Huai-nan into an integral piece of territory, which would have altered the whole phase of the Anhwei military situation. The nature of the Nien organization prevented any effective Taiping-Nien cooperation.

That the union composed of earthwall communities decided the nature of the Nien organization does not mean that the earth-wall itself stood for everything. From the military point of view, the earthwalls and cavalry served the Nien merely as the basis of their tactics. The government commanders, however, took the

1. Anhwei t'ung-chih, 103/4.
2. Fang-lüeh, 30/21. Hsü-hsiu Lu-chou fu-chih even records that the Taipings, who had already seized that city, invited the Nien to help defend it. (20/12)
3. Fang-lüeh, 43/2, 22.
4. Ibid., 42/9-10; 127/8.

133

fortresses for the essence of the Nien strength and formulated policy accordingly. As they saw it, wrecking the earthwalls would lead to the destruction of the Nien nests and then to the eradication of the Nien. To achieve this, in the commanders' opinion, a joint attack from three provinces was the most advisable strategy, because it would finally bottle up the Nien nests. As for the Nien cavalry, the officials thought the invincible Manchurian and Mongolian horsemen would be able to handle it. Hence memorials, requesting mounted forces from outside the Great Wall and regular troops from various provinces, flowed to the Court from the Huai theater. But the degeneration of the military power of the Empire spelled the doom of all the strategies.

The officials overlooked the fact that behind each earthwall a flock of peasants devoted their lives and resources to the Nien cause. Popular support constituted the Nien's real fortress, which was unbreakable so long as the officials could not succeed in detaching the peasants from their leaders. The winning over of the peasants thus should have been the officials' principal concern.

After 1853 the populace of Huai-pei organized themselves into local military forces, the local corps. Once the officials attempted to compete with the Nien for popular support, they could not help but approach the local corps. But since the local corps were forces being developed at the expense of the declining governmental power, it was the influential native persons, instead of the officials, whose call could gain enthusiastic response. Since the Nien were also forces emerging from the Huai-pei localities, they occupied a more favorable position in the contest for local support than did the officials who were appointed from above. The handicaps which impeded the latter, therefore, were understandable.

Yet Yüan Chia-san, an official commissioned to deal with the Nien, was a Huai-pei native; it was, in fact, because of this personal connection that the Emperor sent him to that area. Yüan stayed in Huai-pei for ten years, longer than any of his colleagues, and struggled exclusively with the Nien.[5] From 1853-1856 he did make some attempts to supplement his troops with contingents drafted from local corps, and as late as the fifth month of 1856,

---

5. As for the other two Imperial commissioners, Sheng-pao, a Manchu, spent all his time from 1856 to 1859 in besieging the cities on the Huai banks. In 1860 he fought in Honan, and in 1861-1862 he came to the relief of the long-besieged Ying-chou. During all the terms when he served as commander, he never set foot in the Nien's central area. Prince Seng-ko-lin-ch'in entered Huai-pei in the winter of 1862 and left there in the spring of the next year. From 1864 to 1865 his task was confined to pursuing the Nien throughout several provinces. Yüan, on the contrary, in spite of several interruptions, remained in close contact with the Nien's home area.

the local corps in the Honan-Anhwei border still followed him to attack Chih-ho.[6] After 1856, however, recruits from local corps became a negligible factor in Yüan's army. Even during the period when Yüan was experimenting with the use of local corps, he treated them as an auxiliary force rather than as a power potential worthy of grand-scale mobilization. As Yüan laid stress on the regular army and the cavalry, as a result of his misconception about the essence of the Nien's strength, he considered the local forces, once his zealous supporters, as a thorn in his side.

We know Chang Lo-hsing and Miao P'ei-lin had completed their division of domination in the Huai Basin by 1859. This situation however, was the result of a gradual development. It was not until 1856 that the Nien's banner system came into being, and not until 1859 that Chang Lo-hsing accomplished the integration of the region between the Sha and the Hui into an entity. As late as 1860 Miao P'ei-lin's rival local corps chiefs still held out in Shou-chou. During this long period there were plenty of opportunities for the officials, especially Yüan Chia-san, to gain the support of the local forces. Their failure in this respect left to the local corps only two alternatives: either to go over to the Nien or to gather under the standard of some ambitious local corps chiefs like Miao P'ei-lin.

The utter defeat of the government forces, mainly made up of the regular army and including Prince Seng's cavalry, brought the Huai Army to the Huai theater in 1865. The Huai Army had been established four years before it appeared in Huai-pei and had not been formed for the specific purpose of containing the Nien. Nevertheless, the viewpoint held by its creator on the eve of its appearance merits special consideration. Tseng Kuo-fan, the initiator of the Huai Army, estimated the Huai people in a way different from that of his predecessors. In 1859, two years before the establishment of the Huai Army, he conveyed his opinion to Li Hung-chang, saying that the Huai people were not bandits by nature, and that if the seditious leaders could exploit their vigor, why could not the loyalists exploit their vigor, too? According to Tseng, once the Huai local forces were organized, they would demonstrate no less brilliance than the Hsiang Army. This shows that Tseng neither misunderstood the Huai people's temperament nor underestimated their fighting spirit. In 1861, when the Huai Army was still fighting the Taipings in the south, Tseng had decided that after the suppression of the Taipings, the Huai Army would be preserved to handle the Nien, while the Hsiang Army would be demobilized.[7] At this time Prince Seng was pursuing the

6. Kuang-hsü Lu-i hsien-chih, 8/7.
7. In fact, Li Hsü-i had tried to use the Hsiang Army to pacify Huai-pei in 1861, and T'ang Hsün-fang had followed his example in 1862-1863. Neither of them achieved any outstanding success.

Nien, but Tseng predicted that no good result would be produced by Prince Seng and other Imperial leaders in the north. Tseng's judgment of the other armies, in addition to his decision to disband the Hsiang, his own army, in favor of the Huai Army, indicates that Tseng not only intended to use the Huai people to suppress the Huai bandits but was convinced that the Huai Army, which was drafted from the Huai region, was the most suitable force to cope with the Nien.

But before 1865 most of the Huai Army's recruits were from south of the Huai. Did Tseng's policy of using the Huai people to suppress the Huai bandits include using the people on the north side of the river where the Nien homeland was located? Tseng's answer to this question can be found in a remark he made in 1865 when he came in contact with the Huai-pei area. He believed that if the Huai Army could incorporate the Huai-pei elements, it would have good prospects for successful development.

Yet, before Tseng could use the Huai-pei people, he had to separate them from their leaders. To accomplish this, the work of "investigating the earthwall communities" was commenced. Of course, the success in separating the Nien's supporters, and then in destroying the Nien nests, was in itself a condition leading to the Nien's suppression. But since Tseng stressed the usefulness of the Huai-pei people, the work done in Huai-pei may also be considered as a preliminary step in the mobilization of the Huai-pei peasants; this work made it possible to use the leadership of the new earthwall community chiefs for the loyalist cause.

After 1865 the commanders of the Huai Army continued to recruit their troops from the Huai-pei peasants and the surrendered Nien. In the concluding stage of the Nien campaign, the new recruits from Huai-pei increased to such a degree that a vast majority of the Huai Army was composed of the Huai-pei natives and the ex-Nien. We know that the paramount issue in the contest between the Nien and the loyalists was the winning of the local forces. The Nien owed their ascendancy before 1865 to their success in organizing their native communities into a regional force while their adversaries failed to do the same thing. Now the policy initiated by Tseng Kuo-fan and carried out by Li Hung-chang reversed the whole situation. It challenged the Nien by mobilizing the populace right in the heart of their dominion. Tseng and Li

---

(Wang Ting-an, Hsiang-chün chi, 7/6, 17) In 1861, Yen Shu-sen, governor of Honan, drew volunteers from Hunan, organized them on the model of the Hsiang Army, and entrusted their command to a Hsiang general called Li Hsü-t'ao (李續宜). But this new force displayed none of the brilliance of the other Hsiang forces in the Yangtze Valley. Finally, revenue shortages compelled the governor to dissolve it. (Yü-chün chi-lüeh, 9, Wan-fei 9/8-9; Wan-fei 10/9-11; Fang-lüeh, 110/23; 131/1-8; 187/11)

distinguished themselves from their predecessors by two achieve-
ments; they not only detached the Huai-pei peasants from the Nien
but also formed a new army in which the Huai-pei peasants fought
against their former leaders.

With another regional force, the Huai Army, becoming the
master of Huai-pei, it was now the Nien's turn to be beaten about
as they continued their wandering. Yet the Nien were still capable
of action, and they swore to fight to the death. Before the utter
annihilation of these veteran Nien, additional genuine military
efforts were necessary. Therefore the quality of the Huai Army,
its leadership and strategy, its utilization of modern weapons and
facilities, and its store of adequate provisions, should all be
counted as main factors in the ultimate elimination of the Nien.

Before 1865 the Nien's success in raising a regional force
yielded them their hegemony in Huai-pei. Events subsequent to
that year went just the other way around. The realization of
Tseng's and Li's policy of revitalizing the Huai Army with the
local forces of Huai-pei completed the conquest of that area, and
finally subdued the Nien. So the victory of the Huai Army marks
the triumph of one regional force over another.

Because it was the triumph of a regional force, the pacification of the rebellion did not mean the recovery of the declining
power of the dynasty. On the contrary, the dynasty's power continued to descend. One may say that the emergence of regional
forces was a general tendency after the Taiping and other rebellions. Yet, as far as military power was concerned, the triumph
of the Huai Army over the Nien directly extended the former's
influence in North China. We know that Tseng Kuo-fan began to
disband the Hsiang Army after the capture of Nanking in 1864. But
such was not the case with the Huai Army in 1868. Out of its eighty
thousand men, only thirty thousand were disbanded.[8] Ying-han
(黃 翰), governor of Anhwei, even proposed to substitute the
Huai Yung for the Chihli lien-chün.[9] Mao Ch'ang-hsi (毛 昶 熙),
the president of the censorate, and Tso Tsung-t'ang, who shared
Ying-han's opinion, recommended that Liu Ming-ch'uan, the
prominent Huai commander, should be appointed to the vacant
post of Chihli provincial commander in chief.[10] Ying-han was a
Manchu, and Tso was usually at variance with Li Hung-chang.
None of the proponents had any personal interest in the preserva-
tion of the Huai troops. Yet in view of the weakness of the Chihli

---

8. Chou Shih-ch'eng, Huai-chün p'ing-nien chi, 11/8-9.
9. Fang-lüeh, 317/24. The lien-chün (練 軍), meaning "trained
army," was started in Chihli in 1861. The provincial authorities
picked strong men from the Peking Field Force and the Green
Standard Army for more drastic training. (Ch'ing-ch'ao hsü-wen-
hsien t'ung-k'ao, 217/9635)
10. Fang-lüeh, 319/9, 25-27.

137

lien-chün, exposed during the Nien campaigns in 1867-1868, they favored replacing it with a new army in order to safeguard the Imperial capital. Li Hung-chang rejected this offer on the ground that Liu's "inexorable temperament would not fit the service under the princes and nobles in the capital."[11] But on hearing that Tseng Kuo-fan had been transferred from Liang-Kiang to Chihli, Li changed his mind; he permitted the Ming-chün, the division under Liu Ming-ch'uan and the strongest of the Huai Army, to be stationed at Chang-ch'iu, a town at the junction of the Yellow River and the Grand Canal. According to Li, this change was intended to strengthen Tseng Kuo-fan's position in Chihli.[12] This story tells us that it was personal advantage instead of the Imperial interest which decided the site where the army was stationed.[13]

The triumph of one regional force over another in no way exterminated the root of rebellion. Tseng Kuo-fan decided to win over the Huai-pei peasants because he evaluated them in a different way from his predecessors, that is, he appreciated the usefulness of their potential power. His decision, indeed, achieved the suppression of the Nien. The emphasis on usefulness, however, reduced the winning of the people to a military expedient. We admit that Tseng had the good intention to "save the Anhwei people from the chaotic and catastrophic situation,"[14] but it was beyond the scope of his imagination to work out any new method for solving the century-old problem of rebellion. It is regrettable that detailed records concerning the work he did with the Huai-pei earthwall communities are not available. But from the instructions he gave to his commissioners on that occasion, we know his policy did not go beyond isolating the rebellious leaders from their followers and tightening the governmental control over the latter. The conditions, enumerated at the beginning of this essay, which could engender rebellions, remained intact. The rise, thirty years later, of the Boxers, another branch of the White Lotus, in the old Nien area on the borders of Anhwei, Shantung, Kiangsu, and Honan, testifies eloquently to this fact.[15]

---

11. Li Hung-chang, Letters to Friends and Colleagues, 8/51-52. In his answer to the Court, Li only said that the climate in the north did not suit the southern soldiers. But in his private letter to Tseng Kuo-fan, he disclosed this real reason.

12. Idem.

13. A discussion of the subsequent development of Li Hung-chang's power and the Pei-yang (北洋) clique can be found in Spector, "Li Hung-chang and the Huai-chün."

14. Tseng Kuo-fan, Tseng Wen-cheng-kung ch'üan-chi, Memorials, 11/4.

15. Feng-chin I-ho-ch'üan hui-lu (封禁義和拳寶錄), p. 1; collected in Ch'üan-luan san-chung.

BIBLIOGRAPHY

Chang Chung-li, The Chinese Gentry, Studies on Their Role in Nineteenth-Century Chinese Society, University of Washington Press, Seattle, 1954.

Chang Te-chien (張德堅), Tsei-ch'ing hui-ts'uan (賊情彙纂), Nanking, 1932.

Ch'en Kung-lu (陳恭祿), Chung-kuo chin-tai shih (中國近代史), Shanghai, 1936.

Chiao-p'ing Nien-fei fang-lüeh (剿平捻匪方署), ed. Chu Hsüeh-ch'in (朱學勤) and others, collected in Ch'i-sheng fang-lüeh (七省方署), Peking, 1875-1907.

Ch'ing-ch'ao hsü-wen-hsien t'ung-k'ao (清朝續文獻通考), ed. Liu Chin-tsao (劉錦藻), Shanghai, 1936.

Ch'ing shih-kao (清史稿), ed. Chao Erh-sun (趙爾巽), Mukden, 1937.

Chou Shih-ch'eng (周世澄), Huai-chün p'ing-nien chi (淮軍平捻記), Shanghai, 1877.

Ch'üan-luan san-chung (拳亂三種), compiled by Lao Nai-hsüan (勞乃宣), 1901.

Fan Wen-lan (范文瀾), Chung-kuo chin-tai shih (中國近代史), Hongkong, 1949.

Hirayama Amane (平山周), Chung-kuo pi-mi she-hui shih (中國秘密社會史), Shanghai, 1935.

Hsiao I-shan (蕭一山), Ch'ing-tai t'ung-shih (清代通史), Shanghai, 1928-1935.

Hsiao Kung-chuan, Rural China, Imperial Control in the Nineteenth Century (manuscript in preparation, Modern Chinese History Project, University of Washington).

Hsü K'o (徐珂), Ch'ing-pai-lei-ch'ao (清稗類鈔), Shanghai, 1917.

Hsüan-tsung ch'eng-huang-ti sheng-hsün (宣宗成皇帝聖訓), ed. 1856.

Hsüeh Fu-ch'eng (薛福成), Yung-an pi-chi (庸庵筆記), collected in Ch'ing-tai pi-chi ts'ung-k'an (清代筆記叢刊), Shanghai.

Hu Lin-i (胡林翼), Hu Wen-chung-kung ch'üan-chi (胡文忠公全集), Shanghai, 1936.

Huang-ch'ao ching-shih wen hsü-pien (皇朝經世文續編), ed. Sheng K'ang (盛康), 1897.

Huang-ch'ao ching-shih wen-pien (皇朝經世文編), ed. Ho Ch'ang-ling (賀長齡), 1886.

Huang Chün-tsai (黃鈞宰), Chin-hu ch'i-mo (金壺七墨), collected in Ch'ing-tai pi-chi ts'ung-k'an.

Hummel, Arthur W., Eminent Chinese of the Ch'ing Period, U.S. Government Printing Office, Washington, D.C., 1944.

Kuo T'ing-i (郭廷以), T'ai-p'ing t'ien-kuo shih-shih jih-chih (太平天國史事日誌), Shanghai, 1947.

Li Hung-chang (李鴻章), Li Wen-chung-kung ch'üan-chi (李文忠公全集), ed. Wu Ju-lün (吳汝綸), Shanghai, 1921.

Li Ting-sheng (李鼎聲), Chung-kuo chin-tai shih (中國近代史), Shanghai, 1948.

Lo Erh-kang (羅爾綱), Hsiang-chün hsin-chih (湘軍新志), Hongkong, 1929.

Michael, Franz, Military Organization and Power Structure in Nineteenth Century China (manuscript in preparation, Modern Chinese History Project, University of Washington).

Ming-shih (明史), ed. Chang T'ing-yü (張廷玉), Shanghai, 1930-1937.

Nagano Akira (長野朗), Shina no shakai soshiki (支那の社會組織), Tokyo, 1926.

P'ing-ting Yüeh-k'ou chi-lüeh (平定粤寇紀畧), compiled by Tu Wen-lan (杜文瀾), 1869.

Sano Manabu (佐野學), Shin-chō shakai-shi (清朝社會史), Tokyo, 1947, 1948.

Shantung chün-hsing chi-lüeh (山東軍興紀畧), editor unidentified, Shanghai, 1875-1908.

Spector, Stanley, Li Hung-chang and the Huai-chün, doctoral dissertation, University of Washington, 1953.

Suemitsu Takayoshi (末光高義), Shina no himitsu kessha to jizen kessha (支那秘密結社と慈善結社), Dairen, 1932.

Ta-ch'ing hui-tien shih-li (大清會典事例), ed. Li Hung-chang, Shanghai, 1908.

Ta-ch'ing lü-li hui-chi pien-lan (大清律例彙輯便覽), compiled by the Board of Punishment, 1876.

T'ai-p'ing t'ien-kuo shih-wen ch'ao (太平天國詩文鈔), Lo Yung (羅邕) and Shen Tsu-chi (沈祖基), Shanghai, 1934.

T'ing-chün chi-lüeh (霆軍紀畧), ed. Ch'en Ch'ang (陳昌), Shanghai, 1882.

Ting Pao-cheng (丁寶楨), Ting Wen-ch'eng-kung chou-kao (丁文誠公奏稿), 1899.

Ts'ao Po-han (曹伯韓), Chung-kuo hsien-tai shih tu-pen (中國現代史讀本), Hongkong, 1947.

Tseng Kuo-ch'üan (曾國荃), Tseng Chung-hsiang-kung ch'üan-chi (曾文襄公全集), 1903.

Tseng Kuo-fan (曾國藩), Tseng Wen-cheng-kung ch'üan-chi (曾文正公全集), Shanghai, 1928.

_____, Tseng Wen-cheng-kung shu-cha (曾文正公書札), Nanking, 1945.

Tso Tsung-t'ang (左宗棠), Tso Wen-hsiang-kung ch'üan-chi (左文襄公全集), 1897.

_____, Tso Wen-hsiang-kung shu-tu (左文襄公書牘), Nanking, 1945.

Wang Hsien-ch'ien (王先謙), Tung-hua lu (東華錄), 1899.
Wang K'ai-yün (王闓運), Hsiang-chün chih (湘軍志), Chengtu, 1886.
Wang Ting-an (王定安), Ch'iu-ch'üeh-chai ti-tzu chi (求闕齋 弟子記), Peking, 1876.
_____, Hsiang-chün chi (湘軍記), 1889.
Wei Yüan (魏源), Sheng-wu-chi (聖武記), 1842.
Wen-hsien ts'ung-pien (文獻叢編), a monthly publication by the Palace Museum of Peking, 1930-1937.
Yin Chia-ping (尹嘉賓), Cheng-chiao chi-lüeh (征勦記畧), 1900.
Yü-chün chi-lüeh (豫軍紀畧), ed. Yin Keng-yün (尹耕雲), 1872.
Yüan Chia-san (袁甲三), Yüan Tuan-min-kung chi (袁端敏公集), collected by Ting Cheng-to (丁振鐸) in Hsiang-ch'eng Yüan-shih chia-chi (項城袁氏家集), 1911.
Yüan Pao-heng (袁保恒), Yüan Wen-ch'eng-kung chi (袁文誠公集), collected in Hsiang-ch'eng Yüan-shih chia-chi.

GAZETTEERS

Anhwei t'ung-chih (安徽通志), ed. Ho Shao-chi (何紹基), 1877.
Ch'u-chou chih (滁州志), ed. Hsiung Tsu-i (熊祖貽), 1899.
Ch'üeh-shan hsien-chih (確山縣志), ed. Chang Chin-huang (張瑨琪), 1931.
Feng-yang fu-chih (鳳陽府志), ed. Chiang Shih-ch'e (蔣師徹) and Chu K'ung-chang (朱孔彰), 1908.
Ho-tse hsien-chih (荷澤縣志), ed. Yeh Tao-yüan (葉道源), 1880.
Honan t'ung-chih (河南通志), ed. Sun Hao (孫灝), supplemented 1866, reprinted 1917.
Hsiang-ch'eng hsien-chih (項城縣志), ed. Shih Ching-shun (施景舜), 1911.
Hsin-hsien chih (莘縣志), ed. K'ung Kuang-hai (北廣海), 1885.
Hsin-hsiu Nan-yang hsien-chih (新修南陽縣志), ed. Chang Chia-mou (張嘉謀), 1899.
Hsü-chou fu-chih (徐州府志), ed. Liu Hsiang (劉庠), 1874.
Hsü-hsiu Lu-chou fu-chih (續修廬州府志), ed. Wang Tsung-i (汪宗沂), 1885.
Hsü-hsiu Meng-ch'eng hsien-chih (續修蒙城縣志), ed. Huang Yü-shou (黃與綬), 1914.
Hu-hsien hsiang-t'u-chih (鄠縣鄉土志), compiler unknown, 1937.
Hupeh t'ung-chih (湖北通志), ed. Yang ch'eng-hsi (楊承禧), 1912.
Kuang-chou chih-li-chou chih (光州直隸州志), ed. Ma P'ei-chiu (馬佩玖), 1886.
Kuang-hsü Lu-li hsien-chih (光緒鹿邑縣志), ed. Chiang Shih-ch'e (蔣師徹), 1896.
Kwangsi t'ung-chih chi-yao (廣西通志輯要), ed. Yang Fu-li (羊復禮), 1889.
Po-chou chih (亳州志), ed. Yüan Teng-yün (袁登雲), 1894.

Shansi t'ung-chih (山西通志), ed. Wang Hsien (王軒) and others, 1892.

Shantung t'ung-chih (山東通志), ed. Sun Pao-t'ien (孫葆田), 1915.

Shou-chou chih (壽州志), ed. Ko Yin-nan (葛蔭南) and Sun En-i (孫恩詒), 1890.

Su-chou chih (宿州志), ed. Ting Hsün-chih (丁遜之), 1889.

Tientsin hsien-chih (天津縣志), ed. Chiang Yü-hung (蔣玉虹), 1870.

Wo-yang feng-t'u chi (渦陽風土記), ed. Wang P'ei-cheng (王佩箴), 1924.

Yung-ch'eng hsien-chih (永城縣志), ed. Meng Kuang-lai (孟廣來), 1884.

A Note on Bibliography

So far I have not found a single record written by the Nien themselves. While the Taipings left us edicts, proclamations, communications, as well as personal accounts, correspondence, and other literary works, the Nien left none. As compared with the Taipings, the Nien were politically less mature, and devoted less effort to military and administrative innovations. This might be considered the major reason for the scantiness of the Nien documents. Of course, this observation does not rule out the possibility that the Nien had intercommunal or interbanner correspondence in written form. However, as the Nien domain was almost entirely confined to the rural areas of Huai-pei, documents circulating there would not have spread too far and would not have been well known to outsiders. At the same time, it was difficult for outsiders to get access to the Nien area to get a sketch of the Nien picture. Finally the Taipings, with their territory stretching to the coastal regions, kept some contact with the foreigners. Thus narratives made by the latter are rather plentiful. Since many Taiping archives were deliberately or accidentally destroyed by the victorious officials, documents preserved by foreigners became precious. In fact, some collections presented by recent scholars are drawn from London, Cambridge, and Paris. But the Nien story does not share this fortune.

Official or semiofficial works then become our main source. To use official sources is no pleasant task. They are almost entirely concerned with battle details. Allusions to, or implications about, the Nien organization, can be brought forth only by reading between the lines and by scrutinizing them in connection with other sources of similar provenance. This work of reconstructing something from scattered materials requires inference and imagination.

The Chiao-p'ing Nien-fei fang-lüeh may be considered the official complete work dealing specifically with the Nien. As early as the eighteenth century, Emperor Ch'ien-lung set up a Fang-lüeh Kuan, an institute for editing the documents concerning the Imperial conduct of war. Actually the issuance of such books was intended to make known the military triumphs of the dynasty. The method used by the compilers was to select a military episode, and then to pile around this subject memorials to the throne and responding edicts from the Court. The same pattern was applied to the Chiao-p'ing Nien-fei fang-lüeh. When it was published in 1872, four years after the end of the Nien campaign, the T'ung-chih emperor wrote a preface to the book, stating the purpose of its publication. He desired "to commemorate and to exhibit" his father's military merits so that the descendants of the Imperial House would have a model to follow. In a book so motivated, exaggeration and concealment become unavoidable. In the memorials themselves, the officials usually disclosed facts with a certain degree of reservation, and occasionally even falsified the story. In some cases, it was the compilers who left out many important parts of the documents, for they purposely expunged the memorials.

Yet no source materials on the government side more complete than the Fang-lüeh can be acquired. For accounts of many officials who were not prominent enough to have their own works collected and published, the Fang-lüeh, the only collection which reserves a space for these, is particularly valuable. Exaggeration and concealment are not an insurmountable obstacle to truth. The pictures hidden between the lines can be drawn out by cautious reading and by checking against conflicting data. Besides, accusations or complaints forwarded by hostile officials and impeachments by censors are the most useful materials with which to examine divergent accounts or opinions.

There are a number of narratives based on official documents but presented in diverse forms. Yin Keng-yün and his cocompilers of the Yü-chün chi-lüeh, instead of piling up memorials and edicts, transformed their materials into chronological accounts. As the Nien affair came to an end, the governor of Honan, Li Ho-nien (李鶴年), congratulating himself on his successful term of governorship, ordered his underofficials to produce a detailed narrative by using the memorials, communications, and proclamations stored in the provincial archives. Since Honan was the immediate target of the Nien's plundering expeditions, seven out of twelve chapters of this book are concerned exclusively with the Nien battles. Here also it was the desire to exhibit military merit which stimulated Governor Li to publish this work, and the genuine official documents which constituted the principal source. Shortcomings prevailing in the Fang-lüeh also appear in the Yü-chün chi-lüeh. However, as the compilers of the latter took as their goal the presentation of the whole Nien movement from rise to fall, they did not hesitate to admit the Nien's strong points which rendered possible Nien ascendancy. Nor did they hesitate to criticize the successive governors and other officials. From these self-reproaching statements it is not difficult for the reader to draw a picture close to the truth.

The Shantung chün-hsing chi-lüeh was a work on the same pattern which dealt with campaigns fought in another province, Shantung. In the period after 1857 Shantung encountered as many Nien invasions as did Honan. Out of the twenty-two chapters in the

Shantung work, eight are on the Nien. The rest--dealing with the
religious bandits, the Fu-fei, the local bandits, and the rebellious
local corps in Shantung--are equally useful in ascertaining the
Nien's activities in that province and their relationship with the
other rebels. The descriptions of the organization of the religious
bandits help a great deal in the understanding of the Nien organization. The chapters on rebellious local corps and surrendered
bandits throw full light on the struggle between the officials and
the local forces, and the rivalry among the latter.

The Hsiang-chün chih, Hsiang-chün chi, and Ch'iu-ch'üeh-chai
ti-tzu chi all attempt to give a complete account of the Hsiang
Army. All three are topically arranged, divided according to
various campaigns and expeditions. The Hsiang-chün chih starts
from the self-defense movement in Hunan against the Taiping and
ends with the suppression of the Nien, with two chapters on
organizational and financial management appended. Chapters nine
and fourteen in particular deal with the Nien story. As a staff
member, and as a countryman of Tseng Kuo-fan, the author, Wan
K'ai-yün, could not free himself from bias. Nevertheless, he does
not always defend the Hsiang Army. He does not condone the
weakness of the Hsiang divisions sent to the Huai theater before
1865.

The Hsiang-chün chi covers the same events but gives more
space to details. Chapters seven and sixteen concern Miao P'ei-
lin and the Nien respectively. Wang Ting-an, the author, had
served on the staff of Tseng Kuo-fan and had maintained an
intimate friendship with the Tseng brothers for more than twenty
years. When he embarked on the work of writing this book, he
was proud that he could supplement the official documents by
drawing data from his own eyewitness experiences, his personal
contacts with the top figures, and the first-hand information given
him by the participants. Trying to be cautious, he excluded hear-
say which could not be verified. He also preferred to call his book
a yeh-shih (野史), in Wang's case meaning nonofficial history,
pending further investigation. Despite the author's announcement
about the richness of materials, I do not find in this work abundant
information which is additional to, or different from, that supplied
by the Fang-lüeh and other collections of memorials, at least in
the two chapters concerning the Nien.

The Ch'iu-ch'üeh-chai ti-tzu chi is presented as a biography of
Tseng Kuo-fan, emphasizing his military life. Actually it is a
collection of extracts from Tseng's writings, chronologically
arranged under topics. The relationship between the author, Wang
Ting-an (who also wrote the Hsiang-chün chi), and Tseng Kuo-fan
was one of pupil and master. Apparently Wang wrote this book to
exhibit his master's military success. Unlike the Hsiang-chün
chih and Hsiang-chün chi, this book limits its records to Tseng;

145

that is, it commemorates a man rather than an army. The fact
that it covers a narrower realm does not mean that it furnishes
less information. While the former two give only a rough sketch
of Tseng's conduct of the northern campaigns, the latter one has
detailed accounts of Tseng's administrative as well as military
projects.

The main force facing the Nien after 1865, however, was the
Huai Army. The Huai-chün p'ing-nien chi which deals with the
complete story of the Huai Army - Nien combat, has contributed to
this essay more than have the works on the Hsiang Army. The
book begins with the transfer of the Huai Army to the north in
1865, and concludes with the suppression of the West Nien in 1868;
it is supplemented by two chapters on organization, revenue, and
provisions. The author, Chou Shih-ch'eng, was a nephew of Li
Hung-chang, and he approached his task with a purpose similar to
that of Wang Ting-an; that is, he aimed to perpetuate his uncle's
military fame in writing. But it is not the personal affinity
between the author and the hero which makes this book valuable.
Chou was a staff member of Li's headquarters; in this position he
gained direct access to primary sources, which he made use of to
the full extent. Besides the chronological accounts of the battles,
the appendices on organization, revenue, and provisions are of
great importance. They provide the reader with a condensed
picture of those aspects before he goes to detailed documents.

If the books enumerated above give us chronological narratives substantiated by primary sources, the "complete works" of
the leading participants furnish the original documents themselves.
The complete works of Yüan Chia-san, the Yüan Tuan-min-kung
chi and of Yüan Pao-heng, the Yüan Wen-ch'eng-kung chi, are
contained in the Hsiang-ch'eng Yüan-shih chia-chi, a collection of
the writings of the Yüan family. The compiler, Ting Cheng-to,
was acquainted with Yüan Chia-san and his sons, and led a band of
local corps in Yüan's neighboring district in the late 1850's. He
edited this collection at the request of Yüan's grandson. As a
participant in the Nien campaigns, the editor thought he was
qualified and responsible for commemorating the deeds of the
prominent figures of his native place by publishing their writings.

Yüan Chia-san's work includes memorials forwarded to the
Court, and private letters. Besides the first volume, there are
nineteen volumes of memorials concerning the Nien. This emphasis on the Nien is not equalled in the works of other leading
officials who took part in the Nien affair. The private letters are
of equal importance with the memorials, because they reveal
Yüan's private opinions, which could not be stated in such official
documents as memorials. However, some of those which describe
the battles are merely a repetition of the memorials.

When Lü Hsien-chi was commissioned by the Emperor to
direct the local corps of Anhwei, he gained the Imperial permission to bring with him two assistants, Yüan Chia-san and Li Hung-
chang, both natives of Huai-pei. From that time, these two men
rose to higher and higher positions on the front. If one divides the
Nien campaign into two periods, Yüan and Li will each cover one
of them. Hence to couple Yüan's works with those of Li will cover
almost the entire Nien story.

The collection of Li's works, the Li Wen-chung-kung ch'üan-
chi, comprises memorials, communications, letters, and tele-
grams. This essay only relies on the memorials and letters from
the period 1865 to 1868. Besides reading the memorials side by
side with those selected in the Fang-lüeh, I have laid stress on the
private correspondence. In the letters, Li states his mind more
frankly. Opinions conveyed in such a manner help in clarifying
and modifying the evasive, sometimes even deceitful, statements
in the memorials.

The compiler of Li's works is Wu Ju-lün, a well-known
literary man of the late Ch'ing period. While he was serving on
Li's staff, Wu not only drafted most of Li's memorials but also
offered advice on policy-making. To edit Li's memorials was for
Wu nothing more than to edit his own works.

Between the retirement of Yüan Chia-san in 1862 and the
appointment of Li Hung-chang in 1866, Tseng Kuo-fan filled the gap
as commander in chief. Notwithstanding the shortness of this
interval, the measures adopted by Tseng decided the outcome of
the struggle against the Nien. Among the major sources in
connection with the Nien, Tseng's complete works, the Tseng
Wen-cheng-kung ch'üan-chi, have an importance equal to those of
Yüan and Li. Tseng's works comprise fifteen titles, including his
memorials to the throne, his essays and verse, his official and
private correspondence, two anthologies of prose and verse, a
diary, and a chronological biography. Among them, the most
useful for our subject are his memorials, correspondence, and
chronological biography. In his comments or answers to the
reports from below, and in his private letters, Tseng usually
taught his underofficials as an elder would teach his sons and
younger brothers. Thus this correspondence not only discloses
Tseng's policies, observations and convictions, but also his
personality.

The collected works were collated by Li Hung-chang after his
brother, Han-chang, had finished compiling them. The Li brothers,
respecting Tseng as their master, considered this task a part of
their duty as pupils.

There is a separate collection of Tseng's letters, entitled
Tseng Wen-cheng-kung shu-cha. It is better printed and easier to
read than the corresponding section in his complete works.

The third group of materials which I used a great deal is the local gazetteers. A local gazetteer may be considered a combination of history and political geography for a certain local unit. Its origin can be traced back to the third century. In the Ch'ing dynasty, scholars emphasized the production of local gazetteers to such a degree that provinces, prefectures, subprefectures, districts, and sometimes even villages, all had their own gazetteers. Since the purpose of the gazetteers was mainly to provide a reference book for the local administrators, they contained separate treatises on various subjects, such as topography, boundaries, outstanding historical events, the economic situation, local traditions, education, communications, literary works, biographies of eminent personalities, and so forth. Their value lies in their inclusion of contemporary materials collected by the native scholars to describe their native locality. Of course, as the compiling of gazetteers was monopolized by the scholar-gentry --a privileged class--and supervised by the magistrates, they share the defects of other official works, namely, a lack of objectivity and an emphasis on one side, especially in narratives about rebellions.

On the provincial level, the local gazetteers of Anhwei, Shantung, Honan, and Kiangsu would be expected to supply ample primary sources. However, the Chiang-nan t'ung-chih was compiled before the rebellion, and was not revised after it. The Honan t'ung-chih pays slight attention to military affairs, and the Shantung t'ung-chih contributes little to the presentation of the Nien story, because it more or less copies the Shantung chün-hsing chi-lüeh. The Anhwei t'ung-chih then becomes our only source. The ten years' war fought in Anhwei destroyed a great number of records concerning political geography. The governors in the postrebellion period felt the need of a new provincial gazetteer. Since the upheaval was still fresh in their memories, and since they thought it the most significant occurrence in Anhwei history, they ordered the compilers to emphasize military events and the biographies of loyal warriors. The result is that in the new edition of the Anhwei t'ung-chih the compilers spent nine chapters on the rebellious movements rising in the 1850's and laid comparable stress on the loyal personalities. So the Anhwei t'ung-chih, though confined to one province, does not disappoint us. While the Shantung chün-hsing chi-lüeh and the Yü-chün chi-lüeh contribute to the account of Nien activities in Shantung and Honan respectively, the detailed accounts on the same field in the Anhwei t'ung-chih are comparable to the former two works.

Besides the provincial gazetteers, I have used the local gazetteers of the administrative units from prefectures downward, in Anhwei as well as in other neighboring provinces. Probably the scholarship of the local gazetteers on the district level is not as

148

high as that on the provincial level. Yet, as far as the materials are concerned, they are plainer and closer to the truth, because they were collected directly at the spot where they were to be used.

I would like to mention in general terms a number of local gazetteers from the districts where the Nien heartland was located. The Wo-yang feng-t'u chi, the local gazetteer of the arch-rebel Chang Lo-hsing's native town, helped me to determine Chang's family background and the Nien activities on the eve of the rebellion. Especially as the official documents scarcely bring the nonmilitary aspects of the Nien story into the record, fragmentary records, scattered here and there in the local gazetteers of the Nien districts, provide the outline of the picture. Since works which view the Nien story from the Nien's side are not available, the fragments in the local gazetteers are precious to us, no matter how faint a light they throw on the whole picture. In addition to the Wo-yang feng-t'u chi, the local gazetteers of Po-chou, Meng-ch'eng, Yung-ch'eng and Su-chou help us in the same way.

INDEX

Ch'en Te-ts'ai, 58 n., 85
Cheng Ching-hua, 51, 52
Cheng K'uei-shih, 116
Cheng-yang, 95
Cheng-yang-kuan, 122 n.
Cheng Yüan-shan, 61
Ch'eng Erh-lao-k'an, 50
Ch'eng San-lao-k'an, 50
Ch'eng-shan, 125
Ch'eng Ta, 5
Ch'eng Ta-chi, 109 n.
Ch'eng Ta-lao-k'an, 50
Ch'eng Ta-tao, 25, 29 n.
Ch'eng Ta-wei, 63
Cherim league, 83
Chi Hsüeh-sheng, 99
Ch'i-chu (Banner lord), 26, 45, 132
Ch'i-ho, 124
Ch'i-k'e-chin-a, 64
Chia Chen, 41
Chia-i (Eight Diagrams sect designation), 28
Chia-lu River, 59, 105, 123 n.
Chiang Chung-yüan, 90
Chiang-lao-chia, 25, 29 n., 46
Chiang Nin-hsüeh, 100, 109 n.
Chiang T'ai-lin, 25, 46, 63, 133
Chiao-chou, 117
Chiao Hsiang, 47
Chiao-lai Canal, 125, 130 n.
Chiao-lou, 47
Ch'iao Sung-nien, 102
Chieh-ti, 128
Chien Lo-wen, 53
Chien River, 119 n., 128
Chien-sheng (students of Imperial Academy), 50, 51, 53
Ch'ien-tui (Eight Diagrams sect designation), 27 n.
Chih-ho, 17, 21, 22, 23, 24 n., 25, 29 n., 31, 35, 39, 43, 48, 51, 62, 68, 76, 77, 89, 135
Chihli Army, 125, 128
Chin An-ch'ing, 118 n.
Chin-hsiang, 132
Chin-k'ou, 109 n.

Ch'in Chan-ao, 64
Ch'in-wang (Taiping title), 94
Ch'ing-chiang-p'u, 35, 59
Ch'ing-men-chiao, 12
Ch'ing-shan, 120 n.
Chio-tzu-shan, 18
Chiu-fu-chou, 93
Ch'iu-hsien, 27
Chou-chia-k'ou, 59, 104
Chou-chia-lou, 25, 46
Chou Huai-lin, 25, 46
Chou Lao-ming, 26
Chou Sheng-ch'uan, 111
Chou Sheng-po, 103, 111, 115 n.
Chou T'ien-chüeh, 4, 21, 22, 78, 97, 111
Chu K'ai, 17
Chu Yüan-chang, 11
Ch'u-chou, 92
Chuang-ch'i (Nien term), 70
Chung-i T'ang ("Hall of Loyalty and Righteousness"), 19 n.
Chung-yang Wu-chi Tu (Eight Diagrams sect band), 30 n.
Ch'ung An, 51, 77, 82
Ch'ung-en, 97
Ch'ung-hou, 117, 128, 129
Chü-jen (provincial graduate), 53
Chü-yeh, 52
Ch'üan-chiao, 92
Clans, significance of in Nien organization, 45-50, 55, 58, 61
Club Bandits (Fu-fei), 7, 8, 17, 53

Dragon lanterns, 7

Earthwalls, central government's policy regarding, 32, 33, 38, 42, 68, 107, 117, 130, 136; Nien utilization of, 32-44, 45, 48, 55, 56, 59, 67-70, 71, 74, 76, 86-90, 101-104, 131, 132, 133, 134; Tseng Kuo-fan's policy regarding, 101-105, 106, 107, 138
Eight Diagrams sect, 2, 10, 12,

17, 19, 27, 28, 30 n., 45, 53, 56 n.,
62
"Eye of the militia," 21

Fan-hsien, 3, 57
Fan Shao-hsing, 53
Fei-hsien, 53
Fei River, 33, 34, 44 n., 63
Feng Chin-piao, 20, 21
Feng-hsien, 34, 98, 132
Feng-t'ai, 88, 94
Feng-yang, 2, 6, 16, 34, 35, 36,
    44 n., 70, 78, 94, 106, 133
Fou-yang, 89
"Four Deva Kings," 22
Fu (Taiping title), 27
Fu Chen-pang, 79, 81
Fu-chi, 77
Fu-ch'i-chu (Nien vice-lord), 26
Fu-fei, see Club Bandits
Fu-i (policy of pardon), 92 seq.
Fukien, 117

Gordon, General Charles
    George, 119
Grand Canal, 7 n., 44, 104, 104 n.,
    105 n., 117, 120, 122-125, 126, 128-
    130
Grand Canal fleet, 122
"Great Han Prince with the
    Heavenly Mandate," 8, 24, 30, 31
Green Standard armies, 76, 83,
    86, 99, 137 n.

Hai-chou, 60, 126 n.
Han-chuang, 89, 124
Han dynasty, 48
Han He, 47
Han-ko, 47
Hankow, 119 n.
Han Lao-wan, 25
Han Lin-erh, 11 n.
Han Lo-hsing, 53
Han-wang, See "Prince of Han"
Han-yü, 61
Hao (Eight Diagrams sect and
    Nien bands), 28 n.

Hao-chou, 11
Heng-ling, 73
Heresy, government proscrip-
    tions against, 12, 13
Ho-chün, 116
Ho-fei, 16, 108
Honan Army, 69, 105, 113, 124
Hou (Taiping title), 27
Hou Huang-lo, 46, 49
Hou-lao-ying-tzu, 25, 46
Hou-mao, 46
Hou Shih, 23, 25 n.
Hou Shih-wei, 25, 46
Hou Teng-yün, 98
Hsi-hsien, 5
Hsi-huai, 31 n.
Hsi-ling-a, 77, 82
Hsi-yang, 89
Hsia-i, 17, 26
Hsia-tsai, 53 n., 88, 94
Hsiang Army, 67, 73, 75, 82, 90,
    91, 92, 93, 93 n., 95, 96, 99, 100,
    108-110, 113, 114, 115, 121, 135, 136
Hsiang-ch'eng, 62, 97
Hsiang-yang, 2
Hsieh Hai, 47
Hsieh Lin-yün, 9 n.
Hsieh-lou, 47
Hsieh Szu-lao-hu, 47
Hsieh Teng, 47
Hsieh-tou (battles), 15
Hsien-feng, Emperor, 75 n.
Hsien-feng (secret society
    term), 19
Hsing-hsien, 19, 27, 62
Hsü-chou, 2, 10, 11, 34, 35, 61, 63,
    78, 79, 80, 81, 82, 83, 98, 99, 101,
    104, 105, 106, 112, 115 n., 118 n.
Hsü-hai-tzu, 46
Hsü Hua-te, 46
Hsü Hung-ju, 12
Hsü-i, 126
Hsü Ke-shan, 47
Hsü-lao-chia, 47
Hsü Li-chuang, 96, 99, 111
Hsüeh Ming, 64
Hu Hao-shan, 53

Hu-hsien, 66
Hu Lin-i, 56 n., 116
Hunan volunteers, 109 n.
Hupeh Army, 124, 125
Hu-wei-pien, 10
Hu Yü-shan, 25
Huai Army, 67, 73, 82, 89, 100, 103, 104, 108-118, 121-125, 128, 129, 135-137
Huai River valley, 2, 5, 15, 32, passim
Huai-yang fleet, 122, 129
Huai-yüan, 6, 34, 35, 36, 70, 72, 83, 94, 100, 133
Huang I-sheng, 122
Huang-shu-chuang, 104
Hui-ch'ün, 61
Hui-ting-yü, 76 n.
Hui-tsung, Emperor, 11 n.
Hui Yüan, 9 n.
Huo-ch'iu, 5, 92 n., 94, 96, 133

I (Taiping title), 27
I (tribe), revolt of, 2
I-chou, 2, 10
I-ho-ch'üan, see Boxers
I-hsing-o, 84
I-kuan-tao-tsei ("high-society bandits"), 52
I-liang, 33
I-men, 22
Imperial Academy, 50 n.

Jen Ch'ien, 36
Jen Chu, 48, 58 n., 67, 74, 87, 120, 123 n., 126, 127
Jen-kuei (Eight Diagrams sect designation), 28
Ju-chou, 2
Ju-i-chiao, 12
Ju-nin, 51

K'ai-chou, 20
K'ai-feng, 60, 103
K'an (Eight Diagrams sect designation), 27
Kao Ch'eng-hsün, 53

Kao-lu, 26, 89
Keng-hsing (Eight Diagrams sect designation), 27
Kiang-nan Ta-ying, 75 n.
Kiangsu Army, 104
Ko Ch'un, 26, 29 n.
Ku-shih, 90
Kuan-t'ing, 111
Kuan-wen, 128, 129
Kuang-chou, 2, 5, 11, 91
Kuang-shan, 5
Kuei-te, 2, 6, 11, 16, 17, 20, 78, 89 n., 91, 103, 106, 132
Kun-fei (Club Bandits), 7
K'un-keng (Eight Diagrams sect designation), 27 n.
Kung (Eight Diagrams sect unit) 27
Kung-chi-shih, 25, 46
Kung-sheng (senior licentiates), 50 n., 50, 51, 52, 52 n., 53
Kung Te, 16, 22, 25, 34, 46, 72, 133
Kuo Ch'an, 53
Kuo-jui, 65
Kuo Pao-ch'ang, 127
Kuo Shih-heng, 23

Lai-an, 92
Lai Wen-kuang, 27 n., 58 n., 85, 120, 123 n., 126
Lao-shan, 120
Lei Yen, 26
Lei Yüan-chao, 5
Li (Eight Diagrams sect designation), 27 n.
Li Chan, 55 n.
Li Chao-ch'ing, 124
Li Chao-shou, 92, 93
Li-chia-chi, 46
Li Chung-fa, 46, 49
Li Erh-mai, 46, 49
Li Feng, 40
Li Hei-kou, 46, 49
Li Ho-ling, 25, 46
Li Hsiao-ch'e, 46, 49
Li Hsü-i, 44 n., 55, 95, 109, 135 n.

Mao Ch'ang-hsi, 89 n., 137
Mao-erh-wo, 124
Mao Han-yü, 21
Mao Tzu-yüan, 9 n.
Meng-ch'eng, 3, 4, 6, 16, 17, 21, 22, 25, 26, 33, 39, 41, 44 n., 45, 51, 58, 59, 61, 72, 94, 99, 101, 103, 133
Meng-chu, see "Lord of the Alliance"
Meng Shih-chung, 99
Mi River, battle of, 126
Miao (tribe), revolt of, 2
Miao P'ei-lin, 35, 53, 55 n., 56 n., 65, 70, 84 n., 88, 89, 93-96, 99, 100, 111, 112, 135
Ming-chün (Huai Army division), 138
Ming dynasty, 9 n., 11, 15
Mongolia, Inner, 61, 65, 83
Moslems, Northwest, 2, 127
Moslems, Southwest, 2

Nanking, 58 n., 75 n., n., 93, 101, 109, 117, 137
Nan-yang, 2, 4
Nieh-tzu-hui, 9
Nien, meaning of, 7, 8; unit of organization, 7, 8, 18, 19, 20, 30
Nien-shou (Nien leader), 44
Nien-t'ou (Nien leader), 26
Nien-tzu (paper strips), 7; (bandits), 9
Nirvana Sutra, 9 n.
Niu Hung-sheng, 58 n.
Niu-k'eng-li-chuang, 25, 46
Niu Shih-han, 113
"North Corps," Nien, 65

Pa-ch'iao, 66
Pa-kua-chiao, see Eight Diagrams sect
Pai-hao (Eight Diagrams sect and Nien band), 28 n.
Pai-lien-chiao, see White Lotus Society
Pai-lung-wang-miao, 76 n.
Pai-yang-chiao, 12

P'an Kuei-sheng, 120 n.
P'an Ting-hsing, 111, 125
Pao Ch'ao, 109 n., 121 n., 123 n., 127 n.
Pao-chia system, 102 n.
Pei-yang clique, 138 n.
P'ei-hsien, 34
Peking, 97
Peking Field Force, 119 n., 128, 137 n.
Pien-ma (Nien term), 71
Ping-ting (Eight Diagrams sect designation), 28
Po-chou, 3, 4, 6, 10, 11, 16, 17, 20, 22, 25, 26, 33, 34, 39, 41, 44 n., 45, 51, 58, 59, 61, 68, 69, 77, 78, 101, 103, 112, 133
Po-shan, 5
"Prince of Ch'i" (Taiping title), 27 n.
"Prince of Chün" (Taiping title), 27 n.
"Prince of Fu" (Taiping title), 27 n.
"Prince of Han," 9
"Prince of Hsi-huai," 31 n.
"Prince of Liang" (Taiping title), 27 n.
"Prince of Lu" (Taiping title), 27 n.
"Prince of the East" (Taiping title), 28
"Prince of the West" (Taiping title), 28
"Prince of Tuan" (Taiping title), 27 n.
"Prince of Wu" (Taiping title), 27
P'u-chou, 3, 57
P'u-t'ou, 62

"Red Army," 11
Red Beard Bandits, 10

Salt-smuggling, 14, 57
San Fan Rebellion, 1
San-ho-chien, 35

San-kuan-chi, 26
Secret societies, see Ch'ing-men-chiao, Club Bandits, Eight Diagrams sect, Hu-wei-pien, I-ho-ch'üan, Ju-i-chiao, Kun-fei, Long Spear Society, Lung-hua Society, Nieh-tzu-hui, Pa-kua-chiao, Pai-yang-chiao, Shun-tao-hui, Society of Brotherhood, Society of Heaven and Earth, Society of the Rules of Heaven, Ta-ch'eng-chiao, White Feather Society, White Incense Society, White Lotus Society
Seng-ko-lin-ch'in, 44, 58, 63, 65, 67, 71, 72, 73, 75, 79, 82, 83-86, 87, 89, 95, 100, 104, 105, 109, 115 n., 121, 122, 134 n., 135
Sha River, 33, 34, 35, 41, 104
Shan-hsien, 34, 91
Shan-t'ang (secret society term), 19 n.
Shan T'ung, 11 n.
Shanghai, 12 n., 117, 118
Shanghai Machine Bureau, 120
Shantung Army, 104, 123, 125, 128, 129
Shen-ch'iu, 51, 118 n.
Shen-min (gentry and common-ers), 129
Shen Pao-chen, 117
Sheng Chien-ju, 25, 29 n.
Sheng-pao, 35, 36, 43, 62, 78, 79, 80, 81, 87, 91-96, 118 n., 122, 134 n.
Sheng-yüan (licentiates), 50, 50 n., 53, 94
Shou-chou, 6, 16, 35, 53 n., 63, 94, 95, 96, 98, 99, 135
Shu-ch'eng, 133
Shu-t'ung-o, 73
Shui-hu chuan (novel), 19 n.
Shun-tao-hui, 10
Society of Brotherhood, 19 n.
Society of Heaven and Earth, 19
Society of the Rules of Heaven, 12

Ssu-ta-t'ien wang, see "Four Deva Kings"
Su-chia-chai, 26, 47
Su-ch'ien, 105, 124
Su-chou, 3, 6, 9 n., 21, 23, 33, 34, 35, 36, 43, 53, 63, 80 n., 81, 94, 97, 100, 103, 106, 132
Su-k'o-chin, 73
Su T'ien-cheng, 49
Su T'ien-fu, 16, 17, 23, 26, 39, 47, 49
Sui-hsi-k'ou, 43, 44
Sun Chia-t'ai, 96, 99, 111, 112
Sun-ho, 26
Sun Kuei-hsin, 24 n., 25, 46, 64, 133
Sung Kung, 46
Sun-lao-chia, 46
Sun-lou, 46
Sun Pa, 46
Sung Chin-shih, 62, 63
Sung dynasty, 9 n., 11 n., 15, 131
Sung Hsi-chu, 49
Sung Hsi-yüan, 49
Szu-chou, 34, 62, 63, 64

Ta-chang-ko, 46
Ta-chao-chuang, 46
Ta-ch'eng-chiao, 12
Ta-ch'ing River, 3
Ta-Han-ming-ming-wang, see "Great Han Prince with the Heavenly Mandate"
Ta-lo-chia, 26, 46
Ta-ming, 2
Ta-wang-chuang, 46
Ta-wei-chuang, 47
Tai-miao, 125
T'ai-ho, 41, 55, 61
Taiping rebels, absorption into the Nien organization, 27, 28, 85; compared with the Nien, 24 n., 26, 27, 28, 44, 45, 71; government measures against, 39, 75 n., 93; Huai Army against, 110; in Anhwei, 6, 24 n., 77, 96, 97; in Honan, 6; in Kiangsu,

118 n.; in Kwangsi, 2; in
Nanking, 58 n., 97; Miao P'ei-
lin's cooperation with, 94;
Nien cooperation with, 27, 35,
58 n., 89,133; results of rebel-
lion, 7 n., 51, 59,137; suppres-
sion of, 101,107,116,135 (see
also Hsiang Army)
T'an T'ing-hsiang, 37
Tang-shan, 105,132
T'ang-chu (leader), 54, 55
T'ang Hsün-fang, 88, 93 n.,109,
135 n.
T'ang Hua-chün, 64
Te-chou, 129
Te-hsing-a, 66,129 n.
Te-leng-o, 82
Teng-chou, 86
Teng Pao-shan, 53
Teng Tso-jen, 26
T'ieh (Nien term), 13
T'ien-ch'ang, 92
T'ien Ch'un, 47
T'ien Hsien, 25
T'ien-li-hui, see Society of the
Rules of Heaven
T'ien-ta-chung, 47
T'ien-ti-hui, see Society of
Heaven and Earth
T'ien Tsai-t'ien, 79,118 n.
Tientsin, 14, 57,118,120,128
Tientsin Machine Bureau, 120
Ting Hsien-k'ao, 47
Ting-lou, 47
Ting Pao-cheng, 107,109 n.,
122 n.,124,125,126
Ting San-yüan, 47
Ting-ting (Nien term), 13
Ting-yüan, 35, 44 n., 64, 70, 96
Trading fairs, 6,13
Ts'ao-chou, 2,10,20,45,73,86,
105,115 n.
Ts'ao-hsien, 34, 62, 91
Ts'ao-lou, 47
Ts'ao-shih, 25, 29 n.
Ts'ao Sung-hsien, 47, 49
Ts'ao Sung-t'ang, 47, 49

Tseng Kuo-ch'üan, 107,123 n.
Tseng Kuo-fan, 44, 56 n., 59, 65,
69, 71, 73, 74, 75 n., 88, 90, 93,
95,100-112,114,115,117,122,123,
125,127,135-138
Tsi-ning, 2,101,104
Tso Tsung-t'ang, 56 n., 66, 71,
116,119 n., 122 n.,127-129,137
Tsou-hsien, 120
Tu-nien-t'ou (Nien "supreme
leader"), 22
T'u-hsieh River, 129
T'uan-tsung (local corps chief),
38, 45, 91
Tumet, 83
Tung-ch'ang, 119 n.,128
Tung Ch'ien-ju, 53
Tung Wen-chai, 52
T'ung-ch'eng, 133
T'ung-wa-hsiang, 3
Tzu-ch'uan, 9,19

Wan Army, 113
Wang-chia-yü, 64
Wang Huai-i, 25, 63,133
Wang Kuan-san, 23, 26, 46
Wang Lao-p'u, 46
Wang-lou, 26, 46
Wang Mou-yin, 110
Wang San-lo, 45
Wang-shih, 4
Wang Ta-wei, 25
Wang Ting-an, 37, 72
Wang T'ung-t'ien, 64
Wang-yü, 56
Wei Hei, 46
Wei-lu-k'ou, 46
Wei River, 128, 129
Wei Shu-te, 47
Wei Wen-shan, 47
Wen-tsung, Emperor, 15
Weng T'ung-shu, 34, 63, 95, 96,
111,116,119 n.
White Feather Society, 12
White Incense Society, 12
White Lotus Society, 1, 3, 9 n.,
10-13,15,19,27,28,30,45,52,

131,132,138
Wo River, 33,35,36,44 n.,59,
  63,68
Wo-yang, 24 n.,88
Wu Ch'ang-ch'ing, 111
Wu-chi (Eight Diagrams sect
  designation), 28
Wu-chü (military provincial
  graduates), 50,53
Wu-chün, 9 n.
Wu-ho, 92
Wu-lung-o, 77,78
Wu-sheng, (military licentiates),
  53,54
Wu-wang, see "Prince of Wu"

Yamen runners, 5
Yang An, 47
Yang Fang-hen, 53
Yang Jui-ying, 26
Yang-lou, 47
Yang P'eng-lin, 62
Yangchow, 6,14,110
Yangtze River, 11 n.,71
Yao Lo-kuang, 53
Yellow River, 2,3,44,105,126,
  127,128,129
Yen (Taiping title), 27
Yen-chi, 46,50
Yen-chia-chi, 46
Yen Ching-ming, 56 n.,112,
  119 n.,122,122 n.
Yen-chou, 2,10,60
Yen Hsi-ch'un, 46,49,50,53
Yen Hsiao-ch'ien-sui, 49
Yen Hsiu-lun, 19,45,56 n.
Yen Ming, 46,49
Yen Shu-sen, 109 n.,137 n.
Yin Tzu-hsing, 25
Ying-ch'i, 83
Ying-chou, 2,3,10,11 n.,13,16,21,
  39,40,41,44 n.,72,106,111,112,
  133,134 n.
Ying-han, 137
Ying-kuei, 76,77,78,80
Ying River, 59,104 n.,117
Ying-shang, 94

Yung-ch'eng, 6,16,17,20,25,26,
  33,45
Yü (Taiping title), 27
Yü, see Earthwalls
Yü Army (Honan Army), 113
Yü-ch'eng, 17
Yü-chu (leaders of earthwall
  communities), 38,45,55,69,
  102
Yü-t'ai, 132
Yüan An-yü, 53
Yüan Chia-san, 4,10,22,23,
  24 n.,31,34,35,36,39,43,51,
  55,61,64,69,70,75,77-81,83,
  84,87,88,93,93 n.,95,97-100,
  108,108 n.,111,116,122,133,134,
  135
Yüan Chu-ssu, 46
Yüan dynasty, 11,15,125
Yüan-lou, 46
Yüan Pao-hen, 88
Yüan To, 46
Yün-ch'eng, 105